The Socialist Party of Great Britain

The Socialist Party of Great Britain

Politics, Economics and Britain's Oldest Socialist Party

David A. Perrin

Wrexham

The Socialist Party of Great Britain —
Politics, Economics and Britain's Oldest Socialist Party
First published in Wales in 2000
by
BRIDGE BOOKS
61 Park Avenue, Wrexham
LL12 7AW

ISBN 1-872424-80-5

Front cover: SPGB rally, Trafalgar Square, 1974.
Back cover: SPGB orator Clifford Groves campaigning in
Paddington during the 1945 General Election.

A CIP catalogue entry for this book is
available from the British Library

Printed and bound by
MFP
Manchester

Contents

Acknowledgements

The author wishes to extend warm thanks to all those who have helped make this book a reality — to my family, whose stoicism in the face of my eccentricity seems to know no bounds; to my friends whose persistent eccentricity in the face of my stoicism seems to know no bounds either; to Alister Williams for believing in this project; to all those who assisted me so generously at the School of Politics and Communication Studies at the University of Liverpool, particularly Professor Benny Pollack and Tony Beck; to the staff in the Wrexham Business School at NEWI and in the Business Development Unit there; to Adam and Caroline Buick, for consistently good advice, encouragement and hospitality; to Steve Coleman for his helpful suggestions; and also, of course, to all those many and various members of the Socialist Party of Great Britain who have — without exception — shown commendable generosity of spirit towards me as I rummaged around amongst their collective political baggage. Thank you all for your time and thanks, most of all, for putting up with me.

Introduction

When former British Prime Minister Harold Wilson famously commented that a week is a long time in politics one thing is certain: he could not have had the Socialist Party of Great Britain uppermost in mind. While the structure and composition of political movements in Britain has sometimes changed rapidly, the SPGB has stood out, rock-like, on the fringes of the British political scene for nearly a century. One of the oldest political organisations in Britain today, and certainly the oldest surviving party claiming the title 'socialist', a week hardly registers in its long political life.

This situation is all the more remarkable considering that the SPGB can clearly be situated within the Marxist political sector — after all, the life expectancy of political organisations claiming to stand in this tradition is often short. Differences over aspects of theory, sometimes masking clashes of personality, ensure that there is a continual flow of splits and sects whose theoretical delineations can be slight enough to confuse the most avid observers. When a Marxist organisation endures for a century or so with its objective, principles and overall perspective intact, its very uniqueness should be enough to command attention. The very fact that the SPGB is one of the oldest surviving Marxist organisations in the world makes it of more than passing interest to those wishing to develop an understanding of the twentieth century's principal political philosophy of dissent. That the SPGB is an organisation still adhering to 'classical' Marxism while rejecting Leninism in its various guises means this is doubly the case.

Today, the SPGB — with a few like-minded parties in other countries — continues to plough its own distinctive furrow as the century which gave early birth to it closes. With five hundred or so members, steadfastly still publishing its lively and combative monthly journal the *Socialist Standard*, the SPGB can wish for little more than that its aims and views will receive an altogether wider audience in the new century than they did in the last. The twenty-first century may yield resounding proof — one way or the other — of whether the tiny Marxist organisation founded in London in 1904, which has infuriated and exasperated its political opponents in equal measure ever since, was ahead of its time or not.

This is not an exhaustive work about the SPGB, its political life and viewpoints, nor could it be. The SPGB has been around for so long that entire volumes could be written about the many distinctive and fascinating features of the Party and about the political lives of those who have been members of it. It seems almost negligent not to dwell on some aspects of the SPGB's activities or its political culture as they may well be what those who have encountered the SPGB will have mainly remembered it for, sometimes even more so than for its distinctive political viewpoints. There is little doubt that for a great many the SPGB is remembered as the organisation which provided some of the most forceful and entertaining public speakers of the twentieth century. More than any other political group in Britain, the SPGB made outdoor soapbox oratory and formal indoor debates forces of persuasion to be reckoned with. But entertaining though it might be, this is not a work about the oratorical vigour of Alex Anderson and Tony Turner, or the incisive debating skills of Jack Fitzgerald and Edgar Hardcastle. Instead, it is about the political and economic theories with which these dedicated revolutionaries went into battle.

There are two clear reasons why a book exploring the political and economic theories of the SPGB should merit attention. First, little of real political interest has been written about the SPGB, even though much has been contributed about the politics of the wider working class or labour movement to which the SPGB belongs. The greater part of this has been concerned with organisations like the British Labour Party that have dominated the political agenda through force of ideas and mass support. But many other, less outwardly successful groupings on the political left, have still attracted some attention from researchers in the fields of politics, history and economic theory. This has been most evidently the case with organisations which have, to varying degrees, supported the Bolshevik model of social revolution. With relatively little support in countries like Britain, their activities have nevertheless attracted widespread attention when the USSR was a major world power, from Challinor's *Origins of British Bolshevism* to Callaghan's *The Far Left in British Politics*. Those organisations in the labour movement which have been neither exponents of orthodox social democracy nor of Bolshevism have never provoked nearly so much interest. Invariably, the attention they have received has been by way of passing reference and historical footnote. It is in this latter category that the Socialist Party of Great Britain fits.

In some works on the socialist movement in Britain the SPGB has been ignored completely.[1] Such as the SPGB is mentioned in others, many of the references to it have been inaccurate or misplaced. Even Max Beer's otherwise masterful work on the history of the British socialist movement, for example, manages to list the year of the Party's foundation incorrectly.[2] It is tempting to speculate that if such a distinguished scholar could be so mistaken about an elementary fact about the SPGB, there is not much hope for those less thorough in their researches. But a consultation of the literature demonstrates that speculation on this is not needed — myths and inaccuracies about the SPGB abound all too freely.

In much of the literature on the SPGB writers have simply been seduced by apocryphal tales about Party members and their sometimes colourful behaviour. This is most demonstrably the case with Barltrop's *The Monument*, so far the only book-length published work on the SPGB, where anecdotes and tall stories prevail.[3] Challinor's more serious work on the early socialist movement in Britain should be of interest as it is concerned partly with the SPGB's political cousins the Socialist Labour Party, but it contains only fleeting references to the SPGB, the most notable of which refers not to its political stance but — bizarrely — to the alleged attempts of SPGB member Moses Baritz to disrupt a public meeting addressed by his political opponent Henry Hyndman by blowing a clarinet loudly down the ventilator shaft of the meeting hall.[4]

Such serious comments that are attempted about the SPGB in books like Challinor's are often found wanting. For instance, Challinor's own errors range from the relatively trivial — stating that at one time the SPGB's Manchester Branch contained only one member[5] (untrue and illegal under the Party's rulebook) — to the bold claim that the SPGB was never influenced by the ideas of the American SLP theorist Daniel De Leon[6] (as Chapter 1 of this work demonstrates, also untrue). Walter Kendall's volume on the early revolutionary movement in Britain doesn't attempt to tell us anything about the SPGB of interest, simply that it "has retained its political virginity only at the expense of not reproducing anything at all",[7] a comment without substantiation from Kendall, or as will be seen, much basis in fact. Widgery's text *The Left in Britain* is little better, claiming that the SPGB "denounced the Russian Revolution within hours of hearing of it", another assertion based on myth rather than actuality.[8]

These glaring errors by serious analysts have also been reflected in the more prosaic writings on the SPGB, such as in the comments of Bernard Levin who has claimed, among other things, that the SPGB during its political lifetime has actively opposed the introduction of safety measures at work and free heating for old age pensioners,[9] entirely fictional suggestions which demonstrate a fundamental misunderstanding of the SPGB's position on reformism. It should be clear, then, that on this count alone, a serious examination of what the SPGB actually does stand for is in order. By far the best account of the politics of the SPGB is Stephen Coleman's in *Non-Market Socialism in the Nineteenth and Twentieth Centuries* edited by Rubel and Crump,[10] but the treatment of the SPGB's distinctive theories in such a book could of necessity be no more than a brief one. Without doubt, a clear gap still exists in the history of the British labour movement, a gap which this works attempts, in part, to fill by outlining — and tracing the development of — the principal political and economic theories of the Socialist Party.

The second reason why a text of this nature on the Socialist Party of Great Britain must be a worthwhile endeavour is that the SPGB has had much to say that may be of interest to the political observer, including that which has previously gone unnoticed from political commentators and academics. On this level the SPGB principally arouses interest because of its unique analysis of events in the twentieth century. Indeed, the SPGB's history is largely one of how it has developed and applied distinctive arguments on a wide range of subjects, from 'national liberation' struggles to inflation. To this end, its contributions to the development of Marxian political and economic theory rest on its original analysis of events, though given the undisputed influence of classical Marxian ideas on the Party, this concept perhaps needs some explanation.

The SPGB has on occasion been the first to develop a distinctive and highly original argument within a Marxian framework, such as for example on the state capitalist nature of Soviet Russia or with its conception of socialist planning. While this has not always been recognised, especially by its political opponents, once the facts are known there can be little dispute. On these occasions the SPGB has developed arguments that arise from a Marxian perspective, but which are entirely additional to Marxian political and economic theory as it previously existed.

At other times the SPGB's originality and distinctiveness has perhaps been less striking, but still no less real. In these instances the Party has blended already existing strands of Marxian thought into an entirely new mix, such as with its views on the reform or revolution issue where it has entwined two seemingly incompatible theories, thus developing an entirely unique argument.

Taking this into account, this text aims to illuminate the distinctive political and economic views of the SPGB by tracing the genesis of eight specific contributions that it has made to the development of Marxian theory, and a chapter is devoted to each of these contributions. They are all instances of how the SPGB has developed and applied distinctive arguments during its political lifetime in response to events as they unfolded, and demonstrate that the SPGB, while operating within a Marxian framework, has not merely repeated an inflexible Marxist mantra revealed to the world by Marx and Engels in 1848.

This is not primarily a critical analysis, though some critical comments have been included in the conclusion, regarding some of the possible inadequacies of the SPGB's contributions to Marxian theory and how the SPGB may move to rectify them. Its principal task is to provide an academic reference work for those interested in labour history or political and economic theory who may wish, for whatever particular reason, to include reference of their own to the SPGB and its distinctive arguments. No such text has previously been available. It is also anticipated that it may stimulate comment on the politics of the SPGB and non-market socialism in general, where none might otherwise have been made due to ignorance of the subject. It can be added that given the inadequate nature of the remarks about the Party contained in many earlier works, it is especially hoped that it will encourage any future comment on the politics of the SPGB to be based on something altogether more substantial than the myth and apocrypha that have previously characterised it.

Notes

1. See, for instance, *Socialism in Britain* by T. L. Jarman (Victor Gollancz, London, 1972).
2. *A History of British Socialism*, Volume II, by Max Beer (G.Bell and Sons, London, 1921) p.269.
3. *The Monument* by Robert Barltrop (Pluto Press, London, 1975). Although sub-headed "the story of the Socialist Party of Great Britain" this is not an official history of the SPGB and tends to be anecdotal in nature.
4. *The Origins of British Bolshevism* by Raymond Challinor (Croom Helm, London, 1977) p.39.
5. *Ibid.*
6. *The Origins of British Bolshevism*, p.44.
7. *The Revolutionary Movement in Britain 1900–21* by Walter Kendall (Weidenfeld and Nicholson, London, 1969) p.21.
8. *The Left in Britain 1956–68* by David Widgery (Penguin, Harmondsworth, 1976).
9. 'Creda Quia Impossible' by Bernard Levin in the *Observer*, 18 April 1976.
10. See chapter on 'Impossibilism' by Stephen Coleman in *Non-Market Socialism in the Nineteenth and Twentieth Centuries* edited by Maximilien Rubel and John Crump (MacMillan, London and Basingstoke, 1987).

1. Reform or Revolution?

The 'Impossibilist' Revolts and the origins of the SPGB

Although the Socialist Party of Great Britain was not founded until 1904, its political and economic theories have their clear historical background in the radical movements and fledgling socialist clubs of the mid to late nineteenth century, principally those organisations which claimed to follow in the tradition of the Chartists and the First International, propagating the political and economic ideas of Marx and Engels. Of prime significance was the founding of a new British political organisation in 1881, when a disparate collection of radicals, freethinkers, single-taxers and socialists came together under the aegis of the wealthy English capitalist Henry Hyndman to form the Democratic Federation, which within two years had proclaimed its socialist intentions and renamed itself the Social Democratic Federation (SDF). From the start the SDF was an uneasy coalition of radical activists, with the elements advocating the revolutionary ideas of Marxian socialism being but a vocal minority. Much like the Social Democratic parties on the continent, the SDF had a programme that was a compromise between the ideas of two basic camps, one arguing that the movement standing for social transformation could only gain support on the basis of a 'minimum programme' of reforms and palliatives of the existing capitalist system,[1] with the other, smaller group, insisting that the advocacy of reforms was a diversion from the task ahead and that only a full-blown socialist revolution could put an end to the iniquity, poverty and exploitation of capitalism. It is this latter group, the advocates of what came to be known as the 'maximum programme', with which the founders of the SPGB were associated.

Those who eventually went on to form the SPGB were not, however, the first or only group to wrestle with the question of reform and revolution from within the ranks of the SDF. Even though the Federation had not begun to attract workers with its radical programme of reforms in any great numbers, the apparent attempt at securing support by advocating reform measures had already aroused the suspicions of the more serious Marxists of the time.[2] As early as 1884 a number of dissenters including William Morris, Belfort Bax and Eleanor Marx had left the SDF to set up a new organisation called the Socialist League. This organisation did not adopt a series of palliatives to act as 'stepping-stones' to socialism, and, unlike the SDF, had no political leadership. For the Socialist League, the road to socialism was one of open propaganda based around lectures, street-corner meetings and the sale of its journal *Commonweal*.[3]

The League's crucial disagreement with the SDF about the usefulness of reforms of the capitalist system was summed up by William Morris in the following terms:

> The palliatives over which many worthy people are busying themselves now are useless because they are just unorganised partial revolts against a vast, wide-spreading, grasping organisation which will, with the unconscious instinct of a plant, meet every attempt at bettering the conditions of the people with an attack on a fresh side.[4]

To the Marxists of the Socialist League, reform activity was little more than a useless and unnecessary diversion from the real task of achieving a socialist system of society, and would only help the capitalist class prolong their rule. This was a view that was to re-emerge in the SDF less than twenty years later with the so-called 'impossibilist' revolts of 1903-04.

The history of the Socialist League is not a happy one, and will not be dealt with here, but the problems with which the League wrestled — and some of the solutions it put forward — outlasted its own organisational decline. Most importantly, the tensions within the SDF between the reformers and the revolutionaries endured. While the SDF continued to state that its ultimate object was the overthrow of capitalism, the 'immediate demands' took priority, and by the turn of the century the conflict between what came to be called the 'possibilists' and the 'impossibilists' re-emerged with avengence.[5] To the 'possibilists', mass socialist consciousness among the working class was an unlikely outcome of capitalist class domination, so the achievement of socialism had to be a gradual process based around partial, immediate struggles. To this end, the possibilist political party would have to be involved in reform campaigns, immediate 'practical' programmes and electoral activity to build up support. The epithet of 'impossibilism' developed into a term of political abuse, with the possibilists charging those who "advocated the impossible" with impracticality, utopianism and even an indifference to the suffering of the working class occasioned by their opposition to palliatives. Acceptance of impossibilism, they thought, would render the social democratic movement impotent.[6]

For their part, the impossibilists asserting themselves in the SDF at this time took up many of Morris's criticisms of the SDF and added others of their own. In particular, they charged the SDF with being undemocratic, largely because of the increasingly overbearing influence of Hyndman. They were aggrieved by Hyndman's personal ownership of the Party organ *Justice* and his control over much of its contents, concluding that the SDF was not in any meaningful sense under the democratic control of its membership. The Federation's Executive Council became increasingly autocratic and was empowered to control the content of the SDF's electoral platform.[7] It seemed that the Executive, Hyndman and the editor of *Justice*, Harry Quelch, were moving the Party ever closer to compromise with organisations which rejected Marxian socialism and denied the existence of the class struggle — such as the gradualist Fabians. Even worse, the SDF under Hyndman's influence seemed prepared to enter into electoral arrangements with the openly pro-capitalist Liberals and Tories whenever the leadership considered that it would suit their purposes.[8]

From the turn of the century onwards a number of positions were adopted by the SDF that were roundly condemned by the impossibilist minority, such as Hyndman's argument in *Justice* that the Federation's opposition to the Boer War was pointless and that they should hope for a British victory.[9] By way of response to the perceived drift of SDF policy, a motion was proposed at the 1902 Conference by one of the most prominent Scottish impossibilists, George Yates, to bring *Justice* under the democratic control of the membership and to oppose any attempts at linking the SDF with the reformist Independent Labour Party. The motion was defeated but, undeterred, the opponents of the SDF leadership vigorously carried on their campaign to oppose compromise, political trading, undemocratic practices and reformism.

By 1903, the conflict between the bulk of the SDF membership and the small impossibilist minority had reached boiling point, the majority tired with what they took to be the disruptiveness of the impossibilists. The intransigent impossibilist faction around James Connolly, George Yates, Con Lehane and Jack Fitzgerald attacked Hyndman and Quelch for their reformism and willingness to co-operate with non-socialist bodies, and many of the impossibilists wrote to *Justice* criticising the SDF's official position.[10] After having come under the spell of Daniel De Leon's impossibilist American Socialist Labor Party, James Connolly toured England, whipping up dissent in SDF branches, and the impossibilist group consolidated their position to the extent that three of their number were elected to the SDF Executive. In August 1902, the Scottish District Council of the SDF had begun publishing its own journal, *The Socialist*, and Yates was soon attacking the SDF leadership in its pages. Indeed, *The Socialist* did not merely restrict itself to attacking social democracy in Britain — their opposition was a fundamental one aimed at orthodox social democracy in general. They attacked the largest social democratic organisation on the continent, the German SPD, saying that "The German socialist party has ceased to be revolutionary and has become reformatory".[11] By 1903, incensed by the attacks made upon them and their sister parties abroad, the SDF leadership instigated attempts to expel some of the most notable and vocal of the impossibilist rebels.

The impossibilists had some organisational difficulties too. Their support lay mainly in SDF branches in Central Scotland and London, and although representatives of the two groups met informally to discuss the situation at least twice, it would appear that there was a definite lack of cohesion between them, so much so that while the London members were still fighting within the SDF, the bulk of the Scottish impossibilists decided to break away and form a new party of their own.[12] In the spring of 1903 the impossibilist-dominated Scottish

District Council voted to disaffiliate from the SDF and the inaugural conference of the new body — to be called the Socialist Labour Party after De Leon's American group — was held on the 7th June 1903.

While there was little effective unity or useful co-operation between the two groups of impossibilists — caused at least in part by the geographical distance between them — it soon became clear that there were some important political differences as well.[13] Not only were the London rebels unhappy with the secretive and rather exclusive manner in which the Scottish impossibilists had split from the SDF, they were even less content with the new party's decision to include some immediate demands in its programme — and this despite strong opposition from its own strongly impossibilist Edinburgh Branch.[14] There was also a rumour at the time that undemocratic practices were afoot in the SLP, and this made Fitzgerald and the London impossibilists all the more determined to set the SDF on the right course.[15]

The attacks on the remaining impossibilist rebels continued, however, and their attempts to promote the ideas of Marxian socialism were stifled at every turn by the SDF leadership. The first two days of the SDF's 1904 Burnley Conference was devoted to discussing the issue, and on the second day Executive member Herbert Burrows moved that the impossibilists withdraw their attacks on the Party leadership and official Party policy.[16] This motion was carried and six of the impossibilists were asked to recant immediately. When all six refused, another motion was put forward calling for the expulsion of two of the leading protagonists, Jack Fitzgerald and SDF industrial organiser H. J. Hawkins, and this was passed by 61 votes to 8. Immediately there were accusations that the charges made against Fitzgerald and Hawkins were unfair and that the Conference procedure had been rigged in favour of the Party leadership.[17] The impossibilists decided to form a Protest Committee which set about issuing an open statement to members of the SDF, signed by 88 members and ex-members, calling for the construction of a new revolutionary party to expose the degeneration of the SDF and to fight for socialism. By May 1904 a further leaflet was issued advertising "a meeting to formally constitute a new party". The leaflet asked for assistance in the task of building up a new revolutionary organisation:

> We appeal to all comrades who believe that the economic forces working through the development of capitalist society demand the formation of a Revolutionary Socialist Party . . . and who realise that the SDF has ceased to merit the name of such a party, to throw in your lot with us and help us in building up a strong and healthy fighting party, organised on definite class lines for the emancipation of the working class from the wage slavery under which they exist — from the capitalist society of which they are the victims.

At the Printers' Hall, in a little alley off Fetter Lane, Fleet Street, the Inaugural Meeting of the new party was held on 12th June, 1904. Steadfast in their belief that neither the SDF nor the ILP understood the dynamics of the class struggle and the imperative for socialist revolution, one of the first acts of the impossibilists was to give their new party a name — and with typical boldness they agreed, from a short-list of three, upon the Socialist Party of Great Britain.[18] For the founder members of the SPGB, the drift towards reformism and compromise in all the other radical political parties of the time was such that they were the only Socialist Party.

Constitution and Principles

At the Inaugural Meeting one hundred and forty two people gave their names (though three were later thought to have been false)[19] and they voted to adopt a set of rules and an Object and Declaration of Principles, drawn up by the Provisional Committee that had organised the meeting. The rules of the Party were framed in such a way that the membership was firmly in control of Party affairs — a far cry indeed from the Social Democratic Federation, where the personal influence of Hyndman predominated. A democratically elected Executive Committee would administer the day-to-day business of the Party and there would be no leadership, for it was thought that only a Party that did not know where it was going would need to be led. All binding decisions of policy and principle were to be made at the Annual Conference, and if disputes arose provision was made for Party Polls — the ultimate arbiter. Most distinctively of all, Party meetings were, without exception, to be open to members of the public. There were to be no secret cabals or closed meetings as the founder members were certain they did not want to go the same way as the SDF and end up as a leader dominated, undemocratic clique devoid of any real socialist content; unlike the SDF's *Justice*, the Party journal, the *Socialist Standard*, was to be under the democratic control of the members. Membership was to be strictly limited to socialists — those who agreed with the Party on certain issues only were refused membership, as agreement to the Party's case against capitalism had to be total. If the SPGB was to be democratic it had to be an organisation of equals, and that presupposed unity of outlook on fundamental issues and a basic socialist understanding.[20]

The Declaration of Principles adopted at the Inaugural Meeting was intended to be a basic statement of the working class position in capitalist society and a guide to working class action for as long as capitalism lasted. To this day it can be found in most SPGB literature including all pamphlets and every edition of the monthly *Socialist Standard*. The Object and Declaration of Principles is far from being a comprehensive statement of the SPGB outlook, but it is an important document nonetheless and all potential members since have been required to show agreement with it.

Not only does it give a basic — though legalistically precise — outline of the SPGB conception of revolution, it also stands as proof of the influence of Morris's Socialist League on the SPGB founder members. There is a striking similarity between the SPGB's Object and Declaration of Principles and the Manifesto adopted by the League twenty years earlier.[21] This reflects something else that the SPGB and the Socialist League had in common — their belief that "the failures of existing organisations were simply the fruits of false theories".[22] Socialist propaganda had to be based on correct theory backed up by argument and persuasion, and that necessitated a reliance on formal definitions, logic and analysis. It is for this reason that the Object and Declaration of Principles was not thought of as a catechism, but the sheet anchor of the Party reflecting its impossibilist background. Though periodic attempts have been made to update it since 1904, the SPGB's statement of revolutionary intent has remained unchanged since the Inaugural Meeting, and is as follows:

Object
The establishment of a system of society based upon the common ownership and democratic control of the means and instruments for producing and distributing wealth by and in the interest of the whole community.

Declaration of Principles
THE SOCIALIST PARTY of Great Britain holds:

1) That society as at present constituted is based upon the ownership of the means of living (i.e. land, factories, railways, etc.) by the capitalist or master class, and the consequent enslavement of the working class, by whose labour alone wealth is produced.

2) That in society, therefore, there is an antagonism of interests, manifest-ing itself as a class struggle, between those who possess but do not produce, and those who produce but do not possess.

3) That this antagonism can be abolished only by the emancipation of the working class from the domination of the master class, by the conversion into the common property of society of the means of production and distribution, and their democratic control by the whole people.

4) That as in the order of social evolution the working class is the last class to achieve its freedom, the emancipation of the working class will involve the emancipation of all mankind without distinction of race or sex.

5) That this emancipation must be the work of the working class itself.

6) That as the machinery of government, including the armed forces of the nation, exists only to conserve the monopoly by the capitalist class of the wealth taken from the workers, the working class must organise consciously and politically for the conquest of the powers of government, national and local, in order that this machinery, including these forces, may be converted from an instrument of oppression into the agent of emancipation and the overthrow of privilege, aristocratic and plutocratic.

7) That as all political parties are but the expression of class interests, and as the interest of the working class is diametrically opposed to the interests of all

sections of the master class, the party seeking working class emancipation must be hostile to every other party.

8) THE SOCIALIST PARTY of Great Britain, therefore, enters the field of political action determined to wage war against all other political parties, whether alleged labour or avowedly capitalist, and calls upon the members of the working class of this country to muster under its banner to the end that a speedy termination may be wrought to the system which deprives them of the fruits of their labour, and that poverty may give place to comfort, privilege to equality, and slavery to freedom.

Capitalism and Socialism

As the Declaration of Principles emphasises, the SPGB from the outset identified capitalism as being based on a fundamental and irreconcilable class antagonism between the owners and controllers of the means of living and the non-owners. Then as now for the SPGB, "society is more and more splitting up into two great hostile camps, into two great classes directly facing each other: bourgeoisie and proletariat."[23] From its very inception the Party denied the existence of a 'middle class' and associated those who used the term with the great body of confusionists, compromisers and reformists arraigned against it who either refused to acknowledge the reality of the class struggle or were looking for ways to circumvent it. The working class comprised all those who had nothing of any real worth to sell except their ability to work for others (their 'labour power'), whether they be bricklayers or bank clerks. An employee's status as a salaried or office worker was irrelevant — non-ownership of sufficient means of production to be able to live without working was what was always judged to be of central importance.

The SPGB's conception of class clearly had its origins in the two-class model adopted by Marx and elaborated in the *Communist Manifesto*. Marx, of course, used the term 'class' in a number of ways, even on occasions referring to the "middle classes"[24] but this usage has never been acceptable to the SPGB. As it has evolved, the SPGB has recognised differences in income and lifestyle among the working class but has never seen them as important — the Party in modern times scoffs at the academic sociologists who identify more social classes than there are days of the week. In recent years the SPGB has been almost alone in sticking to the two-class model identified by Marx and even in its early years this view of class was not extensively held outside the Party (though significantly, the SLP also held to it). When Marx himself used terms such as the 'middle class' or 'lower middle classes', it invariably reflected the particular need to identify a section of the proletariat for the purpose of the analysis in hand. In Marx's political writings the two-class model was frequently adhered to, else use was employed of a three-class model consisting of landlords, capitalists and proletarians — indeed, it was this model that was discussed briefly at the end of Volume III of *Capital*. This class scheme is little different in reality from the straightforward division between bourgeoisie and proletariat, especially in developed capitalism.

The SPGB never sought to identify the landowners in capitalism as a separate class, but as a section of the capitalist class becoming less and less distinct from the traditional bourgeoisie. At the time when the Declaration of Principles was formulated, the landowners had become just as much a part of the same "master class" as the industrial capitalists who had been slowly wresting political power from them in the seventeenth, eighteenth and nineteenth centuries. For the SPGB, the aristocracy was not toppled, but integrated into the ranks of this one class enemy, and this is reflected in the wording of Principle Number One.

Implicit in the Declaration of Principles is the Marxian theory of surplus value — the idea that the working class collectively produces all the wealth of society and is exploited in order to keep this parasitical minority, the master class, in a position of privilege. The working class is the class which "produces but does not possess", to cite Principle Number Two. Not owning any means for producing and distributing wealth, the working class is forced to sell its mental and physical energies for wages and salaries, the value of which is less than the total value of the wealth created by the workers and received by the capitalists. Again from the outset, the SPGB judged capitalism to be a system of 'legalised robbery', in which the working class is compelled through the operation of the wages system to hand over the products of its collective labour for wages and salaries that are (usually) enough to keep the workers and their families in a fit condition; the unpaid labour (surplus value) given by the workers being the source of the rent, interest and profit of the capitalist class.

Like Marx, the SPGB argued that the vast bulk of social wealth under capitalism takes the form of commodities — that is, articles produced for exchange on a market with a view to profit. These articles of wealth are generally produced and distributed from start to finish by the working class, hence the SPGB's often used statement that the working class runs society "from top to bottom". Following Engels in *Socialism: Utopian and Scientific*, the SPGB contended that the initial technical role that the early capitalists played in the industrial process no longer existed to any real degree in the twentieth century and that their inventive and administrative functions were taken over by salaried employees. The Party, however, has always been quick to point out since that this does not exempt such salaried officials from exploitation. 'Unproductive' workers like accountants and insurance salesmen are also exploited according to the SPGB, and most certainly constitute a part of the working class, giving unpaid labour to their employers. Indeed, it is their unpaid labour which transfers a part of the surplus value produced in the productive sector of the economy to their employer.[25]

The status accorded the working class by the SPGB is important as much of the early propaganda work of impossibilist groups like the SPGB and SLP was aimed at showing the working class how it was enslaved by capitalism, and at demonstrating to the workers the mechanics of their own exploitation. Both the SPGB and SLP built up a fine reputation for their knowledge and exposition of Marxian economics, and this was certainly one aspect of the SPGB's propaganda that the SLP and others were reluctant to criticise.[26]

The SPGB took the view that so long as wage slavery endured, capitalism itself would still exist. The aim of the Party, as stated in the Declaration of Principles, was declared to be the abolition of the antagonism at the heart of society which results from the class division between the capitalists and workers. This can only be accomplished according to Principle Number Three by converting the means of production and distribution into common property. It is noticeable that the Party's Object does not tell us much else about the proposed nature of socialist society, and the Declaration of Principles seems to tell us little that is specific, being more concerned with describing the nature of capitalist society than the proposed new social system. This reflected the desire of the SPGB founder members not to "write recipes for the cook-books of the future", and also demonstrates that the overwhelming emphasis of SPGB propaganda lay, at least in the early years, in exposing the evils of capitalism rather than promoting the Party's positive alternative to it.

While the SPGB's Object and Declaration of Principles does not give a definition of socialism that sounds remarkably different from that given by other organisations of the time, closer examination reveals important differences. Firstly, the Object refers to socialism being a "system of society", in the same sense as capitalism and feudalism, having a distinct organisational framework for the production and distribution of wealth. Elsewhere the SPGB tells us that "a system of society alludes to the sum total of human relationships"[27] and it is clear from this that socialism is not seen by the Party as an island within a sea of capitalism. On the contrary, socialism "is a system in which the means for producing and distributing wealth will be owned by society as a whole"[28] — and by this the SPGB has always meant world society. The founders of the SPGB saw clearly that as capitalism and the division of labour are a world-wide phenomena, socialism could not exist on a national basis, let alone as a small group of co-operatives operating within the capitalist system.

A further important difference since its foundation between the SPGB and most other political organisations on the issue of socialism has been in its use of phrases such as "common ownership of the means of production and distribution". It is tempting to say that there is something missing at the end of this phrase, but the SPGB has always been quite deliberate in its omission. Indeed, one of the most obvious reasons for the unsoundness of organisations like the ILP in the eyes of the SPGB was their talk of "common ownership of the means of production, distribution and *exchange*". The ILP had been formed by a group of radicals who were unhappy with the narrow appeal of the SDF (they were more 'possibilist' than the possibilists) and in 1893 had declared in favour of a "State of Society in which Land and Capital are commonly owned, and the processes of production, distribution and exchange are social functions". To the SPGB this was dangerous, unsound nonsense.[29] Their readings of Marx taught them that there could be no capital in a socialist society as the widespread existence of capital — a sum of values invested in the means of production in order to create further value — was another distinguishing feature of capitalism.[30] Nor could exchange be a social function of a society of common ownership as to the SPGB there was little point in exchanging something if you already owned it. Exchange, for the SPGB as again for Marx, was seen to be a hallmark of private property society, with socialism entailing the "communistic abolition of buying and selling".[31]

If socialism was envisaged to be a society without capital, the SPGB was clear that there could be no wage labour either. So long as there was wage labour there would be a working class that was exploited through the operation of the wages system, giving surplus value to the capitalists. In socialism, work would be given freely and co-operatively. However, it would not be fair or accurate to say that the abolition of the wages system was a concept unique to the SPGB. The various Social Democratic parties of Europe were committed to it, at least on paper, and in 1893 the SDF and Fabian Society had published a joint *Manifesto of English Socialists* which declared:

We look to put an end for ever to the wages system, to sweep away all distinctions of class, and eventually to establish national and international communism on a sound basis.[32]

Where the SPGB differed from most of the other political groups of the time was in seeing the abolition of the wages system, capital and money as integral to socialism. The SDF, ILP and Fabians all saw these things as desirable ends, but this did not stop them presenting nationalisation and reforms in the meantime as 'socialist' measures. The SPGB presented its vision of socialism as the immediate solution to the problems faced by the working class, and shunned reforms and 'tinkering'.

The SPGB's conception of socialism is clearly Marxian, and like Marx and Engels, the party has never at any time sought to make a distinction between socialism and communism, using the words interchangeably to mean common (or social) ownership of the means of living. And with the abolition of class differences and antagonisms, the SPGB — again like Marx and Engels — has seen no place for the state in a socialist society. As will be demonstrated in Chapter 3, the SPGB has also rejected any notion of a 'workers' state' or a 'transitional society' between capitalism and socialism — regarding such ideas as outdated nineteenth century concepts that do not take into account the development of the forces of production under capitalism and the elimination of natural scarcity. From its inception the SPGB argued that the scarcity caused by capitalism with its profit priority was not a reflection of a lack of productive capability in the world,[33] though this has also led it to argue that full socialism was not an immediate possibility when Marx and Engels were writing about the spectre of communism haunting Europe. For instance, the SPGB has stated that the series of measures advocated in the *Communist Manifesto* to "increase the total productive forces as rapidly as possible" are now irrelevant, saying that "we are convinced that political and economic development since their day would have caused Marx and Engels to reconsider their attitude on this question".[34] Indeed, this is the reason why the SPGB has recognised that the reform measures advocated by Marx and Engels may have been applicable in their day, but are no longer.

As the SPGB has developed its thinking about the nature of socialism, it has contended that in the early years of socialism full 'free access' to goods and services may not be possible, requiring a self-imposed system of rationing.[35] It has not considered that this situation would last for any great length of time as it believes that socialism would be able to increase production rapidly when freed from the constraints and wastage of the profit system. Labour-time vouchers, advocated by both Marx and the impossibilists of the SLP, were rejected as unnecessary and impractical by the SPGB at an early stage.[36]

Ever since 1904 the SPGB has viewed socialism as a world-wide moneyless, wageless, classless (and therefore stateless) society of common ownership, democratic control and free access to wealth. Capitalism and socialism have been seen as mutually exclusive systems, and it is precisely because of this that one of the Party's notable objections to reformism arose.

Reformism

The idea that capitalism can be humanised and changed by a series of reform measures is almost as old as the capitalist system itself, but it was the attempt by the parties affiliated to the Second International to assert the primacy of reform measures as 'stepping stones' to socialism that really brought the epithet 'reformism' into the political vocabulary. Moreover, it was the undoubted success of this attempt to promote reform programmes which led to splits in Social Democratic parties throughout Europe and North America. The SPGB itself washed its hands of the Second International in 1904 after two of its delegates reported back from the Amsterdam Congress with tales of reformism and organisational chaos. During the Congress the SPGB had sent a telegram calling on all those present to take "an intransigent stand against revisionism"[37] but its delegates, Jack Kent and Alex Pearson, could not get the SPGB opposition to reformism and revisionism across, and from that moment on the SPGB opinion of the parties of the Second International steadily declined.

The earlier opposition of the Socialist League in Britain to reforms has already been noted, and the SPGB took an equally hard-line position. As capitalism was the root cause of the social problems confronting the working class, only its overthrow would do — "Socialism and nothing but" became one of the Party's slogans. Indeed, such was the SPGB's hostility to reform activity that the distinction between opposing reformism and the reforms themselves often became blurred in early Party literature.[38] But the essential position developed by the SPGB was that the Party opposed the political advocacy of reforms in order to gain a position of power or influence so that capitalism could be palliated, or socialism enacted "through the back door". This was what lay behind the thinking of Clause Seven of the Declaration of Principles, the famous 'hostility clause', which declares the SPGB "hostile to every other party". As all the other parties had some form of reform programme designed to patch up the social ills of capitalism rather than remove their cause, from an SPGB perspective they had to be opposed.

Throughout its political life the SPGB has advanced a number of reasons for its opposition to reformism, including the belief that no series of reforms can alter the fundamental nature of capitalist society. At root, the SPGB has seen reform activity as being ultimately of more benefit to the capitalists than the workers (in its early years the Party even showed scepticism regarding the possibility of workers' being able to significantly increase their real wages through trade union action).[39] The SPGB has never viewed governments as 'neutral' bodies consciously attempting to act in the interests of the great majority in society, but instead as the guiders and manipulators of the capitalist state attempting to create the best possible conditions for the functioning of the profit system. To the SPGB, reform measures are judged in this light by governments and any possible benefit for wage and salary earners will generally be an incidental rather than central consideration for "the executive committee of the capitalist class". By way of example, the early members of the SPGB saw the SDF's willingness to co-operate with the Liberal Party — then largely representing the industrial sectors of the capitalist class — as the gravest error.[40] As a party of open support for capitalism, the Liberals, so the SPGB contended, would only be interested in those measures designed to strengthen and maintain the capitalist system, and to promote the interests of the section of the capitalist class they represented.

The Marxian theory of wages has also played a major role in moulding the SPGB's view of the efficacy of reform measures and attempts to better the conditions of the working class within capitalism. This theory claims that at any one moment in time the accumulation of capital forms an upper barrier or limit which no increase in the price of labour power can break through. Furthermore, as capital accumulates, and though the absolute level of wages may increase within the parameters capitalism itself imposes, the workers tend to get back a smaller part of the value they produce in the productive process, there being a tendency towards an increase in the rate of exploitation of the working class. Until the 1930s, the SPGB, like many other parties heavily influenced by Marxian economics, took a rather doom laden view of the absolute impoverishment of the workers (see Chapter 4). This impoverishment was allegedly caused by capitalism driving down the price of labour power ever nearer to its lowest limits. While in its early years it seemed too willing to uncritically accept this highly mechanistic argument — largely derived from some of Marx's earlier and rather more prosaic writings — the SPGB could at least claim that it was always clear, in a way the SDF and others never were, of the overall limitations placed by capitalism on reform activity designed to improve the lot of the workers.

Certainly, the fundamental basis of the SPGB's opposition to reformism has remained intact throughout decades of reform activity and its opposition to reform campaigning today lies on the same basis as its opposition to the reform proposals of the Liberals, Fabians, and others at the beginning of the century. One of the SPGB's more recent pamphlets outlined some salient points to be taken on board by those groups and parties determined to engage in reformism:

1) Their campaign, whether directed at a 'right-wing' or a 'left-wing' government, can only hope to succeed if it can be reconciled with the profit-making needs of the system;
2) The measure they have supported, even if implemented, may well have consequences they did not foresee and would not have wanted;
3) Any reform can be reversed and eroded later if a government finds it necessary;
4) Any number of reforms bearing on a problem rarely, if ever, actually solve that problem.[41]

The SPGB has stated that the history of capitalism in Britain and other countries demonstrates the essential validity of this position, with the major social problems of the early twentieth century still around decades later despite the fact that many, if not most, of the social reforms advocated by the Liberals and the Fabians have long been enacted. What is more, the SPGB has since claimed that new and unforeseen social problems have arisen alongside the old ones, bidding for the attention of new generations of reformers. Radical attempts — such as in Russia — to remove apparent capitalist problems like unemployment and poverty through state planning have created more problems than they have actually solved, so interfering with the capital accumulation process as to jeopardise the system's long term survival.[42] To the SPGB, piecemeal reform measures with the best chance of ordinarily being implemented have been those most readily harmonised with the capital accumulation process that is the driving force of the capitalist mode of production. Such reforms, however, are generally those measures of least use to the workers, particularly in the social and economic fields.

From 1904 to the present day the SPGB has reserved a special hostility for those parties that have advocated reforms in the name of socialism — initially the Fabians, the ILP and the SDF, and then later the Labour Party itself. These parties were the organisations in Britain which took social democracy down the road to reformism. As has been seen, the idea that reform measures could act as 'stepping stones' to socialism was at the heart of the 'reform or revolution' debate and from the outset the SPGB was firmly in the camp of the revolutionaries. Its attacks on reform parties became particularly bitter because of its feeling of isolation within the wider working class movement. It felt deserted by former comrades in Britain and any willingness on its part to co-operate with those organisations in other countries that shared some of its viewpoints was short-lived. At the aforementioned August 1904 Congress of the Second International in Amsterdam, the Party's representatives were not only shocked by the reformist tendencies of other delegates but were unnerved by the presence of the ILP, SDF, Fabians and Labour Representation Committee from Britain — all of whom the Party had declared its hostility to.[43]

The success of the reformers in gaining a stranglehold on the Second International, and the effect of this on the SPGB, cannot be over-emphasised. The advocates of the 'maximum programme' were a tiny minority, and organisations like the SPGB and SLP appeared to be insignificant and sectarian grouplets on the fringes of the movement. This situation only served to harden the SPGB's attitude, and since that time the Party has only allied itself with those organisations in other countries that have been prepared to accept its own Object and Declaration of Principles.[44] In its early years the Party attacked the reformist drift of the German Social Democratic Party of Kautsky and Bernstein just as the impossibilist SLP had done — identifying the Erfurt Programme of 1891 as the quintessential reformist muddle, peddling the idea that the party of the working class should struggle in present society for a series of reforms including a change in the system of taxation. The Erfurt Programme was widely translated and used as a model by Social Democratic parties outside Germany, and the SPGB was later to identify it as the major programmatic basis for the reformism that was to grip the entire Second International, saying that "an examination of this programme will reveal the disappearance of all pretence to revolutionary action and an understanding of why the Social Democratic Party lost their way in the bog of reform".[45] The SPGB argued that while the parties of the Second International still mouthed the slogans of the working class, their political practice moved away from propaganda for socialism and entirely towards ensuring the implementation of their reform programmes, by whatever means available. This was, in turn, a reflection of their belief that the working class could never achieve the mass socialist consciousness the SPGB said was necessary for the revolutionary overthrow of capitalism.

The SPGB's specific objections to the reformism of the Second International were twofold. Firstly, it was argued that the reforms advocated by the German SPD (and in Britain by groups like the SDF) would not mean a move nearer the realisation of socialism. According to the SPGB, what the Social Democratic parties were doing was advocating reforms that were in no way incompatible with the existence of capitalism. This had especially been so of the Erfurt Programme. Its proposed reform measures were primarily intended to undermine the foundations of imperial rule in Germany. When the Kaiser abdicated in 1918, capitalism remained intact, as it has done in the years since despite the implementation of a great many of the SPD's initial reform demands. To the SPGB, Bernstein's idea that capitalism could be turned into socialism via reform measures was symptomatic of the confusion of Social Democracy at this time, and a concession to the gradualism of the British Fabians with their well-known views about state ownership and 'municipal socialism'. In response to such ideas, the SPGB contended that reform activity would only serve to bolster the capitalist system and that schemes of 'municipal socialism' were really aiming at municipal capitalism, where the wage labour/capital antagonism and all the other central features of capitalism would still exist.[46] Indeed, the impossibilists who formed the SPGB and SLP had long denounced the 'gas-and-water socialism' of the Fabians and one of the earliest editions of the *Socialist Standard* had proclaimed that "the Fabian Society is not a working class organisation and stands for state capitalism",[47] probably one of the earliest ever usages of the term, certainly in Britain.

The second reason the SPGB opposed the Second International's reformism was because parties with reform programmes would attract the support of people who wished to ameliorate the capitalist system, rather than overthrow it. This was precisely the case with the German SPD, which became the largest political party in Germany on the basis of its reform programme. Those elements within the SPD agreeing with its ultimate aim of socialism were swamped by reformers, or themselves came to put reforms at the head of the political agenda before socialism. The SPGB resolved that this could never be the way forward for a genuinely socialist party, and has since expounded its position on this time and again:

> As Socialism can only be set up when a majority of workers understand and want it, a socialist party must build up support for this aim alone. Support gained on any other basis is quite useless, even harmful.[48]

While this comment was distinctive enough, the SPGB was certainly not alone in recognising the dangers of a supposedly working-class party seeking support on the basis of social reforms. The following passage from Rosa Luxemburg's *Reform or Revolution* shows that the SPGB position had its echoes abroad:

> What will be the immediate result should our party change its general procedure to suit a viewpoint that wants to emphasise the practical results of our struggle, that is, social reforms? As soon as 'immediate results' become the principal aim of our activity, the clear-cut, irreconcilable point of view, which has meaning only insofar as it proposes to win power, will be found more and more inconvenient. The direct consequence of this will be the adoption by the party of a 'policy of compensation', a policy of political trading, and an attitude of diffident, diplomatic conciliation. But this attitude cannot continue for a long time. Since the social reforms can only offer an empty promise, the logical consequence of such a programme must necessarily be disillusionment.[49]

This was precisely the position taken by the SPGB. In the era in which capitalism has ceased to be an historically useful social system, and where socialism has become an historic possibility, reform activity becomes a dangerous diversion for the working class, taking time and energy away from the task of achieving the fundamental social transformation. Once a political party is in the grip of reformists, the ultimate aim of socialism becomes merely a paper promise. To the SPGB and those who took a similar stand on the question of reformist activity, socialism itself was ultimately the only goal worth fighting for.

The Conquest of Political Power: the Nature of Revolution

The number of revolutionaries opposing reform activity may have been small, but they were far from united. This was not because they disagreed about the nature of socialism, or even disagreed about methods of socialist propaganda. The real disagreement lay over exactly how socialism could be achieved. Most of the organisations taking a principled stand against reformism were opposed to socialists entering parliament, and even, in some cases, to standing in elections at all. This was as much the case before the days of the Second International as during it; the Socialist League in Britain took a very sceptical attitude towards parliament and elections, which eventually degenerated into a full-blooded anti-parliamentarism once the League had been taken over by anarchists. The League's advice to the working class was "do not vote at all",[50] although William Morris stated that he did not object to socialists standing for and entering parliament so long as it was understood that they went there as rebels and not as collaborators. This kind of disdain for parliament and electoral activity was common on the continent of Europe and in North America and laid the basis for the vanguardism promoted by Lenin's Bolsheviks that was eventually to infect organisations like the British SLP.

The Socialist League — which never had any pretensions to be a vanguard or anything of the sort — opposed parliamentary activity largely because of its tendency to associate parliament and electioneering with reformism. It saw parliament as the talking-shop of the capitalist class and therefore as the supreme centre of reform activity. The idea that parliament could have any real function in the revolutionary process was dismissed because of its association with palliative legislation and reform activity. In the view of the Socialist League, parliament existed to tinker with the system, not end it, and only the action of a conscious majority of socialists working outside of parliament and elections could establish socialism. Interestingly, when elements within the Socialist League (including Morris) began to look more favourably at the need for a reform programme towards the end of the 1880s, they began to drop their anti-parliamentary stance, thereby serving to reinforce the link between parliament and reformism in the eyes of the rest of the membership. Morris and the others who were eventually prepared to use parliament and advocate some reforms left the Socialist League altogether to co-operate with the ILP, SDF and Fabians.[51]

The insurrectionary tactics favoured by the Socialist League and other groups across the world hostile to reformism never found favour in the SPGB. From the outset, the SPGB saw such ideas as dangerous and mistaken, reflecting what it considered to be a misunderstanding of the nature of the power of the capitalist class. The position taken by the SPGB was unique, and it is from Principle Number Five onwards, where the Party outlines its conception of the socialist revolution, that the SPGB Declaration of Principles is so obviously distinguishable from statements made by other organisations.

The SPGB viewed the state, to use the Guesdist Gabriel Deville's phrase, as the "public power of coercion", arising out of the division of society into classes. Like the conventional social democratic parties it took the view that in developed capitalism the parliamentary system had generally emerged as the most effective way of ensuring the domination of the capitalist class in society, making laws and providing for their enforcement. As such, parliament was seen by the SPGB as the centre of power and the government its executive council, managing the affairs of the various arms of the state machine. The class monopoly of the capitalists was therefore thought to be maintained through parliament, government and their control of the state apparatus, and the final word on setting the coercive apparatus of the state machine into motion rested with the cabinet, backed up by a parliamentary majority.[52]

For the SPGB, the achievement of socialism depended on a majority of conscious socialists organising politically to attain it. With the state machine controlled by the representatives of the ruling class any attempt to take political power by meeting the might of the armed forces head on would be disastrous in an advanced capitalist country. Instead, decisive control of the state would have to be won politically by the working class so that the machinery of government and the coercive apparatus of the state could be "converted from an instrument of oppression into the agent of emancipation". This passage from the Declaration of Principles closely resembles a phrase used by Marx himself in the preamble to the 1880 programme of the Guesdist 'Federation of the Party of Socialist Workers in France', where it was stated that socialism "must be pursued by all the means which the proletariat has at its disposal, including universal suffrage, thus transformed from the instrument of trickery which it has been till now into an instrument of emancipation."[53]

It is certainly the case that the capitalist class had long seen the need to delegate functions to elected bodies,[54] and that ever since the 1880s, the working class possessed the numerical strength to out-vote the capitalists at elections. The SPGB developed the argument that the working class persistently wastes its collective power at the ballot box by continuing to vote in Members of Parliament and governments belonging to the various pro-capitalist political parties who are out to reform the system but do nothing more. In doing this the workers hand decisive control of the state machine over to the capitalists who use it to safeguard their private property and ownership of the means of living. The SPGB judged it to be of vital importance that the working class should stop handing over this power to its class enemy, and instead vote socialist delegates into parliaments (across as much of the world as possible) with the sole mandate of dispossessing the capitalist class and abolishing capitalism. Following this, "the state, with its coercive machinery will be dismantled as its function — the custodian of private property — will have disappeared. New social institutions of administration based on the new social conditions will be democratically formed."[55] In this scenario, the social revolution is carried out democratically by the majority of society, as peacefully as possible, even though the SPGB maintained from the outset that force would have to be used against any undemocratic minority which opposed the will of the mass of socialists and tried to restore capitalism.

It is indisputable that those who have agreed with the SPGB's aim of socialism and its hostility to reform programmes have been foremost in attacking its conception of socialist revolution. It has been argued by anti-parliamentary socialists, for instance, that if the socialist movement grew to the extent that socialism looked likely, then the capitalist class would simply take the vote away from the workers and suspend parliament. The response of the SPGB has been that such an action would be of no long-term benefit to the capitalists and would in fact undermine the basis of their rule — "circumstances have compelled the masters to place administration in the hands of elected bodies. If they withdraw it they will bring their house down about their ears . . . the State machine would be unable to function, owing to the conflicting views among civil and military employees of the Government."[56] As such it is unlikely that there would be much assent to this even among all those who still opposed socialism, as it would serve to stifle their democratic rights too. However, it is probably fair to say that this argument carries more weight in the present era of collapsed dictatorships than it did previously during periods when authoritarianism was rampant.

Another objection to the SPGB conception of revolution has come from those who are unable to agree that the capitalist class could be dispossessed, the world over, in virtually one stroke. The SPGB has responded to this by saying that it is inconceivable to think that given the triumph of capitalism as a world system, eventually turning the world by the advent of mass communications into a 'global village', the socialist movement would only be a mass force in one country. Any suggestion that socialism could be set up in one country is indicative of muddled thinking to the SPGB, and the Party is fond of quoting Marx in support of its case:

> Empirically, communism is only possible as the act of the dominant people 'all at once' and simultaneously, which presupposes the universal development of the productive forces and the world intercourse bound up with communism.[57]

The SPGB position has always been that the socialist revolution must be the conscious act of the world working class electing socialist delegates to parliaments and congresses across the globe with the mandate of dispossessing the owning class and replacing private ownership of the means of living with common ownership. The democratic conquest of the state machine (or, to use Marx's phrase, winning the "battle of democracy") takes away the power base of the capitalist class, removes their claims to democratic legitimacy and ensures that they cannot use the coercive apparatus of the state machine against the socialist movement. Indeed, just as it is envisaged that the growth of the socialist movement will not be confined to one country, the SPGB has argued that it will not be confined to some sections of the working class only — the "workers in uniform" of the police and armed forces are as capable of coming over to the side of the socialist movement as anyone else, it has stated.[58]

At the time of the SPGB's foundation and since, many have seen the Party's conception of revolution with its emphasis on the need for a mass socialist consciousness among the working class, as slow and laborious, and have instead looked towards 'short cuts' to socialism based on minority action. To the SPGB this too has been indicative of a lack of theoretical clarity:

> Minority action is suicidal folly and could not lead to socialism even if successful. For unless the immense majority of the workers want Socialism there is no possibility of it being established. Even if an insurrectionist minority managed to get control of political power, it could not alter the basic problems and processes of capitalism. It would have to contend with the anti-socialist prejudices of the majority and it might be overthrown in another insurrection.[59]

As will be seen in Chapter 3, the SPGB often re-affirms the correctness of its own strategy for revolution when it examines the failed strategies of those who have tried to take a different route. The Party has not of course been successful in achieving socialism either, but it argues that the correctness of its position, combined with the contradictions inherent in the capitalist mode of production will mean that its time will come. The SPGB has certainly been able to demonstrate — on a theoretical if not yet a practical level — that the problem of reform or revolution need not be an endless one, as it is possible for a socialist party to reject the advocacy of reform measures while recognising that political democracy under capitalism can be used for revolutionary ends. As such, the SPGB's political strategy can best be described as 'revolutionary social democracy'. The credibility (or otherwise) of this revolutionary strategy is briefly discussed in the Conclusion.

Challenges to the SPGB's Revolutionary Theory

The idea that the revolutionary party should aim at the democratic conquest of the state machine in order to dispossess the capitalist class did not go unquestioned in the SPGB's early years, including from elements within the organisation itself. Ostensibly the main challenge to its position came from those who saw the Party's revolutionary strategy as being based on a fundamental misunderstanding of the materialist conception of history. To the SPGB's critics, the power of the capitalist class was essentially economic, rather than political, and a strategy based on attaining political power alone to establish socialism was insufficient — what was needed was a recognition that the capitalist class would not allow a majority of socialists to take power unless they could enforce this at an economic level by taking over industry, if necessary to 'lock-out' the capitalists.

Those who took this line against the SPGB saw 'industrial unionism' as the way forward. Emanating from the American SLP under Daniel De Leon, socialist industrial unionism was based on the idea that socialist economic organisations were needed alongside a revolutionary party to rival the existing trade unions. Once the socialist movement was ready to take power, the socialist trade unions would unite into one big industrial organisation which would take economic power as the socialist party democratically took the reins of political power.

The views of the impossibilist American SLP undoubtedly had an influence on both the SPGB and the British SLP.[60] However, the SLP in Britain differed from its American counterpart on a number of issues and was not industrial unionist at its foundation in 1903, preferring, as has been noted, and despite its impossibilist background, a political strategy linked to a reform programme.[61] In the sense that its strategy laid emphasis on the capture of political power for socialism it was similar to that of the SPGB, and one early writer in *The Socialist* even went so far as to suggest that it could "be an act of criminal sectarianism to oppose a union of forces" between the two parties.[62] This attitude to revolution was short-lived, however, and under the influence of its American counterpart the SLP soon adopted industrial unionism. Its key 'Manifesto of the SLP on Trade Unionism' stated:

> If the working class tries to carry through the revolution without a force to counteract the power of the army they will be inviting bloodshed and disaster for themselves ... this force cannot be got by military organisation, and we claim that the Industrial Union alone supplies it.[63]

Only two years after the foundation of the SPGB it became clear that the SLP were not the only ones taking this view — a significant proportion of the SPGB membership did also, and this was to provoke a crisis which almost split the Party in two before it really had chance to make any political headway.[64] The Bexley Heath branch of the SPGB wanted the Party's Executive Committee to approach the SLP with a view to union and one of the Party's founder members, E. J. B. Allen, wrote an article in the *Socialist Standard* called 'Boring From Within' which stated:

We Socialists want to see industrial unionism, that is, we want to see all the workers in each trade organised, and the various trades in each industry affiliated, thus forming one huge, cohesive organisation of the workers.[65]

Although further articles on this line were rejected on the grounds that they merely emphasised industrial organisation and support for the American Industrial Workers' of the World rather than possible future socialist economic organisation, the SPGB actually came remarkably close to supporting the ideas of socialist industrial unionism. A motion at its 1906 Conference on these lines was only defeated by 111 votes to 81. In the eventuality, the SPGB did not entirely reject economic organisation for socialism, even if it primarily emphasised the need to capture political power. Indeed, the SPGB's disagreements with the followers of Daniel De Leon were not so much about the necessity for an economic organisation alongside the revolutionary socialist party — they were more about matters of tactics.

Mindful of the revolutionary shortcomings of the IWW, the SPGB opposed the setting up of an industrial organisation of the workers if it was to contain non-socialists. However, the main dispute concerned the effectiveness of a specifically socialist economic organisation. The SPGB maintained that when the socialist party began to achieve mass support then an economic organisation solely comprising socialists could be formed to pursue the class struggle on the wages front, and eventually to assist in the task of reorganising production on a socialist basis. Until then, a socialist industrial union would only be as large as the socialist political movement, at that time not large enough to make such an economic organisation a viable proposition.[66] The SPGB therefore resolved (after a prolonged dispute centring on the efficacy of trade union action itself) to work within the 'pure and simple' trade unions, advising its members and supporters to expose the unions' acceptance of capitalism and their commitment to reformism.

It was noted in the SPGB that De Leon and the American SLP talked keenly of 'socialist industrial government', and this was a further aspect of industrial unionism as it was imported from the United States that the majority of SPGB members had difficulty in accepting. They felt, perhaps not unreasonably, that to make the industrial union the basis of future socialist society would be to carry into socialism the sectional divisions imposed on workers by capitalism. Eventually, such arguments won the day. The early advocates of industrial unionism in the SPGB either left the Party in disagreement or accepted the majority viewpoint and stayed within it. A fair number of those who had initially been in disagreement came to the conclusion that the Party had been correct all along and that the class rule of the capitalists existed not because of their economic power but because of their control of the political apparatus and the state machine. The kernel of the SPGB argument was this: while the capitalists played a key technical role in the capitalist system's ascendancy, this role had long since disappeared, and capitalism was operated almost in its entirety by wage and salary workers. The capitalist class had come to attain political power because of the essential role it had played as an economic force in earlier capitalist history, but by the time capitalism had raised the forces of production to the level at which socialism became an historic possibility, it was most definitely the political power of the capitalists that ensured their economic domination, rather than the other way around. The development of the forces of production made the capitalist class economically redundant and socially useless, and their control of the means of production now rested on their political control and domination. In any great test of economic strength, such as a mass strike, the capitalist class would be able to win — as it had in the past — because of its control of political power and its domination of the state machine. This meant that although a predominantly socialist working class would need to be organised both politically and industrially, the political organisation and action would be of prime importance when it came to the abolition of the class rule of the capitalists.[67]

As a challenge to the SPGB's view of the mechanics of social revolution, industrial unionism faded away just as it did from the political scene generally, but in the Party's early years another controversy arose, this time concerning parliament and reforms. The basis of this controversy was the dogmatic belief of some members of the SPGB that virtually nothing in the capitalist world could be approved of by socialists, let alone any type of reform. The possibility that the SPGB could distinguish between opposition to reformism and individual reforms was not to their liking, and so in the February 1910 issue of the *Socialist Standard*, a letter from a correspondent called 'W. B. of Upton Park' appeared with the question "what would be the attitude of a member of the SPGB if elected to Parliament, and how would he maintain a principle of 'No Compromise'?". The *Standard's* editors, in a non-committal reply backed by the Executive Committee, stated that this question could not at the time be answered with any degree of certainty, and that the response to each new situation would have to be decided upon democratically, and with regard paid to the merits of each case. This reply, along with a subsequent debate and vote at Party Conference, did not find favour with the small recalcitrant group that had raised the issue. They soon formed themselves into a 'Provisional Committee' and sent out an "Open Letter to the Members of the Socialist Party of Great Britain" which called for the reply in the *Socialist Standard* to be recinded. The Open Letter again raised the question of the actions of an SPGB Member of Parliament once elected, and set out the case of the 'Provisional Committee' as follows:

> We deny altogether that a member of a our Party is elected to Parliament for the purpose of taking part in any kind of legislation, whether by voting for or against it ... To us it is clear that all capitalist legislation is enacted for the purpose of keeping the capitalist system run smoothly in harmony with the economic development and the fact that the capitalist class in pursuance of

such legislation are compelled to dig their own graves is certainly no reason for our supporting them through their measures and thereby admitting that at least at times they can become benefactors of the working class... If it is absurd to talk about suspending the class war it must be equally absurd to insist that there can be a suspension of hostility to the capitalist class by supporting some of their measures.

The Provisional Committee argued that rises in wages were ultimately detrimental to the working class interest as they had the effect of sapping working class discontent and thereby delayed the social revolution. Indeed, according to the Committee, no measure emanating from the capitalist class or their parties could be supported, even one to stop a war. Support for any of the measures brought forward by capitalist parties would not only bolster the capitalist class as a whole, but could lead to the defeat of a government, or the keeping of another one in office. They felt this to be quite intolerable from the working class point of view.

The Executive Committee's reply to the Committee was scathing in its attack on their Open Letter.[68] The SPGB, it said, supported the interests of the working class as a whole and this necessitated supporting those measures which genuinely benefited the working class (and, indeed, supporting the efforts of trade unionism to resist attacks on working class living standards). As for the question of supporting capitalist legislation to stop a war, the reply said that "the declaration of principles shows that the Party is the expression of the material interest of the working class. Further, the attainment of Socialism is dependent on the preservation of the workers in general".

The rebels of the 'Provisional Committee', disgusted with what they took to be the Party's rejection of the principle of 'No Compromise', and its 'reformism', eventually left the SPGB in late 1911. Some later rejoined, but a group around Henry Martin, who had been one of the instigators of the whole affair, left to form a new organisation called the Socialist Propaganda League which survived as a small group until after the Second World War. The Socialist Propaganda League, in fact, represented the first organisational 'split' from the SPGB and it went on to persistently attack the Party in public from the outdoor platform, in pamphlets and in letters to the *Socialist Standard*. Enquirers to the Party's journal continued to ask of its attitude to the reforms brought forward by capitalist parties, and there would always be a measured response, carefully putting the official position; the following reply from the 1930s is as explicit as any answer given:

> While the SPGB is opposed to a reformist policy the socialist delegate in Parliament or on a local council is not, therefore, bound to vote against every particular measure ... [we] do not hold that the measures taken or to be taken by the capitalists are all of them bound to be useless or harmful to the workers, or bound to impede progress towards socialism. Some of the suffrage, factory and trade union legislation in the past, while assisting capitalists immediately or in

the long run, has not been correspondingly harmful to the workers ... a socialist minority in Parliament or on a local council would be required by the socialists who sent them there to criticise from the socialist standpoint all measures brought before them (pointing out their futility in comparison with socialism and so forth), and to refrain from supporting, bargaining or allying themselves with any party for temporary ends, but at the same time would be required to vote for particular measures where there is a clear gain to the workers and the socialist movement in so doing. (The decision, of course, would be in the hands of the Party and not the individual.)[69]

Measures which could directly benefit the socialist movement such as the enfranchisement of the working class would therefore be supported (a modern example would perhaps be the abolition of the electoral deposit, which discriminates against smaller parties). Also, measures designed to alleviate a working class grievance would be considered on their merits.

Though the Socialist Propaganda League predicted the descent of the SPGB into reformism, this prediction was not fulfilled and the Party's position on reforms has never substantially changed from that outlined above. As the SPGB has remained small in size compared to the major political parties, the question of the attitude of socialists MPs to reform legislation was in any case rather premature and not entirely set in its correct context, for the SPGB has maintained that as the socialist movement grows, then the concessions made by the capitalist class in terms of social reforms will increase greatly in an attempt to 'buy off' the workers movement. Opposition to all and every reform in such circumstances, when real gains might be made by the working class prior to the establishment of socialism, would most likely be counterproductive and only alienate the socialist party from the working class whose interests it seeks to further.

The SPGB continues to maintain a hostility to reformism — and the parties that advocate it — rather than individual reforms, and this hostility has never been compromised in the Party's history.[70] Its overriding concern remains the dissemination and propagation of socialist ideas, in the hope that this will help the workers achieve socialist consciousness, thereby bringing about a democratic social revolution in the material interests of the majority class in society. Once political power has been captured by the socialist movement in Britain and other countries, the task of the SPGB will be at an end. As the SPGB sees no role for the state or government in a socialist society, and as political parties are "but the expression of class interests", the SPGB therefore stands as one of the few political parties in the world to have its own non-existence as a prime objective.

Notes

1. The programme of reform measures adopted by the SDF included demands for free, universal education for children, the provision of old-age pensions, the introduction of a heavily graduated system of income tax, and an eight hour day for workers. These demands were intended to "allieviate the evils of existing society". Expressly political demands included electoral reform, Home Rule for Ireland and self-government for the British Colonies and Dependencies. See *A History Of British Socialism*, p.267.

2. *The Origins of British Bolshevism*, p.12.

3. 'Morris and the Problem of Reform or Revolution' in *Socialist Standard*, Feb 1984.

4. 'Art and Socialism' in *The Collected Works of William Morris* (Longmans, London, 1910-15) Volume XXIII, p.208. For further analysis of William Morris's attitude to reformism see 'A Revolutionary Socialist' by Adam Buick in the *Journal of the William Morris Society* Volume VI, Number One, Summer 1984.

5. For a narrative account of the 'impossibilist revolts' from the SDF see 'The Impossibilist Revolt in Britain' by Chushichi Tsuzucki in *International Review of Social History*, Number One, 1956.

6. 'Impossibilism' by Stephen Coleman in *Non-Market Socialism in the Nineteenth and Twentieth Centuries*, pp.83-4.

7. See 'The Founding of the Socialist Party' in *Socialist Standard*, October 1931. The first official history of the foundation of the SPGB appeared in the September and October 1931 editions of the *Standard* in two articles written by Gilbert McClatchie.

8. *The Communist Manifesto and the Last Hundred Years* (Socialist Party of Great Britain, London, 1948) p.28.

9. *Justice*, 20th July 1901.

10. See 'The Founding of the Socialist Party' in *Socialist Standard*, September 1931.

11. *The Socialist*, July 1903.

12. 'The Origin and Meaning of the Political Theory of Impossibilism', unpublished Ph.D thesis by Stephen Coleman (University of London, 1984). See Chapter 1.

13. 'The Founding of the Socialist Party' in *Socialist Standard*, September 1931.

14. *The Socialist*, April 1906. These immediate demands were not unlike those adopted by the SDF and included demands for a minimum wage, an eight-hour day for council workers and free school meals. The SLP's initial reform programme was abandoned when it embraced De Leon's socialist industrial unionism.

15. *The Monument*, p.7.

16. *The Revolutionary Movement in Britain, 1900–21*, p.21.

17. See 'The Death of Comrade Jack Fitzgerald' in *Socialist Standard*, May 1929.

18. 'Socialist Retrospect — the SPGB in 1904' in *Socialist Standard*, April 1954. This is the first in a six-part history of the SPGB's foundation, again by McClatchie.

19. *The Monument*, p.14.

20. See 'Impossibilism' by Stephen Coleman in *Non-Market Socialism*, p.93. All applicants for membership are required to take a short oral or written 'test' assessing their grasp of SPGB positions. Once admitted, the new member stands

in basic equality with all others.

21. 'The Manifesto of the Socialist League' can be found, reprinted, in the *Socialist Standard*, July 1985.
22. *The Monument*, p.9.
23. 'Manifesto of the Communist Party' by Karl Marx and Friedrich Engels in *Marx and Engels: Basic Writings on Philosophy and Politics* by Lewis S. Feuer (Fontana, London,1981) p.49.
24. *The Thought of Karl Marx* by David McLellan (MacMillan, London and Basingstoke, 1986) p.179.
25. On this, see 'The Productive and the Unproductive Worker' in *Socialist Standard*, September 1976, and an editorial reply to a correspondent, June 1990.
26. *The Socialist*, March 1906.
27. *Socialist Principles Explained* (Socialist Party of Great Britain, London, 1975) p.8.
28. *Questions of the Day* (Socialist Party of Great Britain, London, 1977) p.97.
29. 'A Debate With the ILP' in *Socialist Standard*, March 1932.
30. *Capital*, Volume II by Karl Marx (Penguin, Harmondsworth, 1978) p.390.
31. 'Manifesto of the Communist Party' in *Marx and Engels: Basic Writings on Philosophy and Politics*, p.64.
32. *Manifesto of English Socialists*, published on behalf of the SDF, the Fabian Society and the Hammersmith Socialist Society (Twentieth Century Press, London, 1893) p.5.
33. *From Capitalism to Socialism . . . How We Live and How We Could Live* (Socialist Party of Great Britain, London, 1986) p.13.
34. *The Communist Manifesto and the Last Hundred Years*, p.4.
35. 'Marx's Conception of Socialism' in *Socialist Standard*, July 1983.
36. See 'Labour-Time Accounting or Calculation in Kind?' by Adam Buick in *The World Socialist*, Number Two (World Socialist Movement, London, 1984).
37. See 'Some Notes on Party History' in *Socialist Standard*, May 1954. For a detailed analysis of the SPGB's relationship with the Second International see the series of articles by John Crump published in the *Socialist Standard* in May, June and July, 1968.
38. *Non-Market Socialism in the Nineteenth and Twentieth Centuries*, pp.96-7.
39. See *The Origin and Meaning of the Political Theory of Impossibilism*, Chapter 4.
40. See 'An Exposure' in *Socialist Standard*, March 1910.
41. From *Capitalism to Socialism . . . How We Live·and How We Could Live*, p.41.
42. See, for example, 'Economic Crisis In Russia' in *Socialist Standard*, October 1991.
43. 'To the Socialist Working Class' in *Socialist Standard*, January, 1905.
44. The SPGB has long had 'Companion Parties' in other countries. All of the parties and groups adhering to its Object and Declaration of Principles now collectively refer to themselves as the World Socialist Movement. They are, beside the SPGB, the World Socialist Party of Australia, Bund Demokratischer Sozialisten (Austria), the Socialist Party of Canada, the World Socialist Party (India), the World Socialist Party of New Zealand, the World Socialist Party of the United States and Varldssocialistiska Gruppen (Sweden). Small groups and individuals supporting the basic ideas of the World Socialist Movement also exist in other

countries, currently including a growing number in Africa.
45. *The Communist Manifesto and the Last Hundred Years*, p.26.
46. *State Capitalism: The Wages System Under New Management* by Adam Buick and John Crump (MacMillan, London and Basingstoke, 1986) p.119.
47. 'A Plain Statement' in *Socialist Standard*, February 1905. For a detailed analysis of the Party's view of state capitalism, see Chapter 3.
48. *Questions of the Day*, 1977, p.37.
49. *Reform or Revolution* by Rosa Luxemburg (Bookmarks, London, 1989) pp.50-1.
50. *William Morris: Romantic To Revolutionary* by E. P. Thompson (Merlin Press, London, 1977) p.405.
51. 'Morris and the Problem of Reform or Revolution' in *Socialist Standard*, Feb 1984.
52. *Questions of the Day*, 1942, pp.73-4.
53. See 'Karl Marx's Declaration of Principles' in *Socialist Standard*, May 1980. It is more than likely that SPGB founder members knew of Marx's preamble to this Guesdist party programme. Early editions of the *Socialist Standard* contained several articles on history and economics translated from the Guesdist publication *Le Socialisme*.
54. *Questions of the Day*, 1942 edition, p.77.
55. *Socialist Principles Explained*, p.21.
56. *Socialist Principles Explained*, p.22.
57. *The German Ideology* by Karl Marx and Friedrich Engels (Lawrence and Wishart, London, 1970) p.56.
58. *Socialist Principles Explained*, p.21.
59. *Questions of the Day*, 1977, p.12.
60. *Daniel De Leon* by Stephen Coleman (Manchester University Press, Manchester, 1990) p.156.
61. 'The Founding of the Socialist Party' in *Socialist Standard*, September 1931.
62. *The Socialist*, April 1906.
63. *The Socialist*, May 1908.
64. See 'Notes On Party History — The Trade Union Question' in *Socialist Standard*, July 1954, and 'Notes On Party History — the Islington Dispute' in *Socialist Standard*, August 1954.
65. 'Boring From Within' in *Socialist Standard*, November 1905.
66. Editorial reply to correspondent in *Socialist Standard*, March 1987.
67. See transcript of 'Debate With SLP' between Jack Fitzgerald and former SPGB member E. J. B. Allen in *Socialist Standard*, July 1909 and, somewhat more recently, the editorial reply to a correspondent in September 1986.
68. *The Monument*, p.38.
69. Editorial reply to correspondent in *Socialist Standard*, September 1932.
70. Ever since the 'W. B. of Upton Park' controversy there has always been a group within the SPGB which has not sought to make the distinction between opposing all reformism and opposing individual reforms, and its influence has sometimes been reflected in SPGB propaganda. This is discussed further in relation to reforms and political democracy in Chapter 5, note 43.

2. The First World War

War and the Second International

The issues of war and militarism loomed large for the International Socialist Bureau. In an era which saw the rivalries of the major capitalist powers become ever sharper, the attitude of the working class movement towards war was of premium importance to the fledgling International. Indeed, like their predecessor — the First International — the parties of the ISB passed innumerable resolutions condemning both the tendency of the capitalist system towards armed conflict, and the build up of armaments consequent on this.[1] In the year of the Second International's foundation, a resolution had been passed stating that the roots of modern war lay in the competitive nature of capitalism, and that only the final abolition of that system could put an end to the brutal slaughter of armed conflict:

> War, the disastrous product of the present economic conditions, will disappear only when the present mode of production has given way to the emancipation of labour and the international triumph of socialism.[2]

But as subsequent events demonstrated, such early commitments given by the orthodox possibilist parties of social democracy counted for very little when the reality of war was upon them. Far from proving the triumph of international brotherhood and class solidarity, the onset of the First World War served to fracture the Second International and any real hope of working class unity against the spectre of capitalist war, with the major working class parties of Germany, France, Russia and Britain all forsaking their past paper commitments to socialist fraternity by backing their governments' war plans.

That this should have been the case may initially seem surprising, given their early anti-war pronouncements, but evidence that most of the parties of the Second International would vacillate, or even capitulate, when faced with the concrete issue of a capitalist war, existed long before those parties were ever put to a significant test. The practical attitude of much of the labour movement in Britain was reflected abroad: though war was to be abhorred, each war was not to be simply denounced as another manifestation of capitalist barbarity. Wars had to be judged on merit, with attention given to key factors such as who the warring aggressor state was, to the right of nations to 'self-determination', and to the alleged nature of the regimes involved in the conflict.

This general attitude to war — so prevalent among the parties of the Second International — was a direct product of their possibilist theory and practice. As they considered the working class to be incapable of reaching a socialist consciousness and of overthrowing the capitalist system through its own efforts, political leadership and reform of capitalism were needed if any progress was to be made in alleviating working class conditions (see Chapter 1). This applied equally to wars and attempts to restrain the militaristic tendencies of individual capitalist states. Though many of the prominent possibilist leaders of the Second International undoubtedly viewed socialism as the only lasting solution to war and periodically made appeals for the workers of all lands to unite (such as in the resolution passed at the ISB's founding Congress), they saw reform, disarmament and diplomatic efforts to lessen international tensions as the practical way forward. Socialism, they thought, only held out the prospect of a possible distant answer to the problem of armed conflict.

This possibilist outlook found clear expression at the International's 1910 Congress of Copenhagen, which passed a resolution demanding an end to "secret diplomacy", and which called on the organised working class to press for general disarmament in the face of the concerted military build up by the major European powers. In addition, this approved resolution contained references to the nationalities question, claiming the right of autonomy for all peoples, and the need to defend such autonomy against attack and oppression.[3] As early as 1896 the ISB had adopted the idea of the right of peoples to "national self-determination", but the 1910 resolution was clear confirmation to the impossibilists, if any was needed, that the international class struggle had been submerged by the bourgeois outlook on the sanctity of nation states, and that the pursuit of socialism had been overwhelmed by moves towards arbitration, and possible conciliation, with the capitalist class. As the ISB's radical wing pointed out at the time, however, there seemed little point in calling on the imperialist powers to disarm and respect the 'rights' of smaller nationalities if it was clearly not in their interests to do so:

> All demands for complete or gradual disarmament, for the abolition of secret diplomacy, for the dissolution of the great powers into smaller nationalities and all similar propositions, are absolutely Utopian so long as capitalist class rule remains in power. For capitalism, in its present imperialistic course to dispense with present-day militarism, with secret diplomacy with the centralization of many national states, is so impossible that these postulates might more consistently be united with the simple demand 'abolition of capitalist class society'.[4]

Indeed, despite the efforts of the reformers and disarmers, the armaments race continued at a breakneck speed before the First World War, and two different views came to dominate the International on the prospect of war actually breaking out. First there was the belief that world war could not be in the interests of either the capitalists or the workers so "reason would triumph over all" to prevent it from happening. The second view was based on the consideration that war was likely, and that should a conflict break out, then the potentiality for revolution would increase. This second view was held primarily by the more radical elements, including Lenin, Martov and Luxemburg.[5] This group was in a minority, however, and most of the organisations affiliated to the ISB seriously underestimated the danger of a major conflict occuring. Most ironically of all, they underestimated the impact of nationalism on the working class — a nationalism and respect for the sanctity of independent nation states that they themselves had sought to foster in the years immediately before the outbreak of war. ISB leaders like Bernstein, Bebel and Vaillant all supported the concept of a 'defensive war' to protect a national economic structure in which, they alleged, the workers, as well as the capitalists, had an interest of their own to defend from outside marauders. Some elevated the notion of the progressive liberal nation state to such heights that they were able to suggest the conquest of so-called 'backward groups' elsewhere in the name of progress.[6] But in line with the ISB's concessions to nationalism and chauvinism, the workers in Britain and much of Europe needed little prompting to take sides in the war once it came. The actions of the ISB merely intensified the nationalist and bourgeois outlook of the working class that had been developing over the previous decades. In particular, the action of the bastion of European social democracy, the German SPD, in voting war credits, served to disillusion those radicals who had put faith in the ability of the working class and the International to prevent war.

When the conflict finally broke out in August 1914, it soon became clear that none of the British possibilist organisations affiliated to the Bureau would pursue a clear-cut anti-war policy. At best they combined an uneasy disquiet about the war with a desire to support the British workers who had left the mines and factories to volunteer to fight German militarism. Some, like the old SDF (which had relaunched itself in 1912 as the British Socialist Party) capitulated to the war drive completely. Indeed Raymond Challinor's characterisation of their position as "chauvinistic Marxism"[7] seems rather weak in the light of their all-pervading British nationalism, asserted long before the war and then applied with enthusiasm during it. The BSP war manifesto clearly laid out its position:

> Recognising that the national freedom and independence of this country are threatened by Prussian militarism, the Party naturally desires to see the prosecution of the war to a speedy and successful issue.[8]

Their British nationalism was illustrated by none better than Hyndman himself, who wrote:

> Nothing for which the masses of our people have ever striven is more important than that they and all of us should win in this tremendous war against the ruling military caste ... that menaces the rights and freedom of mankind.[9]

Hyndman and other BSP leaders even resolved to set up a Socialist National Defence Committee whose stated aim was to "resist the anti-British, pro-

German pacifist elements in this country".[10] But not all the members of the BSP were prepared to follow this line when it became clear that the war was to be a more prolonged and bloody affair than originally thought. While stopping short of an unequivocal opposition to the war, many in the BSP were unhappy enough with the Party's stance to force a split in April 1916, with Hyndman and the right-wing leaving to form the National Socialist Party. The overall impression remained the same, however — the argument of the impossibilist SPGB and SLP about the SDF's abandonment of the class struggle and its willingness to compromise with the ruling class had been vindicated in a spectacular manner.

The stance taken by members of the ILP and the Labour Party — fast developing into the 'broad church' — ranged from forthright support to pacifist opposition. Most of the leaders rallied behind the flag. Despite some initial misgivings, Keir Hardie, Ramsay MacDonald and George Lansbury all declared their support, and though they identified German militarism as the 'enemy' to be defeated, this did not prevent the Labour leaders eventually giving their blessings to major elements of that self-same militarism in Britain, principally the introduction of conscription. Labour's initial capitulation was so complete that the ILP's radical paper, the *Labour Leader*, declared within a month of the war's commencement that "the head office of the Party, its entire machinery, are to be placed at the disposal of the Government in their recruiting campaign".[11] Even so, despite the official line, most of the opposition to war from within the official Labour movement came from the ILP ranks, though it is true enough that much of that did not depend on Marxist analysis so much as the religious convictions of individual members. Unlike the 'Marxist materialists of the SPGB', the ILP declared religion a 'private matter' and allowed all manner of religious believers into its membership.[12] Whatever the intentions of the ILP's anti-war elements, its relationship with the Labour Party and the trade unions meant that it was not able to put up effective, detached, opposition to the war especially after its leaders had been lost on the pro-war bandwagon. The anti-war ILP faction was entirely overwhelmed in the wider Labour movement and their delegates on the Labour Executive were powerless to stop Labour's support for Kitchener's recruiting campaign and impotent in the face of the Party's later co-option into government.

The SPGB's Opposition to the War

While the parties affiliated to the Second International compromised their earlier anti-war positions, there was little doubt about the position the Socialist Party of Great Britain would take. Indeed, when the Party's Executive Committee met to discuss the outbreak of war, there was no dispute whatsoever. The attitude of the members had always been known — it would be one of outright hostility to the war and to the governments determined to send workers to their deaths in bloody battle. The SPGB's view on the role of the armed forces in society had been clearly stated in the Declaration of Principles adopted at the Party's foundation:

> ... the machinery of government including the armed forces of the nation, exists only to conserve the monopoly of the capitalist class of the wealth taken from the workers ...

According to this, the armed forces were an instrument used to protect the interests of the capitalists — they did not exist, and they were not sent into battle, for the benefit of the workers. With the outbreak of hostilities, the Party's EC issued an immediate anti-war statement, carried on the front page of the September *Socialist Standard* under the headline 'The War and the Socialist Position'. Drafted in the main by SPGB propagandist Alex Anderson, it began as follows:

> Whereas the capitalists of Europe have quarrelled over the questions of the control of trade routes and the world's markets, and are endeavouring to exploit the political ignorance and blind passions of the working class of their respective countries in order to induce the said workers to take up arms in what is solely their masters' quarrel, and
> Whereas further, the pseudo-Socialists and Labour 'Leaders' of this country, in common with their fellows of the continent, have again betrayed the working class position, either through their ignorance of it, their cowardice, or worse, and are assisting the master class in utilizing this thieves' quarrel to confuse the minds of the workers and turn their attention from the Class Struggle,
> The Socialist Party of Great Britain seizes the opportunity of re-affirming the Socialist position ...

The statement then reiterated the role played by the armed forces in capitalist society before going on to say that:

> These armed forces ... will only be set in motion to further the interests of the class who control them — the master class — and as the workers' interests are not bound up in the struggle for markets wherein their masters may dispose of the wealth they have stolen from them (the workers), but in the struggle to end the system under which they are robbed, they are not concerned with the present European struggle, which is already known as the "BUSINESS WAR", for it is their masters interests which are involved, and not their own.
> The Socialist Party of Great Britain pledges itself to keep the issue clear by expounding the CLASS STRUGGLE, and whilst placing on record its abhorrence at this latest manifestation of the callous, sordid and mercenary nature of the international capitalist class, and declaring that no interests are at stake justifying the shedding of a single drop of working-class blood, enters its emphatic protest against the brutal and bloody butchery of our brothers of this land and other lands, who are being used as food for cannon abroad while suffering and starvation are the lot of their fellows at home.
> Having no quarrel with the working class of any country, we extend to our fellow workers of all lands the expression of our goodwill and Socialist

fraternity, and pledge ourselves to work for the overthrow of capitalism and the triumph of Socialism.
THE WORLD FOR THE WORKERS!

The SPGB, it should be noted, rejected the idea that the conflict was 'a war for democracy' or that it was necessary in order to stop the tide of German militarism. These were the arguments of Britain's reformist social democrats and they were dismissed by the SPGB for having abandoned any semblance of a class analysis. Years of reform activity aimed at the effects and instruments of capitalist rivalry had served to dilute the view that capitalism itself was the root cause of military conflict, and possibilist groups had focused instead on one of the necessary consequences of capitalist rivalry — militarism and the preparation for war. This had periodically degenerated into the view of the bourgeois press that the war was being fought simply to defend "liberty, righteousness and democracy" from the aggression of a foreign tyranny.[13] In a special leaflet entitled 'The Call Of the Patriot', the SPGB set out to answer the charge that Germany had to be defeated because of the threat it represented to British traditions of liberty and peacefulness:

This Government, the "defenders of freedom, the upholders of justice and right", endorsed martial law, the denial of all liberty and the firing on defenceless crowds in South Africa, batoned 700 men in Dublin, turned out the military against YOU at Belfast, Llanelly, Leith, the Rhondda Valley and elsewhere; they callously refused to give underfed children sufficient food; they mock with pretty words but cynical, brutal inaction, the condition of the ever growing army of unemployed; they have sanctioned wholesale imprisonment, exile and butchery in India, Persia, Egypt and the New Hebrides, and allied themselves with the infamies perpetrated in Russia and Japan: in a word they reek with lying pretence and self-satisfied pharasaism, for in very truth, they are the ever willing tools of autocracy, capitalism and class rule everywhere.

The SPGB scorned the Belgian capitalists who were said to have suffered in the German invasion of their country, saying that they themselves had committed brutal acts against defenceless people in the Congo to secure supplies of rubber and other raw materials.[14] Moreover, the *Socialist Standard* contended that Britain's ally Portugal was still tacitly involved in the slave trade.[15] In such circumstances, the SPGB held that the workers should not be fooled by the appeals to their better nature. The working class should not, the Party said, come to the aid of those who had been the aggressors in previous wars simply because they now found themselves in conflict with a more substantial foe.

The SPGB was adamant that the real cause of the 1914 war lay in the late arrival of Germany in the imperialist scramble, rather than in any natural aggressiveness or tendency towards militarism on behalf of the German people as a whole. The 'evil men' argument, depicting the Hun as the vicious butchers of Belgian babies, was a successful propaganda ploy by the British capitalists that swayed many in the labour movement behind the 'defenders of humanity' in the British armed forces. But not only did the SPGB see it as propaganda — it was the worst sort of obfuscation.

The SPGB contended that the root of the conflict lay in real economic forces rather than in the mystical 'traits' of the enemy. Germany had joined the colonial scramble late when the best territories and trade routes had been taken by the other imperialist states, and was determined to flex its military power for economic gain. Its aim was to move through the Balkans, across the Dardanelles and onwards towards India and the oil-rich Persian Gulf. This meant removing Russian influence in the Balkans and cutting Russia off from the Mediterranean through control of the Dardanelles passage. Britain, with its Suez Canal lifeline to India and beyond, was threatened, as was France with its African interests.[16] (France also had an oustanding interest in Alsace-Lorraine, annexed by Germany in 1871.) Territorial disputes notwithstanding, it was evident that Germany sought to ape the established imperialist powers in other ways too — just as Britain had planned a colonial Cape to Cairo railway line, so Germany made lavish proposals for a Berlin to Baghdad railway. This only served to prove that war did not come overnight with an assassin's bullet, it was the outcome "of years of conflicting capitalist interests".[17]

Despite the role attributed to the capitalist class by the SPGB, there was never any hint of a conspiracy theory. As the Party was later to state:

> In saying that capitalism is the source of modern wars Socialists do not mean that capitalism's wars are deliberately and wantonly plotted by individual capitalists or groups for the purpose of making money, even though some individuals may do this. Normally it would be more accurate to say that Governments, in trying to handle the problems and antagonisms created by capitalism, turn to war when other means fail.[18]

To the SPGB capitalism was the cause of the war and the Party was confident that there was no issue at stake for the working class. It dealt with the view that even if the war was being fought for economic gain rather than for noble ideas of democracy and anti-militarism, then the workers would still benefit.[19] It was being argued by some of the more cynical supporters of war that the British working class would reap the benefits of the success of the capitalists in securing raw materials, trade routes and markets. Living standards would dramatically rise, and unemployment would fall. The Party pointed out in response that the reserve army of labour would not go away (despite the possible deaths of hundreds of thousands of young men), that capitalism would remain the same in fundamentals after the war, and that it was of no concern to the workers if one section of the international capitalist class improved its position in relation to the others. Whether the British or German sections of that class had control of the oil, rubber, coal and other materials was of no matter to the SPGB — those resources would continue to be owned by that class and not by society as a whole. The living standards of the working class would still be restricted by the rationing of the wage packet, set at a sufficient level to keep the workers and their families in a fit working condition but little more. Bad housing and poverty would equally still be there to haunt the wages slaves.[20]

Though these arguments were derided by those who viewed the conflict as "a war to end all war", and who held out for the possibilty of peace and affluence to come, the position taken by the SPGB proved to be essentially correct. Without even considering all the war deaths and the heartbreak of those at home, the position of the working class during and after the war did not significantly improve at all. The early 1920s was a period of deflation in which wages fell by even more than prices largely because of the relative ineffectiveness of a weakened trade union movement.[21] And far from there being a period of full employment, with levels of production being restored after the destructiveness of the war, by 1921 there was a deep slump and within a decade there was the onset of the greatest depression capitalism in Britain had ever seen.

The war itself had been intended to be a short, glorious affair, but as it continued, so enthusiasm diminished and the more difficult it became for the British state to recruit young men willing to go and fight. The more able and willing had long since volunteered, most never to be seen in their home towns again. When conscription was introduced, the SPGB could not help but make the obvious comparison with the actions of the 'enemy':

> The grim humour of the claim that Britain is fighting to "crush Prussian militarism" is clearly shown by the fact that a Bill is being passed through the liberty-loving, democratic British Parliament establishing 'Militarism' in a far worse form than either the present Prussian or the late Russian rulers ever attempted. Men who have crossed the seas because they refuse to accept military service are to be forced into the army of the "allied" country they may be in or brought back to serve in the army here![22]

Throughout the conflict the SPGB never ceased to emphasise the importance of the working class, not only as the source of unpaid labour, but as operators of the state machine, now being forced to do the 'dirty work' of the capitalists at a time of war. In one of the SPGB's most eloquent statements, the Party appealed to the working class in the following terms:

> ... you, fellow workers, are today (as you always are) indispensible to the bosses, both for the production of profits in the "piping times of peace"(!) and for cannon fodder and the slaughter of the enemy in time of war.
> Without you the masters are helpless, without you the State collapses and the rulers of one country cannot hope to win in the struggle against the rulers of another country. And knowing this, and recognizing YOUR supreme importance, the bosses have been moving heaven and earth, pouring out money like water, lying like Christians, combining cajolery with economic pressure, and ringing the changes on every form of cant, from 'stirring' appeals to your manhood to virulent denunciation of your indifference or backwardness, in order to make YOU go and fight battles from which you will receive the usual

rewards of empty honour, broken health, wounded bodies, or the eternal silence of the grave.[23]

The SPGB pledged itself to fight in the "greater war at home", the class war, and to institute its own recruiting campaign for the socialist revolution. As Clause Six of the Party's Declaration of Principles makes clear, the SPGB is not a pacifist organisation and was prepared from its inception to use force, if necessary, to establish socialism. Its grounds for opposing the war were not pacifist ones, and were based on three basic propositions. Firstly, that war was not an 'accidental' occurence under capitalism but an inevitable product of that system's social and economic organisation; secondly, that the working class had no interests at stake in supporting one section of the capitalist class against another section, and consequently, that only the working class, organised to establish socialism, had the conscious self-interest and power to put a lasting end to war.

The SPGB and SLP: Common Difficulties, Uncommon Approach

While the SPGB stands out as the one British political organisation to take an unequivocal stance of opposition to the war throughout its duration, the position taken by the impossibilist Socialist Labour Party is also worthy of note. The SLP too stated its opposition to the war and refused to take sides in the conflict, stating:

> Our attitude is neither pro-German nor pro-British, but anti-capitalist and all that it stands for in every country of the world. The capitalist class of all nations are our real enemies, and it is against them that we direct all our attacks.[24]

However, the attitude of the SLP differed from that of the SPGB in several noticeable respects. Indeed, unlike the SPGB, a section of the SLP's membership vacillated in their opposition to the conflict and were prepared to support a war for 'national defence'. This was the argument put by leading SLPer Arthur Macmanus[25] and by the then editor of *The Socialist*, Johnny Muir.[26] Contradictory statements about the war appeared in early editions of *The Socialist* and doubt about the SLP's exact attitude to the conflict was illustrated in an article by Muir in the November 1914 edition of *The Socialist* when, referring to the pro-national defence and anti-war factions, he wrote "I have not been able to find out what support each side has, and consequently I cannot say definitely what the official attitude of the Party is." Though this confusion certainly tainted the SLP in the eyes of the SPGB, the anti-war faction soon asserted itself, with the bulk of the SLP eventually taking an anti-war stance including some of the initial doubters.

The main disagreement between the two impossibilist groups lay, not for the first time, in the matter of tactics. A dispute between the two organisations about the actions socialists should take in the event of war had broken out as early as 1912, when the National Secretary of the SLP wrote to the SPGB outlining his party's fears of a war in the Balkans. The SLP indicated that it wanted to form joint committees in all areas of the country to disseminate anti-war material and stated that effective anti-war agitation "could only be brought about by the co-operation of all sections of the Working Class Movement."[27] A. L. Cox, the pro tem General Secretary of the SPGB, wrote back on behalf of the Party in the following terms, saying that the SPGB:

> refuses ... to join with those who may be prepared to 'shout' against wars far away, yet are ready to deny the existence of the greater war — the Class Struggle — here at home. The Socialist Party knows that wars are a feature of capitalism. When the Socialist Party is strong enough to prevent war it will be strong enough to overthrow capitalism; meantime it can only protest against both, but it does not betray Socialism by uniting with defenders of Capitalism to protest against a feature of that system.[28]

The SPGB, the letter said, would not suspend the class war by uniting with what it judged to be pro-capitalist organisations. Any alliance with the Labour Party, the ILP or the BSP was unthinkable. But this move by the SLP was significant as an early British example of attempting to form a 'united front', a tactic which the SLP was to put into practice when the war came to the express disapproval of the SPGB. Indeed a sinister tactic resurfaced in the 1930s, and the SPGB response to it then is discussed in Chapter 5. In the eventuality, the SLP allied itself for 'anti-war' purposes with factions of the Independent Labour Party and British Socialist Party as well as some syndicalist elements in Clydeside. It was noticable that at the same time the SLP also relaxed its rigid membership procedure and found many new recruits who did not, by any means, agree with everything the SLP stood for. These actions had positive benefits in terms of membership and sales of *The Socialist* (which increased from 3,000 in 1914 to about 20,000 by the end of the war)[29] but arguably had less positive effects in terms of the type of members who typically found their way into the organisation, many of whom abandoned the SLP within two or three years to join the Communist Party of Great Britain, leaving only a small rump of industrial unionists behind. Though the SPGB lost members in the turbulent war years it was to eventually emerge intact and organisationally stronger.

Another conflict of opinion between the SLP and SPGB centred around the question of whether socialists should join the armed forces. The social coercion to enlist was tremendous, reinforced by employers eager to encourage enlistment so they could replace male workers with women at lower rates of pay. But despite the pressures, very few SPGB members enlisted and those who did generally left the Party first. The position of the SPGB from the very start of the war had been that anyone who enlisted was not fit to be a member of the Party. The attitude of the increasingly vanguardist SLP was rather different, at least in theory if not always in practice. The SLP had adopted Herve's idea of workers joining the regular armed forces and of using them as a training ground for a revolutionary militia, though its small size, combined with a need to keep the organisation together in the face of extreme adversity, meant this tactic was not generally applied in reality. It was probably just as well — army 'troublemakers' invariably ended up in front of a firing squad.[30]

It is worth noting that the SPGB deserves recognition for one matter during the conflict that surprisingly bypassed the SLP, and has been remarkably ignored by most historians since. In 1915 a conference in London was called of the various social democratic parties of the 'allied' states — Britain, Belgium, France and Russia. The Russian Bolsheviks, not having been invited, sent a 'Declaration to the London Conference' to leftist and anti-war political organisations outlining their opposition to the actions of the European social democrats. All the British organisations refused to publish it, with the sole exception of the SPGB. The March 1915 edition of the *Socialist Standard* carried the communication, officially signed by M. Maximovich for the Bolshevik Central Committee, but most probably written by Lenin,[31] on its front page under the heading 'A Russian Challenge', stating "We have received the following and publish it in order to show the trickery resorted to by the pseudo-socialists responsible for the London Conference in endeavouring to exploit the Russian Socialists, whose challenge they dared not face". The Declaration argued that:

> The German and Austrian Social Democrats have committed a monstrous crime against Socialism and the International by voting war credits and entering a domestic truce with the junkers, the priests and the bourgeoisie . . . We fully understand that conditions are possible when Socialists as a minority have to submit to a bourgeois majority but under no circumstances should Socialists cease to be Socialists or join in the chorus of bourgeois chauvinism, forsake the workers' cause and enter bourgeois ministries.

In the light of the SPGB's response to subsequent events in Russia, this action in 1915 may seem odd, but in reality the SPGB (like most other British political groups at the time) knew little about the Bolsheviks other than their stated opposition to the war and their evident hostility to the orthodox social democratic parties. The SPGB view was precisely summed up in the phrase "under no circumstances should Socialists cease to be Socialists", a charge the Party frequently laid at the door of the SLP.

It is certainly true that throughout the conflict the SPGB viewed its fellow impossibilists in the SLP — and their tactics — with some scepticism. Not only had the SLP wavered at the outbreak of war, but it showed itself willing to work with non-socialist organisations and was seemingly prepared to adopt suicidal tactics of infiltration into the armed forces. Indeed, as late as 1917, the SPGB's distrust of the SLP was such that it was even sceptical about its opposition to the war itself.[32] But the undoubted differences between the two organisations apart, their situation during the war meant they had much in common. This was certainly the case after the introduction of conscription, when members of the SPGB and SLP would often find themselves side by side at the objectors' tribunals, ringing out their denouncements of the capitalist system. In order to escape the tribunals and likely imprisonment, many took to the 'flying corps', the groups of men on the run from the authorities who relied on the goodwill of others for their safety.[33] Some even left the country — this was most notably the case in the SPGB, with two of the Party's most forceful orators, Adolf Kohn and Moses Baritz fleeing to the United States, where Baritz was eventually imprisoned.

SPGB and SLP members who remained in Britain to help run their party organisations also faced common difficulties, particularly over public meetings and the sale of literature. Both organisations relied on the existence of a bare minimum of democratic rights, and when these were curtailed, socialist agitation became difficult. The Defence of the Realm Regulations introduced in November 1914 provided for the life imprisonment of active anti-war agitators; Regulation N°. 27 ran as follows:

> No person shall by word or in writing or in any newspaper, periodical, book, circular, or other printed publication spread false statements or reports likely to interfere with the success of His Majesty's forces by land or sea or prejudice His Majesty's relations with foreign powers, or spread statements or make reports likely to prejudice the recruiting, training, discipline or administration of any of His Majesty's forces, and if any person contravenes this provision he shall be guilty of an offence against the regulations.

SPGB and SLP meetings in the early months of the war were broken up by pro-war demonstrators, and speakers were physically attacked. By the time the Regulations came into operation the SPGB had already been forced to cut its lecture list because of this, and in January 1915, an article in the *Socialist Standard* entitled 'Under Martial Law' announced that the Party had decided to suspend its public meetings for the forseeable future. For its part, the SLP continued its outdoor propaganda only with great difficulty and a number of its members were prosecuted under the Regulations, many being sent to prison. The state had asserted the power attributed to it by the SPGB, and there was little any anti-war group could do but make propaganda as best they could in difficult circumstances, ever mindful of the possible penalties of transgression. In the *Socialist Standard*, the SPGB commented on the restrictions placed upon it:

> We shall be told perhaps that we should have gone on in defiance of the powers that be till we went down in a blaze of fireworks. Our view, however, was the same one dictated by our avowed principles. We have always held that the supreme power is in the hands of those who control the political machine. The most we could hope for by going on was to prove our contentions by acting in opposition to them.[34]

Distribution of both the *Socialist Standard* and *The Socialist* became difficult, and copies were prevented from being sent abroad. Individual members of both organisations suffered great hardship, and the SPGB's Head Office was raided by the police. The SLP in particular came regularly to the notice of the authorities because of its industrial agitation, especially in turbulent Clydeside.

Organisationally, the SPGB was at least able to carry on a bare existence — though for a time greatly depleted in numbers and run by a small group of dedicated women members — with the state not always choosing to exercise the full powers at its disposal. Partly because of its relatively small circulation, the *Socialist Standard*, like *The Socialist*, was not censored by the authorities and was allowed uninterrupted publication throughout the war, despite the fact that virtually every issue contained some comment illegal under the Regulations.[35] One of the greatest ironies of the war years for the SPGB lay in the fact that the only article prevented from appearing in the *Socialist Standard* was omitted because the printer refused to handle it. This was in the February 1916 issue, when the following appeared in an otherwise blank column:

Lld. George and the Clyde Workers.
The firm who machines this paper has refused to print the article which was set up to appear under the above heading. We are therefore compelled to withdraw the article. We congratulate the Government on the success of their efforts to preserve the 'freedom of the Press'.

Despite all the hardship and difficulties of the war, the fact that the SPGB was able to come through the experience intact, and rather better prepared for the troubles to come was certainly no mean achievement, and that the SLP was able to do the same while boosting its membership is not be dismissed either. But to say that the SPGB and SLP faced similar difficulties as objectors to the war does not mean their divergences of outlook and disparity of actions should be readily overlooked. That the SPGB should have been prepared to print declarations by the Russian Bolsheviks while choosing to spurn the SLP was more a product of its understandable ignorance of Bolshevik tactics than any gross sectarianism towards the SLP, whose political differences with the SPGB had been evident for over ten years before the outbreak of war. Any potential hope of co-operation between the two organisations finally vanished when the SLP failed to come out unequivocally against the war when the killing began in 1914.

The SPGB, Marxism and War
As has already been demonstrated in other contexts, much of the ideological baggage carried by the SPGB, SLP and others emanated from the political and economic theories developed during the nineteenth century. The attitude adopted by Marx and Engels, in particular, had a significant impact on the thinking of the 'Marxist' parties of the entire Second International, including those, like the SPGB, which effectively left it. Their attitude to war was no exception. Of special significance was that Marx, Engels and other early pioneers of the socialist movement judged that it was possible for socialists to support 'progressive' wars that could conceivably hasten the establishment of socialism. But if this perspective is to be understood — together with its influence on

parties like the German SPD and its implications for the robustly anti-war SPGB — it cannot be separated from the actual historical circumstances which gave rise to it.

At the time Marx and Engels developed their position on the possibility of 'progressive' wars, feudalism had not been swept away in much of Europe, and the entrenched absolutist monarchies of Tsarist Russia and the Austro-Hungarian Empire were stifling the future development of capitalism. Opposition to these reactionary forces came from capitalists and workers alike. The capitalists wished to overturn the feudal restrictions placed on the developing capitalist relations of production, while the workers demanded political rights and freedom to organise in trade unions. In much of Central and Eastern Europe, the peasantry also opposed the old ruling class, aiming at the dispossession of the feudal landowners. Because of the stifling power of the centralised great empires, developing anti-feudal conflicts inevitably took the form of struggles for national independence and autonomy, with capitalists, workers and peasants putting forward common demands for independence and political democracy. In this context, Marx and Engels supported wars against reaction, arguing that national independence struggles could serve to break up the old feudal regimes and hasten their replacement with liberal democratic bourgeois republics which could, in turn, be swept away by the workers' movement.

The perspective held by Marx, Engels and other early socialists in this period was that it was possible, and necessary, for the workers — at least on a temporary basis — to ally themselves with the bourgeoisie against feudal reaction. They did not support movements for 'national liberation' because they considered 'national autonomy' to be a desirable end in itself, but because they considered it vital to promote the development of capitalist relations of production as quickly as possible. Indeed Marx and Engels opposed some national independence struggles, such as the Czech national movement, on the grounds that they would more likely serve to strenghthen the forces of feudal reaction than promote bourgeois development.

Crucially, Marx and Engels realised that socialist revolution could only be achieved when capitalism had created a world market and an international division of labour.[36] Capitalist relations of production at the time were the only basis for the progressive development of the productive forces and national movements and wars against absolutism were seen primarily in terms of the contribution they could make to the victory of capitalist production and liberal democracy. Marx and Engels looked particularly favourably on movements which could challenge the power of reactionary Russia. Writing after Marx's death, Engels summarized their position during the turmoil of 1848:

> Our foreign policy was simple; support for every revolutionary people, call for a general war of revolutionary Europe against the great mainstay of European reaction Russia ... [if] Germany could be drawn into war against Russia, the

Hapsburgs and Hohenzollerns were done for and the revolution would triumph all along the line.[37]

During the Crimean War they exhibited the same opposition to Russian reaction, hailing the war because the three major reactionary forces in Europe had fallen out, and choosing to take the side of the Western powers.[38] Similarly, the Address adopted by the General Council of the International Workingmen's Association after the outbreak of the Franco-Prussian War, and drafted by Marx, stated:

> On the German side, the war is a war of defence but ... whatever sympathy the Germans may justly claim in a war of defence against Bonapartist aggression, they would forfeit at once by allowing the Prussian Government to call for, or accept the help of, the Cossack.

After Marx and Engels's deaths, socialists — often uncritically — attempted to apply their views on war to the more economically and politically developed conditions of the early twentieth century. Indeed, Marx and Engels's particular idea that a German war of defence could be justified against Tsarist Russia played no small part in influencing the strongest European workers' organisation, the German SPD, to support a war for 'national defence' in 1914. On 31st July of that year, the SPD's *Frankfurter Volksstime* commented:

> The German Social Democracy has always hated Czarism as the bloody guardian of European reaction from the time that Marx and Engels followed, with far-seeing eyes, every movement of this barbarian government, down to the present day... the time has come when we must square accounts with these terrible scoundrels, under the German flag of war.

On the Allied side, the French Social Democrats used Marx to justify their support for the more 'progressive' bourgeois democracy of Britain and France in opposition to reactionary Prussian militarism. Others in the European workers' movement made a different, and less crude, application. While agreeing with the progressive nature of the wars supported by Marx and Engels in the nineteenth century, Lenin argued that the rise of imperialism meant that it was no longer true that a war between the European powers, at least, could have a progressive character. In his *Socialism and War* he wrote that:

> Whoever refers today to Marx's attitude towards the wars of the epoch of the progressive bourgeoisie and forgets Marx's statement that 'the workers have no fatherland', a statement that applies precisely to the epoch of the reactionary, obsolete bourgeoisie, to the epoch of the socialist revolution, shamelessly distorts Marx and substitutes the bourgeois for the socialist point of view. [39]

This being so, Lenin did not abandon Marx's perspective from the nineteenth century entirely, and his particular theory of imperialism led him to argue that it was legitimate for socialists to support wars where the victory of the oppressed, non-sovereign states against the imperialist nations was possible. As early as 1903 the Bolsheviks had already incorporated the ISB's 'right of nations to self-determination' into their programme.

Rosa Luxemburg, who opposed the 1914-18 war on similar grounds to Lenin and whose internationalist credentials were such that she had long criticised Marx's view that an independent Polish 'buffer state' needed to be set up between Russia and Germany, went even further, questioning the very 'right' of nations to self-determination as if 'the nation' was a homogenous social and political entity.[40] But even though Lenin, Luxemburg and other prominent figures in the Second International opposed the war, none of them showed an entirely clear understanding of the changed world situation since the days of Marx and Engels. Indeed, before the First World War Luxemburg had been arguing that the task of the working class was not immediate socialist revolution but the establishment of a unified and democratic Russian and Polish republic.[41]

One group of people who pioneered a coherent understanding of the reasons why Marxian socialists could no longer consider supporting wars, even apparently progressive wars for national independence and 'self-determination', was the tiny group of Marxists in the SPGB. Among the various Marxist groups and parties throughout Europe and North America, it was the SPGB which claimed that capitalism had already triumphed over feudalism, and that there was no question that capitalist war could any longer perform a progressive function for the development of the socialist movement or in any way could serve to hasten the establishment of socialism. In fact, even though the SPGB recognised the earlier necessity of removing the influence of feudalism and autocracy as a prelude to capitalist development, it became doubtful about the validity of Marx and Engels's views on encouraging the working class to do battle with one another for the sake of capitalist liberal democracy against feudal reaction, and in subsequent years was critical of Marx over the issue of 'national defence'. Having learnt through experience that progression towards socialism would be slow and hampered by bourgeois illusions such as nationalism, the SPGB stressed the need to develop socialist understanding in the working class:

> Anything which in the slightest way encourages the workers to retain the blighting and poisoning belief in nationalism and so-called national interests, perpetuates the dangerous illusion of class harmony and plays into the hands of the capitalist class.
>
> Only class-conscious socialists can speak across the frontiers of the capitalist nations to the working class of the world and they can do so only because they are free from the taint of so-called national interests which can be none other than capitalist interests ... We are a Marxist party but we recognise that the conditions of the time, when Capitalism was relatively young and Feudalism had not yet been completely swept away, led Marx and Engels into a false position on war in the course of pursuing their pioneer work.[42]

And referring to Leninist support for anti-imperialist 'national liberation struggles' and the strategy of 'revolutionary defeatism' whereby the working class of one country strives for the defeat of its 'own' bourgeoisie, rather than the capitalist class as a whole:

> Those who continue to hold nineteenth century conceptions about the possibly 'progressive' nature of war are refusing to learn the bitter lessons of experience. They fail to see that the instrument of war that served the rise to power of the capitalist minority cannot be used to achieve the emancipation of the working class. Armed force cannot make up for the backward political development of the working class.[43]

The stance taken by the SPGB in the First World War was a clear rejection of the view that the working class could have anything to gain by compromising with the capitalists either in pursuit of 'national defence' at home or 'national autonomy' for those abroad, even if, at that precise time, the Party had relatively little to say about Marx's earlier attitude to wars.[44] That the SPGB should have been almost alone in standing out against this clearly confirmed its previous characterisations of the abandonment of the socialist and internationalist position in the other workers' groups, to whom it had declared its hostilty in 1904. As the SPGB was later to argue with vigour, these organisations failed to realise that the triumph of capitalism as a world system and the development of a real global market for commodities meant that the economic preconditions for socialism had already been satisfied. Socialism had become a definite historic possibilty, held back only by continuing working class support for capitalism — in itself fostered by the misplaced nationalism, reformism and compromise of the BSP, ILP and the Second International as a whole. Virtually alone among the parties standing in the broad Marxist tradition at the time, the SPGB had addressed itself to the practical question that Marx himself had never really had to face: what should be the attitude of socialists to war once capitalism had triumphed as a world system?[45] The answer given by the SPGB was crystal clear — socialists had to oppose all sections of the capitalist class and all capitalist wars.

The SPGB contended that for their part, the reformist bodies, having identified 'national self-determination', anti-militarism and a host of other causes to be pursued before socialism, deserted the only progressive course of action left and the only one capable of lasting success. It was in this context that the relevance of the exact perspective held by Marx and Engels in supporting 'progressive' wars emerged, in that the former positions of the workers' movement in the conditions of the nineteenth century had been used to justify the capitulation of much of the workers' movement in the twentieth century to the side of capitalist interests. In the conditions of 1914, the SPGB was left to denounce that capitulation and to reassert, as best it could, its opposition to the senseless, systematic butchery of the working class. As it itself commented, "Our object was not to bid defiance to a world gone mad, but to place on record the fact that in this country the Socialist position was faithfully maintained by the Socialists."[46]

Notes

1. *Socialism and the Great War* by Georges Haupt (Oxford University Press, London, 1972) Chapter 1.
2. *The Revolutionary Internationals 1864-1943* by M. Drachkovitch and M. Milorad (Oxford University Press, London, 1966) p.108.
3. *A History of Socialist Thought*, Volume III by G. D. H. Cole (MacMillan, London, 1956) p.84. The infamous 'Kautsky Resolution', on allowing socialist MPs to join cabinets at times of 'national emergency' such as war, had been passed by the ISB as early as 1900.
4. 'The Junius Pamphlet' in *Rosa Luxemburg Speaks*, (Pathfinder Press, New York, 1970) p.324.
5. *The Bolsheviks and the World War — the Origins of the Third International* by O. H. Gankin and H. H. Fisher (Stanford University Press, Stanford, 1940) pp.55-65.
6. See *The Communist Manifesto and the Last Hundred Years*, p.30.
7. *The Origins of British Bolshevism*, p.161.
8. *Justice*, 17 September 1914.
9. *Daily Dispatch*, 7 July 1915.
10. *Justice*, 24 June 1915.
11. *Labour Leader*, 3 September 1914.
12. The SPGB attitude towards religion and armed conflict was elaborated in the November 1914 *Socialist Standard* in an article called 'War and Religion'.
13. *Sunday Chronicle*, 30 August 1914.
14. 'War and Religion' in *Socialist Standard*, November 1914.
15. See 'Allies in Slavery' in *Socialist Standard*, February 1915.
16. *The Socialist Party and War* (Socialist Party of Great Britain, London, 1950) p.60.
17. 'Economic Causes of the Great War' in *Socialist Standard*, August 1964.
18. *The Socialist Party and War*, p.27.
19. 'The War and the Socialist Position' in *Socialist Standard*, September 1914.
20. *Ibid.*
21. See, for instance, *A Textbook of Economics* by W. J. Weston (Pitman and Sons, London, 1930) p.223.
22. 'Manifesto of the Socialist Party of Great Britain to the Proposed International Congress' as published in the *Socialist Standard*, July 1917.
23. SPGB leaflet 'The Call of the Patriot', February 1916.
24. *The Socialist*, September 1914. Also quoted in *The Origins of British Bolshevism*, p.125.
25. See *The Friends of Alice Wheeldon* by Sheila Rowbotham (Pluto Press, London, 1986) p.27.
26. *The Socialist*, December 1914.
27. 'Ourselves and the SLP' in *Socialist Standard*, January 1913.
28. *Ibid.*
29. *The Friends of Alice Wheeldon*, p.18.
30. A full list of those executed under the British Army Act, together with the offences with which they were charged, is given in *Shot At Dawn* by Julian Putkowski and Julian Sykes (Wharncliffe Publishing, Barnsley, 1989).

31. See 'Lenin and the *Socialist Standard*' in *Socialist Standard*, April 1970. 'M. Maximovitch' was in fact Maxim Litvinoff, the Bolshevik representative to the ISB, later appointed Soviet Commissar for Foreign Affairs, 1930-9.
32. See, for instance, 'Manifesto of the Socialist Party of Great Britain to the Proposed International Congress' in *Socialist Standard*, July 1917.
33. *The Monument*, p.52.
34. 'Under Martial Law' in *Socialist Standard*, January 1915.
35. See ' Fifty Years Too Late' in *Socialist Standard*, August 1964.
36. See 'Manifesto of the Communist Party' in *Marx and Engels: Selected Writings*, pp.67-9 and 'Socialism: Utopian and Scientific', pp.147-52.
37. *Social Democrat*, 13 March 1884.
38. See, for instance, the *New York Tribune*, 12 April 1863.
39. *Socialism and War* by V. I. Lenin (Lawrence and Wishart, London, 1940) p.17.
40. *The National Question* edited by Horace B. Davis (Monthly Review Press, London, 1977). See Appendix.
41. An analysis of this is contained in 'Rosa Luxemburg and the National Question' in *Socialist Standard*, April 1978.
42. *The Socialist Party and War*, pp.92-3.
43. *Ibid*.
44. It would be true to say that the SPGB didn't realise the full implications of Marx's views on some of the wars of the nineteenth century until it was confronted with the question of a 'war for democracy' in the 1930s. For a brief explanation of this, see 'Some Theoretical Questions' in *Socialist Standard*, September 1954.
45. 'The National Question' in *Socialist Standard*, July 1969.
46. 'Under Martial Law' in *Socialist Standard*, January 1915.

3. Russia and State Capitalism

The World's First Socialist Revolution?

When Jack Fitzgerald of the SPGB wrote in the *Socialist Standard* that the Russian upheavals of March and November, 1917 were by far the most important events of the First World War, he was stating an opinion which, with hindsight, seems a self-evident truth.[1] But the extent to which these important upheavals would actually affect the SPGB itself, and the entire political tradition which had spawned it, could hardly have been appreciated or predicted at that time. As has already been noted, the practical debate within the working class movement before the Bolshevik seizure of power had centred on the efficacy of reformist and revolutionary strategies for the achievement of a social transformation. The Russian Revolution, however, seriously muddied these waters and brought to the world's attention a political theory — Leninism — which, perhaps for the first time, sought to systematically reappraise and reinterpret Marxism rather than simply reject it outright in the pursuit of piecemeal reforms.

There had certainly never been any doubt that there was room for interpretation — indeed the SPGB showed at its foundation the type of synthesis possible between various strands of broadly Marxist thinking, its outlook and political strategy bearing the influence of such diverse elements as Kautsky and De Leon, Engels and Morris. But the Bolshevik Revolution went further than this and challenged some of the very foundations on which pre-1914 Marxism had been built. The perceived need to achieve mass socialist consciousness among the working class, the role of a mass socialist party as both a spur to, and an expression of, that consciousness, and the necessity of a developed economic basis of society for a successful socialist revolution, all came into question.

The apparent triumph of the Bolsheviks in backward Russia sent the Marxist movement into turmoil. Moreover, previously impotent political organisations across Europe and North America showed themselves to be more impressed by the sudden and unexpected success of revolutionaries in the midst of bloody world war, than concerned for the event's potential impact on core elements of Marxist theory as they had always understood them. Contrary to legend,[2] the tiny SPGB was initially affected by this feeling like other radical parties.

The SPGB's reaction to the Bolshevik seizure of power contrasted with its position on the earlier, openly pro-capitalist, March Revolution. On that occasion the *Socialist Standard* clearly said that the revolution was:

... but another example of the capitalists using the discontent and numbers of the working class in Russia to sweep away the Feudal rules and restrictions so strongly symbolized in the Czar and the Council of Nobles, and to establish a system of government in line with modern capitalist needs and notions.[3]

The *Socialist Standard*'s first editorial commenting on the Bolshevik Revolution, however, did not proceed on the basis that the working class was being used or manipulated in any way for the benefit of higher forces. Having prefaced its remarks with a note of caution regarding the scanty and possibly misleading information available to it, the *Standard's* praise was fulsome enough:

> Whatever may be the final outcome, the Bolsheviks have at all events succeeded in doing what all the armies, all the diplomats, all the priests and primates, all the perfervid pacifists of all the groaning and bleeding world have failed to do — they have stopped the slaughter, for the time being at all events, on their front.
>
> How much more than this they intended to do the future may reveal. They may have higher aims, yet to be justified by success or condemned by failure; but it is an astounding achievement that these few men have been able to seize opportunity and make the thieves and murderers of the whole world stand aghast and shiver with apprehension.[4]

The ending of the war, at least on the Eastern Front, was considered by the SPGB to be the principal success of the Bolsheviks, and an act directly in the interests of the working class. But as for the nature of the Bolshevik seizure of power itself, the SPGB was noticeably more cautious than its political rivals in assessing its supposedly socialist content. The Socialist Labour Party in particular, which had long harboured vanguardist ambitions, saw itself as the British embodiment of the Bolshevik revolutionary strategy, possibly even before its Russian success. Along with Sylvia Pankhurst's Workers' Suffrage Federation (WSF), the SLP had been represented at the Leeds Soviet Convention of June 3, 1917, and joined with the WSF in calling for workers' and soldiers' councils to be set up in Britain. After the Bolshevik takeover, *The Socialist* ran pieces such as 'The Triumph of SLP Tactics in Russia',[5] claiming that its industrial unionism and desire to educate the mass of the working class in socialist ideas rested easily with the spirit of Lenin and the Bolsheviks.

The SLP and the anti-parliamentary WSF were not alone in their admiration for the Bolsheviks and their declared aim of constructing the first socialist state — the conference of the British Socialist Party in the spring of 1918 also expressed support for the November revolution together with initial Bolshevik measures for the "reorganisation of Russia under the control of the working classes".[6] That the SPGB did not share many of these attitudes towards the new Russian regime soon became clear when the Party's early praise for the Bolshevik anti-war strategy had run its course.

What focused the SPGB's attention above all were the lavish claims made on the Bolsheviks' behalf by their supporters in Britain. The first detailed analysis of the Russian situation, written by Fitzgerald, appeared in the August 1918 *Socialist Standard* under the heading 'The Revolution in Russia — Where It Fails'. It tackled the claims of the SLP by outlining why the Bolshevik takeover could not lead to the establishment of socialism in Russia. The article asked:

> Is this huge mass of people, numbering about 160,000,000 and spread over eight and a half millions of square miles, ready for socialism? Are the hunters of the North, the struggling peasant proprietors of the South, the agricultural wage-slaves of the Central Provinces, and the industrial wage-slaves of the towns convinced of the necessity, and equipped with the knowledge requisite, for the establishment of the social ownership of the means of life?
>
> Unless a mental revolution such as the world has never seen before has taken place, or an economic change has occurred immensely more rapidly than history has ever recorded, the answer is 'No!' ... What justification is there, then, for terming the upheaval in Russia a Socialist Revolution? None whatever beyond the fact that the leaders in the November movement claim to be Marxian Socialists.

In fact, as Buick and Crump have noted,[7] the SPGB identified as many as five key reasons why the establishment of socialism in Russia by the Bolsheviks was impossible. First, as indicated above, the mass socialist consciousness demanded by the SPGB before a successful socialist revolution could take place was noticeably absent in Russia, as elsewhere. Fitzgerald seized on a remark by Litvinoff which suggested that the Bolsheviks did not really know the views of the entire working class when they seized control, only some sections of it such as the factory workers of Petrograd. Second, it was not even the case that the working class was in a numerical majority in Russia, a society dominated by its peasant economy. How could a majority socialist revolution be carried out when the workers were still in a minority and when the largest social class were the largely illiterate peasantry? While illiteracy did not entirely preclude the spread of socialist understanding, it certainly made it more difficult. In any event, the peasants had long shown themselves more interested in ridding themselves of the heavy tax burden on land, and increasing the size of their plots, than in demanding common ownership. Third, socialism could not exist in an economically backward country where the means of production was not sufficiently developed to support a socialist system of distribution. Fourth, and crucially, it was not possible to construct socialism in one country alone, given the nature of capitalism as a world system with a world-wide division of labour. Isolated 'socialism in one country' would be doomed to failure, no matter how honourable the intentions of the revolutionaries involved. The fifth reason advanced for the non-socialist nature of Bolshevik Russia by the SPGB went to the very root of its political differences with Bolshevism: socialism could not be achieved by following leaders.

Leninism and the Politics of the Vanguard

Lenin's conception of the role of the political party in a proletarian revolution differed fundamentally from that of the impossibilist SPGB, and from the social democratic movement out of which it had emerged earlier in the century. While the Bolsheviks initially claimed to be part of this same social democratic political current, and though Lenin frequently used the terminology of Marx, Bolshevik theories on political tactics and party organisation owed far more to the various strands of nineteenth century Russian revolutionary thinking embodied in the Populist movement.[8] Underlying these Populist theories was the basic assumption of vanguardism — "the doctrine that a given group's emancipation depends crucially on some other, much smaller group's leadership, guidance, or domination in some stronger form".[9] That such a vanguardist approach was deemed necessary was a product of Lenin's belief that the achievement of a mass socialist consciousness in the working class was impossible before a proletarian revolution, when the dead-weight of capitalist ideology could be lifted. (In this sense, the basic assumption of Bolshevism was the same as that of reformist social democracy, differing only in the means adopted to achieve working class power.) Lenin strove to justify this assumption in *What Is To Be Done?*:

> The history of all countries shows that the working class, exclusively by its own effort, is able to develop only trade-union consciousness, i.e., the conviction that it is necessary to combine in unions, fight the employers, and strive to compel the government to pass this or that necessary labour law, etc. The doctrine of socialism, however, grew out of the philosophic, historical and economic theories elaborated by educated representatives of the propertied classes, by intellectuals ... in Russia, the theoretical doctrine of Social-Democracy arose altogether independently of the spontaneous growth of the working-class movement; it arose as a natural and inevitable outcome of the development of thought among the revolutionary socialist intelligensia.[10]

Throughout his political life, Lenin refused to accept that the working class "in the mass" could achieve a socialist understanding, arguing that socialist consciousness could only come "from without". At the Congress of Peasants' Soviets in 1918 he claimed that if revolutionaries had to wait for the intellectual development of the working class they would not see socialism for at least five hundred years. To avoid this calamity, a centralised and politically mature core of revolutionaries was necessary to initiate social change when the working class in the mass was not yet conscious of its interests — "the Socialist political party, that is the vanguard of the working class, must not allow itself to be halted by the lack of education of the masses."[11] This outlook, which undoubtedly reflected the undeveloped condition of the working class in Russia, was eloquently expounded by the Bolshevik apostle Karl Radek in *Socialism From Science to Practice*:

In no country can the revolution begin as the act of the majority ... the most active are always the first to rise ... the creative and impulsive force of the revolution is required to rouse the great body of the people to liberate them from their intellectual and spiritual slavishness under capitalism, and to lead them into a position where a defence of their interests can be made.[12]

This 'minority action' perspective clearly mirrored the nineteenth century anti-Tsarist view of Russian Populism, as elaborated, for instance, by Peter Tkachev:

A real revolution can only be brought about in one way: through the seizure of power by revolutionists ... The revolutionary minority, having freed the people from the yoke of fear and terror, provides an opportunity for the people to manifest their revolutionary destructive power.[13]

Commenting on the apparent triumph of Bolshevik principles from its position in Britain, the SPGB claimed that the Bolshevik vanguardist outlook reflected the political and economic immaturity of Russia, and the minority position of the Russian working class. The Bolsheviks had taken their opportunity to seize power in a war-ravaged country promising 'peace, land and bread', but contrary to the rhetoric of their fervent admirers in Britain, Bolshevik tactics had evidently failed to establish socialism and were most certainly inappropriate for the more developed capitalist states in Western Europe. Unlike groups such as the British SLP, who considered Bolshevism an exciting confirmation of the Marxist theory they had sought to promote in Britain, the SPGB recognised the theoretical dangers inherent in the Bolsheviks' vanguardism and denied the applicability its supporters contended for it in Britain.[14] It was a hostility spurred by the knowledge that key elements of orthodox Marxist theory were really being fundamentally challenged, rather than developed, and from a hitherto unexpected source. In 'A Socialist View of Bolshevist Policy' the SPGB commented:

Ever since the Bolshevik minority seized the control of affairs in Russia we have been told that their 'success' had completely changed Socialist policy. These 'Communists' declare that the policy of Marx and Engels is out of date. Lenin and Trotsky are worshipped as the pathfinders of a shorter and easier road to Communism.

Unfortunately for these 'Bolsheviks', no evidence has yet been supplied to show wherein the policy of Marx and Engels is no longer useful, and until that evidence comes the Socialist Party of Great Britain will continue to advocate the same Marxian policy as before ... We shall insist on the necessity of the working class understanding socialism and organising within a political party to obtain it.[15]

The SPGB saw Lenin's vanguardism as a fundamental denial of the basic socialist — and Marxist — proposition enshrined in Clause Five of the Party's Declaration of Principles, that the emancipation of the working class "must be the work of the working class itself". The SPGB was adamant that for a society of social ownership and truly democratic control to exist, the co-operation of the majority of society was necessary, and there could be no co-operation without both understanding and agreement. There was certainly no question that a co-operative socialist society could be created by a minority vanguard party, and so Bolshevik tactics were quite useless from the socialist perspective — even dangerous, given the violent insurrectionary scenario promoted by Lenin and then fatally attempted by the Spartacists in Germany.

Almost alone in the years after the Bolshevik Revolution, the SPGB set about countering the view, supposedly hidden in the writings of Marx and Engels and revealed to the world by Lenin, that the correct path to working class emancipation lay in the vanguard of the working class rising up to smash the bourgeois state, then creating a 'proletarian dictatorship' replete, if necessary, with press censorship and the banning of other political parties. To the SPGB, Lenin's 'Dictatorship of the Proletariat' was not, as Marx had envisaged in his *Critique of the Gotha Programme*, an expression of the democratic will of the great mass of the majority class in society, but a dictatorship of the vanguard party over the working class and the peasants. Lenin was equated with the minority, conspirational theorists of the past — Blanqui, Buonarroti and Weitling — men who thought it madness to wait for mass political consciousness when revolutions could be created by hardened tacticians and conspirators. In an article in the *Socialist Standard* on 'Democracy and Dictatorship in Russia', the SPGB sought to demonstrate the Blanquism of the Bolsheviks by quoting Lenin's proud claims from *The New International* of April 1918, that "Just as 150,000 lordly landowners under Czarism dominated the 130,000,000 Russian peasants, so 200,000 members of the Bolshevik party are imposing their proletarian will in the interest of the latter."[16] The SPGB counterposed these views with the warnings of the mature Marx and Engels, who themselves had flirted with minority tactics as politically inexperienced individuals in the 1840s. Engels in particular had become explicit in his warnings against the type of vanguardism and elitism identified by the SPGB to be at the root of Bolshevik tactics, stating in his Introduction to Marx's *Class Struggles in France 1848-50*:

> The time is past for revolutions carried through by small minorities at the head of unconscious masses. Where it is a question of the complete transformation of the social organisation, the masses themselves must participate, must understand what is at stake and why they must act. That much the history of the last fifty years has taught us. But so that the masses may understand what is to be done, long and persistent work is required ... even in France the Socialists realise more and more that no durable success is possible unless they win over in advance the great mass of the people.[17]

Its arguments against the Bolsheviks' vanguardist conception of revolution notwithstanding, the SPGB had to deal with a Bolshevik-inspired resurrection of the view that its 'parliamentary' road to socialism was outdated. Having studied the methods of the Bolshevik takeover, the opponents of the SPGB's revolutionary strategy in Pankhurst's WSF and in the groups that went on to found the Communist Party of Great Britain in December 1920, put an old argument in a new, improvised form — namely that the Russian example had shown that attempts to take over parliament and the capitalist state machine were almost entirely useless. Russia had demonstrated that the working class could set up its own organs of power in the form of workers' councils (soviets). A justification for this view was given by Marx, it was said, in *The Civil War in France*, where notice was given that "the working class cannot simply lay hold of the ready-made state machinery, and wield it for its own purposes".[18]

The SPGB did not dispute, and had never disputed, this particular dictum of Marx. Its own Declaration of Principles expressly stated that the state machine that had been used by the capitalists to ensure their class domination of society would have to be "*converted* from an instrument of oppression into the agent of emancipation" (emphasis added). What the SPGB disputed was the new interpretation put on Marx's words in the light of the events in Russia. To the SPGB, creating new organs of working class power in opposition to the might of the capitalist state would be folly and was certainly not what Marx had in mind. Engels had settled the issue for the party in a letter to Bernstein, saying it was "simply a question of showing that the victorious proletariat must first refashion the old bureaucratic, administratively centralised state power before it can use it for its own purposes".[19]

In recognising the unique role played by the soviets in Russian society in the absence of legitimate bourgeois parliamentary government, the SPGB argued that they were a specific product of backward political conditions, and were used by the Bolsheviks, as the best organised and most effective political group, for their own purposes. They did not in themselves constitute bodies that could be of use to the working class in all situations. In an article entitled 'Parliament or Soviet? A Critical Examination', the *Socialist Standard* argued in the manner of the *Communist Manifesto* that the precise application of socialist principles would vary according to the degree of political and economic development reached in various countries, saying that it was absurd "to condemn or uphold the Soviet system irrespective of the conditions out of which it arose" and that by adopting the Soviet model for their constitution, the Bolsheviks had not invented a grand new system but had accepted an already established fact.[20]

Though the SPGB pointed out the electoral disparities that could make the soviet system open to manipulation[21] and denied its similarity to the Paris Commune,[22] it is noticeable that the SPGB was not as hostile to the idea of the working class organising soviets in conditions of backward political development as were some of its opponents at the thought of using parliament and 'bourgeois elections' for socialist purposes in countries like Britain. To the SPGB, Russia did not prove its opponents' contentions that soviets could be successfully set up in opposition to an established bourgeois parliamentary state, only that they could function as a partial substitution for one in a backward country lacking the means for democratic expression. As the Menshevik leader Martov had written, the Bolsheviks and their supporters had sought to detach the rise of spontaneous working class organs of democracy from the undeveloped political conditions that spawned them, proclaiming them as a 'universal form' to be used by socialist parties in all future revolutions:

> As soon as the slogan 'soviet regime' begins to function as a pseudonym under the cover of which the Jacobin and Blanquist idea of a minority dictatorship is reborn in the ranks of the proletariat, then the soviet regime acquires a universal acceptation and is said to be adaptable to any kind of revolutionary overturn. In this new sense, the 'soviet form' is necessarily devoid of the specific substance that bound it to a definite phase of capitalist development. It now becomes a universal form, which is supposed to be suitable to any revolution accomplished in a situation of political confusion, when the popular masses are not united, while the bases of the old regime have been eaten away in the process of historical evolution.[23]

For the SPGB, the ultimate irony (and justification for its position) occurred when Lenin and the Bolsheviks — by now dubbed "the opportunist weathercocks" — abolished the power of workers' councils in the factories in January 1920, and instructed their followers in the more advanced capitalist states to adopt the tactic of 'revolutionary parliamentarism', aiming not to smash the bourgeois state and transfer power to malleable councils of workers, but to capture control of the state machine without specific recourse to the 'universal form' of the soviet.[24] This proved to the SPGB that the real 'universal form' for the Bolsheviks was the dictatorship of the vanguard party. The soviets, originally thrown up as products of popular will and democratic intent under autocratic Tsarism, proved to be the dispensable means to this end.

The Economic Basis of Soviet Russia

The SPGB's analysis of the economic foundation of Soviet Russia under the Bolshevik dictatorship rested on a firmly materialist basis. As socialism could not be established in backward, isolated Russian conditions where the majority of the population neither understood, nor wanted, socialism, the position of the Bolsheviks was judged to be a necessarily precarious one. A precipitous takeover of power had put the them in a position where the achievement of their ultimate goal of a communist society was not a realistic prospect. The *Socialist Standard* commented in 'A Socialist View of Bolshevist Policy' that with socialism necessarily absent from the immediate political agenda in such a situation, "the minority in power in an economically backward country are forced to adapt their program to the undeveloped conditions and make continual concessions to the capitalist world around them",[25] thus echoing the words of Marx in his Preface to the First Edition of *Capital*:

One nation can and should learn from others. Even when a society has begun to track down the natural laws of its movement ... it can neither leap over the natural phases of its movement nor remove them by decree. But it can shorten and lessen the birth pangs.[26]

In the absence of world socialist revolution, there could only be one road forward for semi-feudal Russia — the capitalist road. With the virtual elimination of the small Russian bourgeoisie, it would be necessary for the Bolsheviks to develop industry through the state ownership of enterprises and the forced accumulation of capital. In *The Impending Catastrophe and How to Combat It*, written before the November revolution, Lenin had envisaged just such an approach to the Russian crisis. According to this document, Lenin saw that immediate measures required included nationalisation of the existing banks and the formation of a single state bank, together with the nationalisation of all insurance companies, the nationalisation of the monopolies and all other key industrial concerns. The *Socialist Standard* took the opportunity to again cast doubt on the supposed general applicability of Bolshevik actions — in this instance, the development of 'state capitalism' as a precondition for the establishment of socialism:

> If we are to copy Bolshevik policy in other countries we should have to demand State Capitalism, which is not a step towards Socialism in advanced capitalist countries. The fact remains, as Lenin is driven to confess, that we do not have to learn from Russia, but Russia has to learn from lands where large scale production is dominant.[27]

Lenin's essential claim was that state-monopoly capitalism provided the necessary technical conditions for the advance to socialism. (The SPGB's ire was raised further by apparent references from Lenin to the already 'socialist' nature of Russia, though such references were later exposed to have usually been incorrect renderings by over-enthusiastic translators of occasions when Lenin actually talked of 'state capitalism'.)[28] In fact Lenin made the nature of the economic structure to be developed in Russia quite clear in April 1918:

> What is state capitalism under Soviet power? To achieve state capitalism at the present time means putting into effect the accounting and control the capitalist classes carried out. We see a sample of state capitalism in Germany. We know that Germany has proved superior to us ... state capitalism would be our salvation; if we had it in Russia, the transition to full socialism would be easy, would be within our grasp, because state capitalism is something centralised, calculated, controlled and socialised, and that is exactly what we lack ... Only the development of state capitalism, only the painstaking establishment of accounting and control, only the strictest organisation and labour discipline, will lead us to socialism. Without this there is no socialism.[29]

As the SPGB took great pains to point out to its opponents, Lenin here admitted that the social formation in Soviet Russia was essentially state capitalist, albeit under the guidance and control of an imperfect 'proletarian state'. For Lenin, the nature of the revolutionary polity in such circumstances was the crucial determinant of the type of social system in existence. Without what Lenin termed "revolutionary democracy", state capitalist monopoly would remain state capitalism. With workers' control of production and control of the proletarian state by the vanguard party of the working class, however, socialism would be a reality. According to *The Impending Catastrophe and How To Combat It*, socialism was merely "state-capitalist monopoly made to serve the interests of the whole people", a definition generally accepted by the organisations of orthodox, possibilist social democracy, who also viewed state-monopoly capitalism based on the nationalisation of industry and state planning of the economy to be the foundation of a socialist system of society. Indeed, out of this arose the peculiar situation whereby Lenin attacked the 'parliamentarist' social democrats for advocating state capitalism without working class control, while Kautsky for the social democrats threw the charge back by accusing the Bolsheviks of advocating state capitalism in the form of a nationalised economy under the stifling rule of a vanguardist dictatorship.[30]

As Lenin had commented, the precise aim of the Bolsheviks was to build up a form of state-monopoly capitalism on the German model, under the political control of a 'revolutionary democratic' state. Nationalisation of key productive and distributive units was judged to be an essential prerequisite for the advance towards socialism, with Lenin writing in *The State and Revolution* that a "witty German Social-Democrat of the seventies of the last century called the postal service an example of the socialist economic system. This is very true ... To organise the whole economy on the lines of the postal service ... under the control and leadership of the armed proletariat — is our immediate aim."[31] The SPGB viewed this as state capitalism, no matter what political conditions appertained. To the SPGB, nationalisation and state direction of the economy was state capitalism in Germany, state capitalism when advocated by the British Labour Party, and most certainly state capitalism under the dictatorship of the Bolsheviks. The existence of supposedly benevolent governments and 'workers' states' could not in itself change the exploitative character of the economic basis of society. As for the German postal service under Bismarck being an example of embryonic socialism, Engels in *Socialism: Utopian and Scientific* had ridiculed Bismarck's extension of state ownership in the economy as "spurious socialism",[32] a description the SPGB was happy to endorse.

More than twenty years after the Bolshevik seizure of power, the SPGB was to show it remained unconvinced that state capitalism was really socialism even if presided over by those who proclaimed themselves socialist:

> ... the chief characteristics of Capitalism [in Russia] have not disappeared and are not in the process of disappearing. Goods are not produced for use but for sale to those who have the money to buy, as in other countries. The workers are not members of a social system in which the means of wealth production are

socially owned and controlled, but are wage-earners in the employ of the State or of semi-State concerns, etc. The Russian State concerns are no more 'socially owned' than is the British Post Office or the Central Electricity Board, or any private company ... The Bolshevik attempt to usher in Socialism by 'legal enactments' and by 'bold leaps' before the economic conditions were ripe, and before the mass of the population desired Socialism, has been a total failure. In course of time that failure will become obvious to the workers inside and outside Russia.[33]

Capitalism, based on the separation of the producers from the means of production had not been abolished, nor could it have been. Production still took place as a system of exchange involving the circulation of capital. Capital was self-expanding at the point of production consequent on the exploitation of wage labour, and articles of wealth were still being produced for sale on the market with a view to the realisation of surplus value. Indeed, much of the SPGB's early analysis of the economic basis of the Soviet system reflected a desire to demonstrate the similarities between Russian state capitalism and the British private enterprise based capitalism the SPGB was most familiar with. Until the late 1920s and Stalin's extensive programmes of forced accumulation and the collectivisation of agriculture, the SPGB tended to cautiously characterise the Soviet system as being a mixture of private and state capitalism. Articles in the *Socialist Standard* seized on official Soviet statements and publications showing the existence of rent, interest and profit in Russia, a striking confirmation to the SPGB that Russia was still a part of world capitalism and that the Russian workers were exploited by capitalists. One such piece in the *Standard* entitled 'Russia: Land Of High Profits' pointed to increased Russian trade with the major capitalist powers, and the "staggering profits", on average 81 per cent for 1926-7, gleaned by the Concession Companies from the exploitation of Russian workers.[34] The SPGB mocked the 1917 Bolshevik slogan of 'Down with the foreign bondholders', saying that though the foreign bondholders had been well and truly 'downed' with the initial repudiation of the National Debt built up under Tsarism, they had been replaced with Russian bondholders — "a distinction without difference from the standpoint of the Russian workers".[35] The right of inheritance and massive income inequality served to further reinforce the Party's view that "Russian capitalism, although administered by the Communist Party dictatorship, reproduces almost down to the last detail the paraphernalia of the capitalist world as we know it here".[36] The SPGB had thought it likely right from the Bolshevik ascension to power that the new Russian rulers would have to compromise with the capitalist world, particularly to attract finance necessary for the schemes of forced industrialisation undertaken, and to obtain much needed foreign currency. But despite the adoption of the New Economic Policy in 1921 and the move back towards some forms of small scale private enterprise, state capitalism in its various forms proved to be well and truly established in Soviet Russia, and the more open compromises with world capitalism entered into by the Communist Party in the 1920s were understandable given the task undertaken by the Russian rulers — to drag backward Russia into the twentieth century through the development of capitalist relations of production after the almost complete destruction of the tiny Russian bourgeoisie in 1917.

It was evident to the SPGB that under the guise of 'proletarian revolution', the Bolshevik dictatorship had taken over the historic role of a largely absent capitalist class. In this sense, the SPGB viewed the Bolshevik ascent to power as not so much a socialist revolution as a coup carried out by a political minority when the rule of Tsarist autocracy had already been overthrown pending the full development of bourgeois political democracy. Lenin and the Bolsheviks had put themselves in a position which Engels had warned against as far back as 1850, and the growth of state capitalism was the necessary consequence:

> The worst thing that can befall the leader of an extreme party is to be compelled to take over a government when society is not yet ripe for the domination of the class he represents and for the measures which that domination implies. What he *can* do depends not upon his will but on the degree of antagonism between the various classes, and upon the development of the material means of existence, of the conditions of production and commerce on which class contradictions always repose. What he *ought* to do, what his party demands of him, again depends not upon him or the stage of development of the class struggle and its conditions. He is bound to the doctrines and demands hitherto propounded which, again, do not proceed from the class relations of the moment … Thus, he necessarily finds himself in an unsolvable dilemma. What he *can* do contradicts all his previous actions and principles, and the immediate interests of his party, and what he *ought* to do cannot be done. In a word, he is compelled to represent not his party or his class, but the class for whose domination the movement is then ripe. In the interest of the movement he is compelled to advance the interests of an alien class, and to feed his own class with talk and promises, and with the assertion that the interests of that alien class are their own interests. He who is put into this awkward position is irrevocably lost.[37]

'Transitional Society' or 'Political Period of Transition'?
While the SPGB certainly took the view that the Bolsheviks were "irrevocably lost", the Bolsheviks, together with their supporters in Britain, argued that those who failed to heed the lessons of the remarkable Russian triumph would be doomed to irrelevance. For a tiny organisation on the fringes of the labour movement, however — and for all its alleged irrelevance — the SPGB's presence in the political arena was an important one. With the devastating split in the Socialist Labour Party in 1920-1, when over a third of the SLP membership joined with the British Socialist Party and other radical left-wingers to form the pro-Bolshevik Communist Party of Great Britain, the SPGB remained the one organisation that could plausibly and persistently challenge the claims of Lenin's followers in Britain to be the bearers of a truly Marxist perspective.

During the politically turbulent 1920s and 30s, the SPGB proved to be the Communist Party's harshest critic, denouncing at every turn the "Leninist distorters of Marx", and in so doing provoking officially sanctioned verbal and physical abuse from Communist Party members.[38]

To the SPGB, nowhere had Leninists distorted Marx more than on the question of the revolutionary transformation of capitalism into the future society based on common ownership. A whole new political vocabulary had arisen with the ascent of Lenin, Trotsky and then Stalin, and this had found principal expression in the phrase 'transitional society', a term employed with increasing frequency by the would-be Bolsheviks in the Communist Party of Great Britain. As the Russian experience had apparently demonstrated the impossibility of immediately replacing capitalism with communism, the CPGB argued for the necessity of a society in transition from capitalism to communism, which would exhibit features of both systems without being either. In this transitional stage, the working class through the active role of the vanguard party would be the ruling class in society, and would build up a socialist system, which, as frankly admitted by Lenin if not generally by his supporters, was really "state monopoly capitalism made to run in the interests of the whole people". While the wages system would still exist under this 'socialist system', it was claimed that the exploitation of the working class would not, and though buying and selling would continue, commodity production would be abolished with the adoption of a centralised plan of production. By way of justification, it was claimed that this transitional society was what Marx had referred to as the "political period of transition" between capitalism and communism.[39]

The SPGB enthusiastically set about refuting these claims that Marx had advocated such a 'transitional society' or that the creation of such a system was a desirable working class aim in Russia or anywhere else. Nowhere, it was true, had Marx use the term 'transitional society' or referred to socialism as a transitional mode of production between capitalism and communism. On the contrary, both Marx and Engels had used the terms 'socialism' and 'communism' interchangeably to refer to a system of society based on common ownership, democratic control, and production for use. In his 1888 Preface to the *Communist Manifesto*, Engels had described why Marx in particular preferred to use the word 'communism', though there was no real difference in meaning between the two, with 'common ownership' and 'social ownership' being synonyms.[40] Marx had certainly written of the 'higher' and 'lower' phases of communist society, but these were precisely phases of communist, and not some other, society. In both phases of communism/socialism, the wages system would have to have been abolished along with commodity production, the market, money and the state.

Any talk of a 'transitional' mode of production, often called 'socialism' by the Bolsheviks' supporters in Britain, was nonsensical to the SPGB. To them it was simply not true that communist relations of production could permeate capitalism in the same way that capitalism had slowly evolved out of, and eventually eclipsed, feudalism. Private property societies could permeate one another in such a manner, but the change from private ownership of the means of living to common ownership would have to necessitate a definite break in the form of a social revolution carried out by the working class capturing state power and using it to socialise production. The SPGB considered that the period in which the working class wields state power in order to establish socialism/communism corresponds to the "political period of transition" referred to by Marx in the *Communist Manifesto* and elsewhere, in which the economic basis of society is implicitly still capitalist. The length of this expressly political transition period would depend primarily on the level of development of the forces of production. Marx and Engels envisaged a lengthy political period of transition in their early years and a much shorter one when the productive forces had already developed to a sufficient degree to make the introduction of socialism/communism (initially with the labour-time voucher system of rationing) immediately possible.[41]

The basically state capitalist programme of measures advocated by Marx and Engels in 1848 in the second section of the *Communist Manifesto* was explicitly designed to raise the level of the productive forces "as rapidly as possible", but with the advent of the second industrial revolution Engels could already write in 1888 that no special stress was placed on these measures as "this programme has in some details become antiquated".[42] By the twentieth century, this was most definitely the case, and in the eyes of the SPGB this meant that the political period of transition was reduced to being of a fairly negligible duration. This point was made most clearly by Gilbert McClatchie for the SPGB in an authoritative article in the *Socialist Standard* just after the Second World War.[43] Once a class-conscious proletariat had captured control of the state institutions of the various major countries of the world, common ownership could be almost immediately enacted. Hence the 'transition' to socialism could be said to take place under capitalism itself, with capitalism developing the forces of production to a sufficient degree to make a socialist society based on an abundance of wealth possible, while simultaneously providing the conditions which would give rise to, and then help to power, the socialist movement. The conditions foreseen by Marx and Engels in the *Communist Manifesto* a century earlier whereby a politically mature working class came to power in the major industrial countries before the economic basis of society was ready to sustain a socialist/communist mode of production no longer applied, and therefore neither could the lengthy political period of transition when the working class would develop the productive forces under capitalism before socialising production. In the epoch of the truly world capitalism of the twentieth century, the SPGB judged that although a very short political period of transition between capitalism and socialism/communism was necessary to expropriate the bourgeoisie and socialise production, this no longer needed to be the more lengthy period countenanced by Marx and Engels in the mid nineteenth century.[44] As for a 'transitional society' between the two systems, this was a Leninist distortion never to be found in Marx and without any applicability for the socialist movement whatsoever.

The Capitalist Class in Russia

If, as the SPGB asserted, capitalism existed in the Soviet Union under the political dictatorship of the Communist Party, and not 'socialism' or some sort of 'workers' state', it was reasonable for the Party's opponents to demand who or what constituted the exploiting capitalist class there.[45] Clearly, the fledgling bourgeoisie had been expropriated after the Bolshevik seizure of power and no longer had private ownership rights and property titles to the rapidly developing means of production. As the SPGB pointed out, however, this did not mean that all investment was conducted through state channels and the SPGB devoted much time, especially in the inter-war period, towards publicising the amount of investment by private capitalists in the Soviet economy. As one writer in the *Socialist Standard* commented:

> ... investment, in the National Debt, in the co-operatives, and in the trading concerns, etc. are forms of exploitation of the Russian workers. They, like the workers everywhere, carry on their backs a class of property owners, receiving incomes from property ownership.[46]

In the early years of the SPGB's analysis of Soviet Russia, the Party concentrated on the more peripheral, though not insignificant, forms of non-state ownership in the Soviet economy and the manner in which the Communist Party rulers were forced to compromise with investors and financiers from both inside and outside Russia. More significantly, the SPGB also argued that the capitalist nature of Soviet Russia and its necessary trading and investment relations with the rest of the capitalist world meant that it had a developing internal class system that was far removed from the amicable relationship between "the only two classes in Russian society, workers and peasants" referred to by Stalin in his statement on the new Constitution of 1936. The *Socialist Standard* claimed:

> ... this statement ... dismisses the cleavage of interests between peasants and workers, and it leaves out of account, as if they did not exist, the elaborate arrangements by means of which an officially favoured minority of Russian citizens can enjoy a very high standard of living, which stands in increasing contrast to the conditions of the great majority. In this, and in the investment system, and in the laws which permit the inheritance of property, Russia is facing a progressive differentiation into classes.[47]

Ammunition for the SPGB's view of the class nature of Soviet Russia was provided by supporters of the Russian dictatorship such as Reg Bishop in his book *Soviet Millionaires*,[48] where it was claimed that the existence of 'rouble millionaires' was proof of economic success and the rapid progress of Russia under the Communists.

Inequality of wealth was a chief target of the SPGB and as the Russian state became even more centralised and dominant this increasingly necessitated an analysis of what under Stalin became the most noticeable source of privilege — the party/state machinery itself and the nomenklatura system based on it. The SPGB was not slow to attack the privilege and riches accruing to the top Communist Party bureaucrats, military officials and factory managers who were variously referred to as "the ruling clique", the "new bureaucracy" and "the ruling class". This latter term became the SPGB's standard reference to a Russian elite clearly privileged both in control of the means of living and in consumption. Strangely, however, it was not until well after the departure of Khrushchev that the SPGB systematically referred to this ruling elite as a specifically capitalist class. In earlier SPGB texts this was sometimes implied,[49] but the Party always stopped short of actually labelling this privileged group openly 'capitalist'. This was, in fact, a fundamental contradiction in the SPGB's analysis that tended to mar the Party's otherwise clear critique of Soviet state capitalism. How could, for instance, a privileged ruling class in a major capitalist country, in the very epoch of world capitalism, not be a capitalist class? A ruling class, taken to mean a social class exercising control of the state machine through its hold on political power, could not rise to its dominant position in society divorced from the material conditions of production. Given the by now large-scale development of capitalist industry in Russia, the ruling class certainly was not the peasantry and explicitly not the working class, which had not in Russia or anywhere else won the "battle of democracy" and was not in a position to socialise production. As the SPGB itself had affirmed early on, the Bolsheviks in Russia had been forced by circumstances to take the capitalist road and to perform the historic functions of the capitalist class in their attempts to defeat backwardness through the development of industry and the forced accumulation of capital.

The failure of the SPGB to identify the Soviet ruling elite as a specifically capitalist class paradoxically stemmed from the view that capitalists lived off unearned income accruing from the exploitation of the working class which was consequent on their ownership of the means of living. The Russian ruling elite did not possess legal property titles to the means of production in Russia, and furthermore appeared to receive their income in the form of wages and salaries rather than in the 'holy trinity' of rent, interest and profit. To compound the Party's theoretical contradiction, many SPGB members therefore judged that the Communist Party bureaucrats were members of the working class dependent on the sale of their labour power — who also constituted a privileged 'ruling class' keeping the working class as a whole in subjection.

This issue of the nature of the Russian ruling class was not resolved until the SPGB's Annual Conference in 1969, when a motion was carried that "the ruling class in state capitalist Russia stands in the same relationship to the means of production as does the ruling class in any other capitalist country (viz. it has a monopoly of those means of production and extracts surplus value from the working class) and is therefore a capitalist class".[50] The proponents of the motion, generally younger members who had entered the Party in the 1960s, argued that the Communist Party bureaucrats, enterprise managers and other top officials performed the functions of a capitalist class in that they monopolised the means of living by only allowing others access to it via the operation of the wages system, and also accumulated capital out of the value created in the sphere of production by wage labour, a value greater in magnitude than that paid in wages and salaries as the price of labour power. Although it was not essential to their status, capitalists invariably had greater incomes on average than workers because of their privileged position in the productive process as the "functionaries of capital". These SPGB members argued that the state capitalist class, like the privately owning capitalist class in the West, was privileged in consumption, receiving bloated 'salaries' that were not the price of labour power but a portion of the total surplus value created by the working class. The state capitalist class in Russia was also judged to be privileged because of the multitude of benefits and perks open to them, including access to exclusive consumption outlets such as expensive shops and restaurants from which the working class was physically denied access.[51]

The opponents of this view in the SPGB pointed out the extent to which private enterprise operated in Russia, with 'non-official' economic activity accounting for up to one quarter of the total. These members claimed that a private enterprise capitalist class certainly existed in Russia, and that to say that it was the bureaucracy who were the collective capitalists overlooked this. Indeed, it was prophetically argued that the long-term ambition of many in the bureaucracy was probably to convert themselves into a privately-owning capitalist class on Western lines operating in a mixed state/private enterprise economy that would be more efficient than the then already stagnating Soviet system.[52]

Those who took this position and opposed the 1969 Conference motion, largely the older Party members with more formal and legalistically based definitions of the capitalist class, argued that both Marx and Engels had opposed the view that privileged managers and bureaucrats were actually capitalists. Edgar Hardcastle ('Hardy'), a member particularly revered by the membership for his extensive knowledge of economics and who had been an editor of the *Socialist Standard* for most of the period since the early 1920s, said that Marx and Engels had held that under state-owned capitalism the capitalists were forced out of control by salaried officials.[53] Engels had commented that although the transformation of enterprises into state concerns "does not do away with the capitalistic nature of the productive forces" and also that "the more [the state] proceeds to the taking over of the productive forces, the more does it actually become the national capitalist, the more citizens does it exploit", at the same time "All the social functions of the capitalist are now performed by salaried employees. The capitalist has no further social function other than tearing off coupons, and gambling on the stock exchange … "[54] Marx, too, had written of the progressive separation of the functions of the capitalist on the one hand as a manager, and on the other as "a mere owner, a mere money capitalist", saying that "the manager's salary is or should be simply the wage for a certain kind of skilled labour, its price being regulated in the labour market like that of any other labour."[55] In one particularly apposite passage of *Capital* Marx had written that:

> Capitalist production has itself brought it about that the work of supervision is readily available, quite independent of the ownership of capital. It has therefore become superfluous for this work of supervision to be performed by the capitalist. A musical conductor need in no way be the owner of the instruments in his orchestra, nor does it form part of his function as a conductor that he should have any part in paying the 'wages' of the other musicians. [56]

Given the structure of the nineteenth century English industrial capitalism analysed by Marx, it can hardly be surprising that he identified the capitalist class as the private owners of capital with legal property titles to the means of living. There was, though, a definite recognition on Marx's part that even in the 1840s a "new swindle" of dubious management and supervision was arising in joint-stock companies, the remuneration of which was not the price of labour power at all, and 'wages' in name only. Directors and managers were already beginning to use their position of control to command a portion of the surplus value for their own consumption needs, with Marx wryly stating that "the wages of supervision are in inverse proportion, as a rule, to the actual supervision exercised by these nominal directors."[57]

As the majority in the SPGB pointed out, the view that the Russian ruling bureaucracy simply carried out the role of managers and trustees clearly overlooked their emergence as a controlling class holding sole responsibility for the accumulation of capital, making key decisions about what to produce, how much to produce, where to produce it, and, if possible, the rate at which it should be produced. This controlling class could not be equated with the supervisors and managers referred to by Marx who received a wage based on the amount needed to produce and reproduce their labour power. On the contrary, this class of bureaucrats was using its position of control to perform the functions carried out by individual capitalists in earlier phases of capitalism's development and to command a privileged income derived from surplus value. Though it did not have legal title to the means of production, and was not able to bequeath property, it was, as the proponents of the motion at SPGB Conference argued, clearly a possessing class of the type mentioned in the SPGB Declaration of Principles, exercising a "monopoly … of the wealth taken from the workers".

The prevailing view in the SPGB came to be that the nature of a class could not be determined simply by legal forms or even by methods of recruitment (the Soviet possessing class was not recruited via inheritance but by other, more meritocratic methods, that have not been entirely unusual for possessing classes in history).[58] The Party, or certainly the vast body of its membership, ultimately concluded that although the state capitalist class did not have legal property titles to the means of production, it nonetheless constituted a capitalist class exercising a collective ownership of the means of production and distribution. What was judged to be of prime importance, therefore, was the social reality of capitalism rather than a particular legal form. The opponents of the theory of state capitalism, to the SPGB, had never been able to see beyond the latter.

State Capitalism as a Theory

While the SPGB was the first political group in Britain, and possibly the world, to identify the state capitalist direction taken by Russia under the Communist Party dictatorship, many others came to the same conclusion, if not always for the same reasons. Unlike the SPGB, most of these groups stood in the Leninist tradition or at least showed a willingness to identify positive aspects of the Bolshevik takeover that could be applied by the socialist movement elsewhere in the future. In particular, the Leninist conception of socialism as state ownership and direction of the economy under the control of a vanguard party operating through the political medium of workers' councils was readily accepted by most of these groups. Hence they only later ascribed a 'state capitalist' characterisation to Russia when they judged that state ownership no longer coincided with 'proletarian democracy' and the power of the soviets. This was essentially the analysis initially put forward by 'council communists' such as Otto Ruhle who saw in the crushing of the soviets the rise of "commissar-despotism" and state capitalism[59] (Ruhle himself later realised the inadequacy of this position and came to view nationalisation and state regulation as intrinsically state capitalist). The largest 'left communist' group in Europe, the German KAPD, developed a similar perspective. It identified capitalism as the private (specifically non-state) ownership of the means of production, and, like the council communist Workers' Socialist Federation in Britain, praised the Bolsheviks for their construction of socialism in the industrial centres of Russia. Later, the KAPD became critical of the Soviet system with the final crushing of the soviets and the introduction of the New Economic Policy,[60] which it thought heralded a 'reversion to capitalism'.

Despite the initial excesses of left communist and council communist groups who invariably let their early admiration for the Soviet political form dominate their analysis, the worst example from the SPGB perspective of the conflation of socialism with state ownership plus 'revolutionary democracy' came from the Trotskyists. Ironically, the Trotskyist theories of state capitalism, being by far the most fragile, are the most well known. C. L. R. James and Raya Dunayevskaya from the American Socialist Workers' Party were the first Trotskyists to break with Trotsky himself and identify the state capitalist nature of the USSR,[61] though perhaps the most widely known theory was that elaborated by Tony Cliff and circulated as a discussion document within the Revolutionary Communist Party of Britain in the period immediately after the Second World War, before being published as *Russia: A Marxist Analysis*. Cliff's reasons for breaking with orthodox Trotskyism by identifying the Soviet Union as state capitalist were plain enough:

> When I came to the theory of state capitalism I did not come to it by a long analysis of the law of value in Russia ... Nothing of the sort. I came to it by the simple statement that ... you cannot have a workers' state without the workers having power to dictate what happens in society.[62]

Cliff's analysis was firmly rooted in the idea that the USSR was a form of 'workers' state' before Stalin's first Five Year Plan of 1928 established the bureaucracy as a new class consuming surplus value. Like all the Trotskyists that have followed him, Cliff did not identify the USSR as a society developing along state capitalist lines from 1917 but only from Stalin's ascension to power — under Lenin Russia was supposedly a society in transition from capitalism to communism, based on working class power. For Cliff, a perceived change of political control led to a fundamental change in economic structure, to what in fact amounted to a 'reversion to capitalism'. Perhaps surprisingly, those Trotskyists who remained faithful to Trotsky's own view when in exile of Russia as a "degenerated workers' state" made some of the most pertinent criticisms of Cliff's analysis, particularly his conclusion that the economic structure of the Soviet system had changed in 1928 and had assumed a capitalist basis. Foremost among these critics was rival British Trotskyist Ted Grant:

> If Comrade Cliff's thesis is correct, that state capitalism exists in Russia today, then he cannot avoid the conclusion that state capitalism has been in existence since the Russian Revolution and the function of the revolution itself was to introduce this state capitalist system of society. For despite his tortuous efforts to draw a line between the economic basis of Russia before the year 1928 and after, the economic basis of Russian society has remained unchanged ... money, labour power, the existence of the working class, surplus value, etc. are all survivals of the old capitalist system carried over even under the regime of Lenin ... the law of value applies and must apply until there is direct access to the products by the producers.[63]

This conclusion was certainly rejected by Cliff and all the other Trotskyist state capitalist theorists, though not of course by the SPGB.

It should also be recognised that other elements emerged, primarily from the left communist tradition, who revised their analysis of Russia to such an extent that they were able to recognise that Russia under Bolshevik rule had never been anything but capitalist, in their view because of the backwardness of the economy and the isolated nature of the 'proletarian revolution'. This was the view developed by those elements that emerged from the Italian left communist milieu after the Second World War, some of whom in political exile were to group together in the Gauche Communiste de France. The GCF's journal, *Internationalisme*, clearly expressed this perspective, arguing, very much in the manner of the SPGB before them, that events in Russia had shown that it is not enough for socialists to expropriate the private bourgeoisie, and to concentrate capitalist production in the hands of the state, if production itself is to continue on a capitalist basis:

> The most far-reaching expropriation may lead to the disappearance of the capitalists as individuals benefiting from surplus value, but it does not in itself make the production of surplus value, i.e. capitalism itself, disappear. This assertion may at first sight appear paradoxical, but a closer examination of the Russian experience will prove its validity. For socialism to exist, or even a move towards socialism, it's not enough for expropriation to take place: what's essential is that the means of production cease to exist as capital. In other words, the capitalist principle of production has to be overturned. The capitalist principle of accumulated labour commanding living labour with a view to producing surplus value must be replaced by the principle of living labour commanding accumulated labour with a view to producing consumer goods to satisfy the needs of society's members.[64]

Today, many council communist, left communist and Trotskyist political groupings identify Soviet Russia, certainly post-Lenin, as having always been essentially state capitalist, and like the SPGB, they have applied their analysis of Russian society to other 'socialist' countries exhibiting similar features in Asia, Africa and Central America.[65] That the SPGB was not alone in identifying the capitalist nature of the USSR does not of course diminish its status as the one organisation which promoted a state capitalist analysis of the events in Russia at the time of their happening, and not merely with the benefit of hindsight. What is more, the SPGB has remained one of the few organisations committed to such a critique of the USSR and similar regimes, never seeking to adopt or promote the Leninist vanguardism which so clearly led to that state capitalist outcome.

Notes

1. 'The Revolution in Russia — Where it Fails' in *Socialist Standard*, August 1918.
2. See, for instance, *The Left In Britain 1956–68*, p.500.
3. 'Easter 1917 — A Survey and A Statement' in *Socialist Standard*, May 1917.
4. 'The Russian Situation' in *Socialist Standard*, January 1918.
5. *The Socialist*, March 1918.
6. *British Socialists* by Stanley Pierson (Harvard University Press, Cambridge, Massachusetts and London, 1979) p.287.
7. *State Capitalism: The Wages System Under New Management*, pp.119-20.
8. *A History of the Soviet Union* by Geoffrey Hosking (Fontana, London, 1985) p.27.
9. *The Battle of Democracy* by Keith Graham (Wheatsheaf Books, Brighton, 1986) p.206.
10. *What Is To Be Done?* by V. I. Lenin (Foreign Languages Press, Peking, 1976) p.38.
11. *Ten Days That Shook The World* by John Reed (Penguin, Harmondsworth, n.d.) p.263.
12. *Socialism From Science To Practice* by Karl Radek (Socialist Labour Press, Glasgow, n.d.) p.17.
13. *Lenin* by David Shub (Pelican, London, 1966) p.26.
14. 'Where Russia Stands' in *Socialist Standard*, July 1921.
15. 'A Socialist View Of Bolshevist Policy' in *Socialist Standard*, July 1920.
16. 'Democracy and Dictatorship in Russia' in *Socialist Standard*, December 1919.
17. Friedrich Engels's Introduction to *Class Struggles In France 1848–50* by Karl Marx (Progress Publishers, Moscow, 1972) p.18.
18. *The Civil War in France* by Karl Marx (Foreign Languages Press, Peking, 1977) p.66.
19. *Selected Correspondence of Karl Marx and Friedrich Engels* (Progress Publishers, Moscow. 1975) p.345.
20. 'Parliament or Soviet? A Critical Examination' in *Socialist Standard*, April 1920.
21. 'A Socialist View of Bolshevist Policy' in *Socialist Standard*, July 1920.
22. The SPGB addressed itself on numerous occasions to the view that the Bolshevik 'workers' state' mirrored the Paris Commune. See, for instance, the arguments deployed against John Keracher of the American Communist paper *The Proletarian*, published in the *Socialist Standard* in August and December 1930. While the SPGB denied the claims of the Communists on this point forcefully enough, the association of one with the other was enough to deter the Party from celebrating the Commune after 1918.
23. *The State and the Socialist Revolution* by Julius Martov (Slienger, London, 1977) p.14.
24. 'The Super-Opportunists' in *Socialist Standard*, August 1920.
25. 'A Socialist View of Bolshevist Policy' in *Socialist Standard*, July 1920.
26. *Capital*, Volume I, by Karl Marx (Penguin, London and Harmondsworth, 1976) p.92.
27. 'A Socialist View of Bolshevist Policy' in *Socialist Standard*, July 1920.
28. See 'Lenin and State Capitalism' in *Socialist Standard*, August 1990.
29. 'Report On the Immediate Tasks Of the Soviet Government' in *On State Capitalism*

During the Transition To Socialism by V. I. Lenin (Progress Publishers, Moscow, 1985) pp.24-7.

30. *Terrorism and Communism* by Karl Kautsky (George Allen and Unwin, London, 1920) pp.201-2.
31. *The State and Revolution* by V. I. Lenin (Progress Publishers, Moscow, 1985) pp.49-50.
32. 'Socialism: Utopian and Scientific' by Friedrich Engels in *Marx and Engels: Basic Writings*, p.143.
33. *Questions of the Day*, 1942 edition, pp.62-66.
34. 'Russia: Land of High Profits' in *Socialist Standard*, September 1930.
35. *Ibid.*
36. *Ibid.*
37. *The Peasant War in Germany* by Friedrich Engels (Lawrence and Wishart, London, 1969) p.115.
38. 'Impossibilism' by Stephen Coleman in *Non-Market Socialism*, p.97.
39. 'Critique of the Gotha Program' by Karl Marx in *Marx and Engels: Basic Writings*, p.169.
40. 'Manifesto of the Communist Party' in *Marx and Engels: Basic Writings*, p.46.
41. 'The Myth of the Transitional Society' by Adam Buick in *Critique* 5 (Glasgow, n.d.), pp.59-70. This is a detailed refutation, from an SPGB perspective, of the modern applicability of a transitional society.
42. 'Manifesto of the Communist Party' in *Marx and Engels: Basic Writings*, p.47.
43. 'The Transition Period' in *Socialist Standard*, January 1946.
44. 'Marx in His Time' in *Socialist Standard*, September 1973.
45. They often did so. See 'Party News Briefs' in *Socialist Standard*, August 1948.
46. 'Russia: Land of High Profits' in *Socialist Standard*, September 1930.
47. 'The New Russian Constitution' in *Socialist Standard*, January 1937.
48. See 'Local Boy Makes Good' in *Socialist Standard*, February 1944.
49. The furthest the SPGB was prepared to go at this time was to tentatively suggest that the nomenklatura may be "emerging" as a new capitalist class. See the article 'The Russian Capitalist Class' in the *Socialist Standard*, December 1949.
50. SPGB 65th Annual Conference Report. See also *Socialist Standard*, May 1969.
51. See *State Capitalism: The Wages System Under New Management*, pp.56-62. This book was written by two supporters of the motion at the 1969 SPGB Conference.
52. SPGB 65th Annual Conference Report.
53. *Ibid.*
54. 'Socialism: Utopian and Scientific' in *Marx and Engels: Basic Writings*, p.144.
55. *Capital*, Volume III, by Karl Marx (Penguin, Harmondsworth and London, 1981) p.567.
56. *Capital*, Volume III, p.511.
57. *Capital*, Volume III, p.514.
58. *State Capitalism: The Wages System Under New Management*, p.57.
59. *From the Bourgeois To the Proletarian Revolution* by Otto Ruhle (Socialist Reproduction/Revolutionary Perspectives, Glasgow, 1974) p.17.
60. *Anti-Parliamentary Communism: The Movement For Workers' Councils in Britain*

1917-45 by Mark Shipway (MacMillan, London & Basingstoke, 1988), Chapter 2.

61. 'Soviet State Capitalism? The History of an Idea' by William Jerome and Adam Buick in *Survey* 62 (Information Bulletin, London, 1967) p.68.

62. Tony Cliff interviewed in *The Leveller* 30 Sept 1979, pp.20-21. Quoted in *The Far Left In British Politics* by John Callaghan (Basil Blackwell, Oxford, 1987) p.88.

63. 'Against the Theory of State Capitalism' in *The Unbroken Thread* by Ted Grant (Fortress Books, London, 1989) pp.199-220.

64. 'The Russian Experience' from *Internationalisme* 10 (1946) as published in the *International Review* 61 (International Communist Current, London, 1990) p.17.

65. A comprehensive, critical survey of theories of state capitalism is provided by Neil C. Fernandez in his *Capitalism and Class Struggle in the USSR: A Marxist Theory* (Ashgate, Aldershot, 1997), Chapter 2.

4. Economic Crises and the 'Collapse of Capitalism'

Collapse Theory

To many, the massive slump which had occurred in America and Europe during the early 1930s served to confirm what they had believed for some years — that Marxism had predicted capitalism was heading for a cataclysmic economic collapse heralding the onset of socialism, and that it had been right to do so. Among those convinced of impending disaster were the remnants of the old Independent Labour Party including its well-known orator and Glasgow M.P. James Maxton. Maxton, indeed, went further than most, actually giving the collapse of capitalism a date. As the *Daily Record* reported, on 21st August 1931 he told an audience of his constituents:

"I am perfectly satisfied that the great capitalist system that has endured for 150 years in its modern form ... is now at the stage of final collapse, and not all the devices of the statesmen, not all the three party conferences, not all the collaboration between the leaders, can prevent the system coming down with one unholy crash. They may postpone the crash for a month, two months, three months, six months," he cried, forefinger pointing at his audience, and body crouched, "but collapse is sure and certain".[1]

"Sure and certain", also, were the views on the pending collapse of capitalism of at least one prominent member of the Communist Party, who, when invited to take part in a debate with the SPGB replied to the effect that there was no point in arranging a meeting as capitalism would have collapsed before it could have time to take place.[2] Unlike the initially more circumspect ILP, the theory of capitalist collapse was at the centre of the Communist Party's revolutionary strategy from the outset. *The Communist* of 22nd October 1921 stated that those who had founded the CPGB were already "impelled by the conviction that the capitalist system had broken down". Later, the Wall Street Crash and its aftermath merely seemed to confirm capitalism's irreversible decline and descent into chaos. That capitalism had survived the intervening years was no matter — to the Communists its mechanical breakdown was assured.

The reasons why the British Communist Party and eventually much of the ILP held this view were numerous. Cataclysmic views of capitalist crises were adopted by several influential theoreticians of the Second International era, and later many of the overt justifications for capitalist collapse theories were provided by Leninist writers. Third International figures such as Trotsky pointed to the impossibility of an economically restructured Europe after the First World

War[3] while Bukharin was among many identifying the possible collapse of capitalism through a combination of economic crisis and war. It is also likely that the CPGB and ILP picked up much of their belief in economic catastrophe from the rather less well-known figure of Herman Cahn, an American Communist writer who made an impact on the English-speaking revolutionary world after the 1914-8 war with his book *The Collapse of Capitalism* (1919). Cahn argued that the development of a "new force" since Marx's day — the world credit system — had fundamentally destabilized capitalism:

> in the economic world since his time … a new force has grown up which no longer leaves the downfall of capitalism to the vague future, or of its earlier ending to the spread of a high degree of intelligence among the real proletariat, but makes the coming of that great event a matter of figures and entirely independent of the collective will of men. The war has enormously hastened the development of this force, and the catastrophe is imminent.[4]

The apparent instability at the heart of capitalism seemed to indicate to Cahn that it was incapable of survival, with or without the conscious efforts of the working class to overthrow it. Most earlier revolutionary writers and propagandists tempted by collapsist notions had stopped short of this conclusion, instead relying on mechanistic beliefs in the inevitability of the working class rising up to overthrow the system at a time of devastating economic crises, huge unemployment and widespread poverty. Among the generation of late nineteenth century revolutionaries, Engels had taken this latter view when writing during the crisis of the 1880s that it was almost possible "to calculate the moment when the unemployed, losing patience, will take their fate into their own hands".[5] Henry Hyndman of the SDF wrote at the same time that "it is quite possible that during this very crisis … an attempt will be made to substitute collective for capitalist control".[6] Their view, at the time of Britain's first Great Depression, had been that the crisis of capitalism was not only severe but probably fatal because of its galvanising effects on the working class. Karl Kautsky, whose writings had a profound impact on both the reformist and revolutionary elements in the international social democratic movement, took a similar stand, arguing that capitalism would probably be overthrown by the working class before it reached its final stage of stagnation and economic collapse. He did, at times, however, indicate the belief, later taken up by Cahn and many of the Bolsheviks, that even without the necessary revolutionary action of the mass of the working class, capitalism was incapable of prolonged survival. His expectation of working class action to overthrow capitalism was firm until the latter periods of his political life, but in arguing against the openly revisionist elements in the Second International he nonetheless claimed to identify purely economic barriers standing in the way of capitalism's future development:

... it is clear that the capitalist mode of production becomes impossible from the historical moment when the market can no longer extend in the same tempo as production; that is, as soon as overproduction becomes chronic. Bernstein understands historical necessity to mean a situation of constraint. Here we have such a situation which, if and when it appears, will infallibly lead to socialism.[7]

The meaning of this particular passage is clear — even if the working class fails to rise up to establish socialism, capitalism as a mode of production becomes "impossible" and is finished, with socialism as the only possible alternative rising pheonix-like from the ashes.

To the British Communist Party, arguments such as this, and the later views of Leninists like Trotsky, Bukharin and Cahn, testified to their belief that economic collapse was imminent. Though the working class did not follow their cause to any great measure during times of relative capitalist expansion, the economic crisis would at last give the vanguard of the working class its chance, and capitalism — either directly overthrown by the vanguard in the first stirrings of crisis or fatally broken by the total collapse of production — would be gone forever.

The SPGB's Political Refutation of Collapse Theory

The Socialist Party of Great Britain responded to these claims by the CPGB and ILP with a mixture of scepticism and derision — scepticism when they were first forcefully put forward during the slump of the early 1920s, and derision when they were repeated with equal force in the next slump ten years later. During the crisis of the early 1920s, the SPGB noted in the *Socialist Standard* Communist predictions of a total collapse of capitalist production within a decade and was quick to remark after the first five years, and then the full ten, that such a collapse had not taken place and that moreover it did not look likely.[8] To the Communist Party, only the timeframe for the projected collapse had altered — the underlying soundness of their collapsist position remained intact.

Whatever the precise predictions of economic disaster on offer, the SPGB saw great dangers to the cause of socialism in the collapse-based politics of the CPGB and ILP. The SPGB view of social revolution was, after all, one based on mass understanding of the failings of capitalism and the necessity of socialism, and before the 1930s its opposition to collapse theories was primarily political. The idea that capitalism could physically collapse and socialism somehow appear without the conscious action of the majority of workers was anathema. In 1932, when prophesies of capitalist collapse had reached a peak during the major world economic crisis, the SPGB set out to specifically counter the arguments of its opponents with a short pamphlet entitled *Why Capitalism Will Not Collapse*. This pamphlet, which sold out its initial print run of 10,000 in just over a year, set out to address the most important political aspect of the issue:

... our work has been made more difficult by the idea that Capitalism may collapse of its own accord. It is clear that if Capitalism were going to collapse under the weight of its own problems then it would be a waste of time and energy to carry on socialist propaganda and to build up a real socialist party aiming at political power. If it were true, as is claimed, that Capitalism will have broken down long before it will be possible for us to win over a majority for the capture of political power, then, indeed, it would be necessary to seek Socialism by some other means. Workers who have accepted this wrong and lazy idea of collapse have neglected many activities that are absolutely essential. They have taken up the fatalistic attitude of waiting for the system to end itself. But the system is not so obliging![9]

Having stated the essential point of contention, that of the necessity of organised working class action to achieve socialism, *Why Capitalism Will Not Collapse* went on to examine the views expressed by senior politicians, economists and industrialists during the various capitalist crises from 1829 onwards. This was because it was clear that each crises had brought out its own prophets of doom. These ranged from William Huskisson, President of the Board of Trade in 1829, to Lord Randolph Churchill, who, when commenting on the Great Depression in Britain in the 1870s and 1880s said "Turn your eyes where you will, survey any branch of industry you like, you will find signs of mortal disease." The pamphlet asked its readers to note how alike many of these comments from the capitalist past were and "how each one falsifies the preceding ones. The fact of another crisis taking place is proof enough that the earlier crises did not turn out to be insoluble — the patient cannot have more than one fatal attack."[10] As a result, those who were foretelling disaster in the early 1930s were no more to be believed than those who had foretold collapse in previous crises. Past experience alone had shown collapse theories to be wrong and lacking historical perspective, and there was nothing to indicate that the crisis following on from the Wall Street Crash was going to be significantly different from any of the others, except perhaps in terms of its global spread, with capitalism becoming more interconnected and capital itself more centralised. Ironically enough, Lenin had been closer to the view of the SPGB than most of the British Communists in stating that "no situation for capitalism is without a way out"[11] and Marx had repeatedly referred to the repetitive capitalist trade cycle — "capitalistic production moves through certain periodical cycles. It moves through a state of quiescence, growing animation, prosperity, overtrade, crisis and stagnation".[12] Indeed, Marx had written that "There are no permanent crises",[13] only transitory curtailments of production.

A factor which tended to complicate the entire issue was the precise meaning of such words as "collapse" and "breakdown" — earlier figures in the working class movement had sometimes used these phrases, and so for that matter had one or two of the early writers in the *Socialist Standard*. Unlike the Communists however, they had not usually meant an absolute physical stoppage to production which would signify the "psychological moment" when a vanguard of socialists could seize political power. This point had to be made clear by the SPGB in 1934 in an article entitled 'The Collapse of Capitalism — Attitude of the SPGB' where it was stated that, particularly in the years prior to the First World War, such words were simply intended to be colourful descriptions of normal capitalist crises and that whenever an SPGB propagandist had used these phrases "it would always be against the background of the ... contention that there could be no Socialism without an organised Socialist working class".[14] This comment, interestingly, reiterated an earlier statement in the *Socialist Standard* designed to refute the arguments of a correspondent who had stated that the policy of the SPGB was to "Preach economic consideration as the sole factor in social development, and wait until the crash comes!" On that occasion, in 1905, the Party had given what could be said to be its definitive reply on the political ramifications of economic crises:

> It is inevitable that economic development will bring things to a crisis, but whether from out of this crisis will arise the Socialist Commonwealth depends upon whether sufficient of the working class have been made Socialists, and have been class consciously organised. Obviously, then, to "wait until the crash comes" may be the policy of reform pedlars, but it is decidedly not the policy of the Socialist Party of Great Britain.[15]

The SPGB took the view that while the slump may be the time when the working class is galvanised into action to expropriate the capitalists, the crucial factor in the social revolution still had to be mass socialist consciousness, not the kind of collapse of production later envisaged by Herman Cahn and the Communists:

> A period of revolution begins not because life has become physically impossible, but because growing numbers of workers have their eyes suddenly opened to the fact that problems which they hitherto accepted as part of man's unavoidable heritage have become capable of solution.[16]

The SPGB and the Economic Bases of Collapse Theories

Necessary though it was for the SPGB to deal with the important political ramifications of collapse theory, and to put the lurid claims of the Communist Party and others in historical perspective, a part of the SPGB's opposition to the various collapse theories propounded by its opponents during both the slump of the 1930s and the subsequent economic crises of the post-Second World War period came to rest on what the Party considered to be their gross theoretical inadequacy from the standpoint of Marxian economics. What made the SPGB's task on this front more difficult was the fact that some of the unsound economic theories utilised by proponents of capitalist collapse to justify their case emanated not only from Bolshevik propagandists and rather peripheral figures like Cahn but, as has been seen, from some of the most respected writers and propagandists of the socialist movement — figures such as Kautsky, Luxemburg and even Engels, who had all at some time made statements which were at least implicitly collapsist. A situation thereby developed whereby the SPGB was in the position of challenging some of the claims and pronouncements of the key exponents of Marxian economics, pronouncements that could be — and frequently were — used against it by its opponents.

Kautsky's talk of the capitalist system becoming "impossible" because of the inability of markets to keep pace with production has already been noted. There can similarly be little doubt that while Engels took the same view as the SPGB on the necessity of mass political action to establish socialism, towards the end of his life he developed a very different attitude towards the nature of capitalism's crises. During most of the time of his involvement with the socialist movement, Engels, like Marx, had referred to capitalism's trade cycle as being "periodic", with the cycle judged to complete its course every seven, and then later, every ten years. But by the time of the Great Depression of the late nineteenth century Engels had clearly abandoned this view of capitalism's "periodic" crises. In his 1884 Preface to Marx's *Poverty of Philosophy*, for instance, he talked of the boom after the slump failing to appear and stated that "If it should fail altogether, then chronic stagnation would necessarily become the normal condition of modern industry, with only insignificant fluctuations".[17] In the same Preface Engels refers to Marx basing his communist demands on "the inevitable collapse of the capitalist mode of production which is taking place before our eyes to an ever greater degree".[18] His view that capitalism had by then reached a stage of chronic stagnation and possible collapse was repeated in his 1892 Preface to the English Edition of *The Condition of the Working Class in England*:

> Capitalist production cannot stop. It must go on increasing and expanding, or it must die. Even now the mere reduction of England's lion's share in the supply of the world's markets means stagnation, distress, excess of capital here, excess of unemployed work-people there. What will it be when the increase of yearly production is brought to a complete stop?
>
> Here is ... the heel of Achilles, for capitalistic production. Its very basis is the necessity of constant expansion, and this constant expansion now becomes impossible.[19]

This view was undoubtedly impelled by the depth and duration of the 1873-95 'Great Depression', and in some ways prefigured the arguments of the Communist Party and others in the 1920s and 30s. But what increasingly came to the attention of SPGB members via the propaganda of the Communists was the implication that capitalism had an 'Achilles Heel' of some sort. Was it really the case, for example, that the cause of capitalism's crises was some great flaw in the system itself that would eventually bring it crashing down? Were there tendencies at work in the capitalist economy which meant that the periodicity of capitalism's crises would give way to permanent, chronic stagnation and the possible collapse spoken of by Engels? Was the further development of the capitalist system becoming "impossible" as many asserted?

Engels himself had clearly been in little doubt as to the root cause of the chronic state of stagnation perceived to be the final state of the capitalist system, pending its overthrow. It was as Kautsky, Luxemburg, Bogdanov and others were later to claim, capitalism's inability to find sufficient markets for the entire product of industry. A more common view in Second International circles had been the explicitly class-based argument that crises were caused by the restricted purchasing power of the working class alone, but Engels had elaborated this 'overall deficiency of purchasing power' view memorably in his Preface to the English Edition of Volume I of *Capital*. Here Engels applied a Malthusian argument on overpopulation to the Marxian concept of overproduction for the market:

> *While the productive power increases in a geometric ratio, the extension of markets proceeds at best in an arithmetic one.* The decennial cycle of stagnation, prosperity, overproduction and crisis, ever recurrent from 1825 to 1867, seems to have run its course; but only to land us in the slough of despond of a permanent and chronic depression. The sighed-for period of prosperity will not come ...[20] [emphasis added]

Capitalism's crises manifested themselves as an overproduction of commodities for the market, and if these crises were becoming permanent, then this must be, so the argument ran, because of an inability to find new markets. Nearly thirty years later, just before the outbreak of the First World War, Rosa Luxemburg was to develop a more detailed version of this crude 'underconsumptionist' justification for economic collapse in her work *The Accumulation of Capital*.

Luxemburg went so far as to assert in her polemics against the revisionists in the Second International that the collapse of capitalism was a central tenet of Marxism, stating that "Without the collapse of capitalism the expropriation of the capitalist class becomes impossible".[21] *The Accumulation of Capital* was her attempt to provide the theoretical underpinnings for this view by an elaboration of the tendencies at work within the capitalist mode of production which would ensure its eventual downfall. Just like Engels, Luxemburg claimed to identify a "deep and fundamental antagonism between the capacity to consume and the capacity to produce in a capitalist society"[22] based on the inability of 'pure' capitalism (consisting solely of workers and capitalists) to find sufficient outlets for an ever-increasing surplus product of industry.

Essentially, Luxemburg took the view that aggregate demand in capitalism was simply a reflection of the combined available consumption fund of the workers and the capitalists. When a part of the surplus value accruing to the capitalist class was reinvested in production, then the total available for consumption, and hence aggregate demand, was reduced. The accumulation of capital in 'pure' capitalism would therefore become impossible when there was no-one able to buy the commodities in which this portion of surplus value was embodied. Indeed, the cyclical expansion of the capitalist system in the nineteenth century was itself only explicable in terms of the existence of a non-capitalist periphery to the world economy which could buy this surplus product. By progressively eliminating this periphery through its own sporadic drive towards expansion, capitalism undermined the basis for its continued advancement and would collapse at the point at which there were no non-capitalist areas on the planet left to buy the surplus product.

Luxemburg's argument was, in common with the latter argument of Engels, a particular enunciation of the idea that crises are caused by the inability of the workers and capitalists combined to buy back the entire social product. When it had developed its views of economic crises more fully in the post-1945 period, the SPGB was to point out that this analysis, like all other crude underconsumptionist theories, was fundamentally flawed because of its mistaken view of what constitutes aggregate demand in capitalism.[23] The SPGB was able to assert that aggregate demand is not, as Luxemburg contended, solely determined by the consumption of the workers and the capitalists, but by their consumption plus the investment of the capitalists. The supposedly 'excess' surplus value can be realised on the market when the capitalists, in the process of converting part of this surplus value into capital, buy means of production such as raw materials and machinery from other sections of the capitalist class — and this can always take place so long as the surplus product is not all owned by the one capitalist who, in such a mythical situation, would be condemned to buy his own goods.[24]

In the period from the Second World War onwards, the SPGB was prepared to tackle these apparently erroneous theories from Luxemburg, Engels and others head on in articles and verbal debate, especially when regurgitated by the Party's opponents in the Trotskyist movement, or by the left communists.[25] In the heady atmosphere of the 1920s and 30s however, when — as we shall see, its own crises theory was not fully worked out — the Party was more circumspect in its attacks, indirect or otherwise, on the economic pronouncements of the 'giant' figures of the socialist movement. Its developing economic opposition to the mechanical and fallacious theories of collapse based on crude underconsumptionism took a rather different, and more obviously propagandistic form. For not only did many opponents of capitalism base their economic theories on overall underconsumptionism, but many of the system's supporters did also, fearing that capitalism was fatally flawed and in need of dramatic assistance if it was to be saved. In the days of massive unemployment and declining production they too thought capitalism to be heading for collapse, while holding that they could make interventions within the framework of the system itself to prevent this from happening. The most obvious example of such a group of underconsumption-inspired capitalist economic reformers was the

Social Credit movement led by Major Douglas, and the SPGB devoted much space in the *Socialist Standard* during the early and mid 1930s to debunking the basis of Social Credit's particular arguments for capitalist reform. In doing so it laid the foundations for a sustained critique of underconsumptionist economic thought in general, which was extended in argument in the post-war era to Marxists and non-Marxists alike.

Major Douglas's particular underconsumptionist case was a simple one. Capitalism, he argued, was beset by a permanent deficiency of purchasing power because all the money paid out by enterprises in the form of wages, salaries and dividends could never be enough to buy back the total amount of products placed in the markets by industry as a whole.[26] Enterprises are unable to provide a sufficient 'consumption fund' for this because they have to make other payments to cover the price of raw materials, the cost of bank charges, and other 'external' costs. While all enterprises have to charge a price for their own goods and services which will be enough to cover both of these types of payments, only one of the two types of payment goes toward making up the total purchasing power in the economy capable of buying back all of the consumption goods produced. Therefore, according to Douglas, there was a permanent 'gap' between the prices charged by industry for their goods and the ability of consumers to pay for them. Hence, consumers in capitalism never had enough money to buy all of the commodities produced at prices that covered the entire cost of production. This apparent deficiency of purchasing power was what, Douglas asserted, led to overproduction of commodities, glutted markets, unemployment, and chronic economic stagnation.

The reformist Social Credit movement, unlike Marxians such as Luxemburg and Engels, considered capitalism's chronic tendency towards crises brought about by underconsumption to be capable of solution, and did not necessitate capitalism's overthrow and replacement with socialism. Social Credit's remedy for this perceived defect was as straightforward as the defect itself seemed obvious. If not enough purchasing power existed in capitalist society, governments would have to step in and provide it, thereby closing the 'gap' between prices and consumer demand. Douglas argued that governments could do this by distributing free credits to supplement consumers' incomes through utilising the alleged power of the banks to create multiples of credit from a given deposit base. Banks, he argued, could create credit "with the stroke of a pen" at no cost to themselves, and in this lay the solution to the problem. The SPGB's response to this alleged ability of the banks to inject purchasing power into the economy out of nowhere is discussed in Chapter 7.

Major Douglas's identification of capitalism's supposedly inherent defect (let alone his solution to it) did not go unchallenged in the world of political economy, and the tiny SPGB was foremost among the critics of his Social Credit movement. Indeed, most other political parties, including Labour and even the Communists, had supporters of Social Credit theories within their own ranks.

As Social Credit gained adherents among the reformist parties during the early 1930s, the SPGB published articles and ran meetings countering the arguments of this new group of capitalist reformers. The SPGB's lengthiest and most serious attack on the underconsumptionism of Social Credit came in a series of articles in the *Socialist Standard* during 1933 by Hardy.[27] On the Editorial Committee of the *Standard*, and also the chief research officer for the Union of Post Office Workers, Hardy had spent some time as part of his employment in discussion with leading bankers and economists such as Reginald McKenna and John Maynard Keynes, trying to find ways of disproving Douglas's various contentions. One of the items of interest was the notion that capitalism was going to automatically break down because of its alleged purchasing power deficiency. Hardy noted Douglas's assertion to the MacMillan Committee on Finance and Industry of 1930 that capitalism's inherent underconsumptionist defect had been in existence for at least one hundred years and also his apparent inability to explain why this "inherent defect" had not gone on causing progressive unemployment and trade depression throughout the whole of the period.[28] Douglas had been clearly unable to explain to the Committee why capitalism's crises and depressions had been essentially periodic, interspersed with years of noticeable expansion.

This empirically-based argument was damaging enough to Douglas, but Hardy's own most devastating assaults on Social Credit's underconsumptionism came from the theoretical standpoint of Marxian economics. Firstly, Hardy attacked the reasoning which lay behind Douglas's underconsumptionist assertions about the inability of consumers to buy all the products of industry at prices that covered their entire cost of production:

> Major Douglas is looking at only half the process of production and sale. It is quite true that the money paid out in the form of wages, salaries and dividends in any week or other period will not be sufficient to buy all the products placed on the market by industry as a whole, but it does not have to do so. In any given week the persons with cash and bank deposits with which they can purchase goods, do not consist only of people holding unspent wages, salaries and dividends. It also includes persons (and companies) who have just received payment for raw materials and finished articles which they sold and delivered some time previously and who are now in the market buying finished products and more raw materials, partly for personal consumption and partly for further production.[29]

Among other things, Douglas had failed to take note of the difference between the markets for consumer goods and for producer goods. Although it was true that wages, salaries and dividends could not be enough to buy back the entire product of industry, they did not have to. What use, for instance, would the working class as consumers have for producer goods such as lathes and pig iron? To Hardy and the SPGB there was no doubt that sufficient purchasing power existed in the capitalist economy to sell consumer goods at prices that covered their costs of production, and also enough purchasing power for the buyers and sellers of producer goods to trade those commodities as well. Two years later the substance of this reply to the Social Credit theorists was repeated by John Strachey, then a Communist, in his book *The Nature of Capitalist Crisis*.[30]

Hardy's second argument for the SPGB, however, went beyond this particular criticism of the Douglas theory and was of special significance for it implicitly attacked the basis of all underconsumptionist theories of capitalist collapse from a Marxian standpoint, and served to underpin most of the SPGB's subsequent economic attacks on collapse theories (such as that propounded by Luxemburg). Taking into account the Marxian notion that the exchange value of a commodity is determined by the amount of socially necessary labour time required to produce it from start to finish, and that all income in capitalism is ultimately derived from this value production, Hardy contended that it was possible to state that:

> although the price of an individual commodity need not be the same as its value, the sum total of all values is identical with the sum total of the prices at which the goods actually sell. The total 'purchasing power' in existence at any given time is the sum total of all the values and, therefore, cannot be more or less than the commodities in existence because the two things are the same. To say that there is a 'deficiency of purchasing power' is like saying that the total values or prices of all the goods in the market is greater than the values or prices of all the goods in the market; or like saying that there are goods in existence which have value but which cannot be exchanged for other goods having value — which is absurd.[31]

From the Marxian perspective outlined by Hardy, what the supporters of underconsumptionism had to ask themselves was how, at the level of the economy as a whole, could there be a serious, long-term discrepancy between the additional values of all the commodities produced on the one hand, and the combined additional purchasing power represented by the wages and salaries of the working class and the surplus value divided between the capitalist class, on the other. If underconsumptionism was correct, there would have to be a definite gap between the living labour-time put into commodities as new value, and the combined income derived from it by the workers and capitalists — income for the workers being equal to necessary labour (the amount necessary to ensure their own reproduction as workers), and income for the capitalists being derived from unpaid labour. Essentially, more labour time would have to go into the production of commodities, determining their exchange value, than ever came out again. But this was demonstrably not the case. If it were capitalism could never have periods of prosperity and boom where all the commodities produced most certainly were able to sell at (or around) their values. The idea — essential to all crude underconsumptionist collapse theories — that new value added in the production of commodities could not somehow find purchasing power and sufficient demand, was therefore false. The demand or "purchasing power" certainly existed, though whether it was always utilised in a manner that prevented crises from breaking out was a different question, to be dealt with below.

The SPGB concluded from this that crude underconsumptionist views of capitalist collapse did not bear close analysis, either in particular or when looked at in general from the Marxian view. In the underconsumptionist sense, there was no great 'flaw' in the capitalist system and crude underconsumptionism, at root, rested on a misunderstanding of the relationship outlined by Marx between productive labour and effective demand. The workers and the capitalists combined could buy back all the products produced for sale on the market, and an inability to realise value created in production was not the cause of capitalism's cataclysmic economic crises. Indeed, the type of purchasing power deficiency supposed by Douglas and Luxemburg would have stifled capitalism's advancement completely.

Underconsumptionism in its various forms provided the basis for most collapse of capitalism arguments, but one other theory which also pointed ultimately towards capitalist collapse was to come to the SPGB's attention. It began to find a limited vogue during the 1930s, particularly in some sections of the Communist Party, though without attracting really widespread interest on the left until well after the Second World War, when it was taken up in various forms in Britain by the International Socialists, the Revolutionary Communist Group and others.[32] This was the contention that capitalism would eventually reach a state of permanent crisis or collapse because of the tendency of the rate of profit to fall as a result of technical innovation. A vigorous analysis based on this theme by Henryk Grossman[33] was published in German in 1929, though the most prominent advocate of the falling rate of profit theory in the 1930s was John Strachey, despite the fact that his rendition of it was rather wan compared to the ones from Trotskyists and others which followed in the 1950s and thereafter.

In distinction to crude overall underconsumptionism, the SPGB accepted the central premise of this theory, which was that the rising organic composition of capital (the ratio of constant to variable capital) would, on its own, reduce the rate of profit as capitalism technically progressed by replacing living labour — the sole source of surplus value — with dead labour. Given a constant rate of exploitation this would point to a fall in the rate of profit on the total capital employed. However, the SPGB observed that the most notable aspect of this theory when applied to the actuality of capitalist development was not the rapidity with which the rate of profit fell, but its slothfulness.[34] In practice, the falling rate of profit acted not so much as a continuous, inexorable law of capitalist development, but a mere tendency which could be — and frequently was — counteracted by a variety of other factors. This had clearly been recognised by Marx:

> If we consider the enormous development in the productive powers of social labour ... then instead of the problem of explaining the fall in the profit rate, we have the opposite problem of explaining why this fall is not greater or faster. Counteracting tendencies must be at work, checking and cancelling the effect of the general law and giving it simply the character of a tendency.[35]

The primary factors offsetting, and even reversing, this tendency, included the plethora of methods (shift work being an obvious example) aimed at increasing the rate of exploitation. Others included the cheapening of the elements of constant capital that went hand in hand with heightened productivity in the producer goods sector of the economy, and the increased rapidity of the turnover of the total capital.[36] The SPGB was certain that the slow tendency for the average rate of profit to fall did not, either on theoretical grounds or on available empirical evidence, point to a breakdown of capitalism in the twentieth century. Nor, according to the SPGB, could this tendential fall explain capitalism's periodic crises and depressions. The rise in the organic composition of capital would have to be extraordinarily rapid to bring on crisis conditions, and neither was it clear that an immediate fall in the rate of profit was the principal factor affecting firms' investment decisions.[37]

So from the 1930s onwards the SPGB's political views on the fallacy of collapse theories were increasingly backed up by the contention that neither underconsumptionist nor falling rate of profit theories supported the claims of those on the left who foretold capitalist collapse. This is not to suggest, however, that the explanations provided by the SPGB for capitalism's recurrent crises were entirely consistent throughout its history or wholly exempt from criticism.

The Development of the Crisis Theory of the SPGB

Given the theoretical influence exerted on the SPGB by the leading figures of the socialist movement of the late nineteenth and early twentieth centuries, it would have been surprising, to say the least, if the ideas of the Party had not in some ways been shaped by their expositions of Marxian economic theory. Hyndman's *Commercial Crises of the Nineteenth Century* (1892), Louis Boudin's *Theoretical System of Karl Marx* (1907), and Kautsky's *Economic Doctrines of Karl Marx* (1925) were all, despite their numerous other merits, expressions of underconsumptionist thought to varying degrees, and all were quite widely read in the impossibilist SPGB and SLP as basic works of Marxian economics. At least partly as a product of this, some forms of underconsumptionist explanations of capitalist crisis were well to the fore in the SPGB in its early years — this being another crucial reason at the time why, at least until the 1930s, the SPGB rarely directly attacked all the underlying economic premises of collapse theories. During its earliest years it was the SPGB's unique impossibilist political stance with its emphasis on mass socialist understanding which prevented the SPGB from lurching towards an acceptance of collapse theory more than any specific consideration of Marxian economics. That Leninist and reformist parties could so easily subscribe to an automatic collapse of capitalism was a reflection of their belief that the working class was incapable of overthrowing capitalism by its own efforts.

The early literature of the SPGB was replete with references to glutted world markets, contracting markets and general overproduction. Though the SPGB did not generally accept the crude total underconsumptionist arguments of Engels and Luxemburg that the workers and the capitalists combined were unable to buy back the entire product of industry, it did affirm that crises were caused in essence by what can be termed 'working class underconsumptionism' — an apparent maldistribution of income arising from capitalism's class character which favoured the economically satisfied capitalist class and restricted the consumption and buying power of the workers. As noted, because of its class flavour this was a particularly common analysis among the prolific writers of Marxian economics in the late nineteenth and early twentieth centuries, and was a viewpoint adopted by other Marxian parties at the time, including the SLP. Justification for it was often given in a rather out-of-context quotation from Volume III of *Capital*, that:

> The ultimate reason for all real crises always remains the poverty and restricted consumption of the masses, in the face of the drive of capitalist production to develop the productive forces as if only the absolute consumption power of society set a limit to them.[38]

A factor held to exacerbate this working class underconsumptionism by most early writers for the *Socialist Standard* was growing unemployment, which they held would rise because of the increasing technical composition of capital, as machinery replaced human labour. This would lead to massive crises of overproduction and slumps as the increased output of industry sought outlets in further reduced markets. It was this argument which formed the basis of the SPGB's very first foray into crisis analysis in the November 1904 *Socialist Standard*. Two decades later, the slump of the early 1920s confirmed it in the eyes of many in the SPGB, and one writer even went so far as to state that with the exception of defeated Germany, "the workers of every country are unemployed to an extent never yet experienced",[39] empirically a grossly exaggerated and incorrect statement which at the time could not even have been justified in relation to Britain alone. This early SPGB perspective on crises and slumps was also aired — for one of the last times — in the Party's *Why Capitalism Will Not Collapse* pamphlet:

> By means of labour-saving machinery and methods the same quantity of goods is produced by fewer and fewer workers, and displaced workers are constantly

added to the army of unemployed. The unemployed man or woman, having only unemployment pay to spend, cannot buy as much as formerly. Thus buying is curtailed while all the time efforts are being made to increase production — a contradiction that is bound to result in over-stocked markets and trade depression.[40]

According to this theory, as capitalism automates this process can only be an ongoing one, and taken logically must lead to crises of ever-increasing severity.

While the SPGB was prepared to endorse the view that crises become increasingly severe because of this process, its political conviction that capitalism would drag on endlessly until the working class consciously put an end to it won through in this period over any idea that capitalism's slumps might become so deep that a recovery was impossible. Some years later one writer in the *Socialist Standard*'s fiftieth anniversary issue submitted that this early position on crises was not entirely consistent:

> many are the explanations of, and prophecies about, crises that have not stood up to the test of events; including some by the SPGB ... Nobody could hold a theory that crises become worse and worse without being at least strongly tempted to believe that this could not go on indefinitely; a time must come when the crisis would be far too great for recovery to be possible.[41]

Without endorsing collapsist notions, the SPGB had held exactly such a theory. Worse and more frequent crises, yes, more unemployment, yes, a great worsening of conditions for the working class, yes, but collapse — no.

Even if the SPGB was correct in its assertions that capitalism would not collapse, it was certainly conceivable that its own initial view of the cause of crises, political considerations notwithstanding, ultimately pointed in that direction. It expected the output of consumer goods to grow rapidly while the share of the workers in the national income declined — because of increasing unemployment and the payment of subsistence wages — and that it seemed, would mean increasingly frequent and severe crises. This was not the collapsist underconsumptionism of Luxemburg or the late Engels, but it was certainly an underconsumptionism of a fashion.

As the SPGB was to eventually recognise, this early explanation for capitalism's periodic crises was far from adequate. Its view that the working class would get a smaller share of the product of its collective labour, concentrating ever more of the social wealth in the hands of an economically satisfied capitalist class, and thereby causing problems for the capitalists as to how to profitably sell an ever-increasing surplus product, had been accepted principally from Boudin.[42] It overlooked that what the workers and capitalists cannot (or in this case, will not) spend on consumption the capitalists can invest in new means of production. If the demand for consumer goods as a proportion of total demand tends to fall because of the mechanisation process, then underconsumption and crisis can be avoided if the proportion of consumer goods in the total output also falls, and at the same rate. In fact the entire tendency of capitalist production is to increase the quota of production goods relative to consumer goods in the total output, so counterbalancing any tendency for the share of wages in total income to fall. This was an aspect of capitalist development curiously overlooked by Boudin, as well, at least for a time, by the SPGB and others.

There are, however, clear signs that the crises analysis of the SPGB began to gradually change with its detailed look at the 1930s slump, when, as has been seen, its first clear economic refutations of collapse theories were also elaborated. Articles in the *Socialist Standard* by Hardy, Raspbridge and other regular writers noted that what might loosely be called a 'general' overproduction for the market was by no means uniform. While many firms and sectors of industry did suffer badly, others continued to expand. Hardy observed in this period that "a minority of firms have made little or no profit or have suffered a loss. Most firms have made profit, although not at the rate of the earlier period. Some firms have prospered exceedingly."[43] While employment in many industries was decreasing in 1930s Britain, such as in the coal mines and the railways, other sectors like electricity generation and some consumption goods industries like motor car manufacturing were expanding and, despite their high technical composition of capital, were taking on more workers. It was clear also that the displacement of workers by machinery took place at a much slower rate than previously imagined.[44] Because of these factors the whole idea that crises were principally caused by the restricted consumption power of the working class, or the workers' inability "to buy back what they have produced" as it was sometimes put, came to be rejected by most of the SPGB's principal writers and speakers on economics, along with an Editorial Committee dominated by Hardy and Gilbert McClatchie which was strong enough to take along most of the rest of the Party. After the 1930s the SPGB came to deride the 'working class underconsumptionist' theory it had once held just as Marx had actually denounced it decades earlier:

It is a pure tautology to say that crises are provoked by a lack of effective demand or effective consumption. The capitalist system does not recognise any forms of consumer other than those who can pay ... The fact that commodities are unsaleable means no more than that no effective buyers have been found for them ... If the attempt is made to give this tautology the semblance of greater profundity, by the statement that the working class receives too small a portion of its own product, and that the evil would be remedied if it received a bigger share, i.e. if its wages rose, we need only note that crises are always prepared by a period in which wages generally rise, and that the working class actually does receive a greater share in the part of the national product destined for consumption. From the standpoint of these advocates of sound and 'simple'(!) common sense, such periods should rather avert the crisis.[45]

For empirical as well as theoretical and political reasons then, working class underconsumptionist explanations of capitalism's periodic crises were replaced in the SPGB by an analysis elaborated by Marx and — in a slightly different form — by some economists of the late nineteenth century including Rudolph Hilferding and the Ukrainian born Social Democrat Mikhail Tugan-Baranovsky.[46] This approach, which had been alluded to though never fully developed by the Party in its early days,[47] was based on the view that economic crises arose out of what Marx had termed capitalism's "anarchy of production", and it did not in itself indicate either that crises would get progressively worse or could prove fatal.

The key element in this new SPGB explanation of capitalism's trade cycle lay in the recognition that capitalist growth is not balanced, steady and sustained, and that the process of accumulation is periodically interrupted by points — corresponding to the onset of an economic crisis — when the circulation and accumulation of capital in key branches of production is severely disrupted. In the competitive drive to accumulate more capital, some enterprises, industries or departments of production find that they have over-extended their operations. In pursuit of future profits they expand their productive capacity beyond what the market they are producing for can absorb. Thus results a sectoral over-accumulation of capital appearing in the form of an over-production of commodities for market demand. Serious consequences follow, particularly if those industries that have over-expanded are central to the economy as a whole. When production is cut back in the main industries affected a chain reaction is initiated with these industries' suppliers now no longer being able to sell all of their commodities, which in turn affects their suppliers' suppliers. Such an overproduction therefore has only to start in a few key industries before the inter-connectedness of capitalist production and the de-stabilizing forces of money and credit get to work, transmitting an initial partial overproduction to other sectors. As Marx put it, "For a crisis (and therefore also overproduction) to be general, it is sufficient for it to grip the principal articles of trade".[48] Once some industries have overexpanded and have been forced to lay off workers, overall market demand contracts leading to general overproduction and slump.

It follows that if capitalist growth is to be achieved in a sustainable and controlled manner, growth has to be balanced in each sector of the economy. But the absence of social regulation in the accumulation process means that this cannot happen for sustainable periods. The growth of an industry in capitalism is not linked with the demands of other industries — instead its growth is determined by the expectation of profit, and this periodically leads to disproportionate investment and a disproportionate expansion between the various branches of production.

This view of the cause of crises was developed by the SPGB throughout the post-Second World War period and has since been applied by the Party to the major economic downturns in Britain of 1974-5, 1980-2 and 1990-2. The basis for it was expanded most clearly by SPGB theoretician Ted Wilmott in a series of articles for *Forum*, the Party's internal discussion bulletin, and then in the *Socialist Standard* in 1957, marking what was then the clearest move yet away from underconsumptionist thought:

> Crises, as Marx pointed out, do not arise through a lack of paying consumption of the mass of the population. They arise because disproportional development in one industrial sector leads to a curtailment of investment (and so production) which by upsetting the balance of the different industrial branches brings about a general slowing down of production. It is this disproportional development which starts the downward spiral of wages and employment with its corollary of shrinking purchasing power... A crisis does not mean there is a total deficit of purchasing power unable to buy back an absolute overproduction of consumer goods.[49]

In this analysis, a contraction of purchasing power and general overproduction are the consequences of a crisis, not its cause, as the under-consumptionists contended. As excess capital is wiped out or devalued in the slump, any purchasing power deficit proves to be only temporary, and production and effective demand move back into unstable equilibrium.

According to this 'disproportionality' argument a crisis could initially break out in a variety of ways, such as the overdevelopment or decline of a sector of the economy, or particular industries within a sector. While this is certainly true, it could also be said that disproportionality theory points to economic crises being usually precipitated by one of two main factors. Firstly, at the height of a boom the reserve army of unemployed labour could disappear causing wages to rise at the expense of profits. A similar result could come about because of shortages of specific types of skilled workers, pushing wages up for particular occupations and thereby cutting the rate of profit. In this scenario, the reinvestment fund of the capitalists would be depleted, precipitating a fall in demand for producer goods, commodities not intended for consumption but for the production of other commodities. An over-expansion of the producer goods sector (or certain industries within it) would then lead to a cut-back in the production of the means of production itself, resulting in lay-offs and wage cuts. As a consequence of this the downturn in demand would then quickly spread to the consumption goods industries as the market for consumer goods shrank.

The second most general type of crisis brought about by disproportionality involves a more direct form of overproduction, and is possibly more common than the first.[50] This is the crisis brought about by the disproportionate expansion of the consumer goods sector. Having ordered new and more efficient plant and equipment during a boom, the output of the consumer goods sector increases more rapidly than the available market for consumer goods can cope with. Precisely because of the high level of investment in new means of production, both wages and the available spending power of the capitalist class on consumer goods cannot keep pace with the rapid expansion of output in the consumption goods industries.[51] Though credit can put off the moment of reckoning, when the expansion of these industries is finally checked it soon spreads to the producer goods sector as demand for further means of production tails off. In this way overproduction sets in, profit rates fall and the crisis becomes generalised. This could be called an underconsumptionist explanation of crisis, but its essential cause lies in disproportionality rather than an overall, inherent deficiency of aggregate demand or purchasing power.

The SPGB has contended that once capitalism has in one of these ways brought the system to the point of slump, with falling production and growing unemployment, it then creates the conditions for recovery, ensuring that no slump is ever permanent.[52] During the downturn enterprises going bankrupt will have their assets bought cheaply by their rivals. This results in a depreciation of the capital invested in them leading to a halt, and eventually a reversal, in the short-term fall of the rate of profit. There is also a decline in the large stocks of commodities that build up towards the end of the boom, during the crisis and in the initial stages of the slump, and a fall in the prices of raw materials.

Additionally, after production is cut-back, the spread of unemployment exercises a downward pressure on wage rises leading to an increase in the rate of exploitation without, at this stage of the economic cycle, damaging the prospects for market sale. Destocking will have already been taking place alongside the curtailment of the production of new commodities.

Interest rates are another factor working to ensure that each slump is only temporary. During the slump interest rates will tend to naturally fall after their peak at the time of crisis. The demand for money capital eases off, having a beneficial impact on the rate of industrial profit, and in conjunction with the other factors, improves the prospects for investment and expansion. By this process, the slump creates the conditions for further capital accumulation and the reappearance of boom conditions before expansion is once again halted (and reversed) by disharmonious, unbalanced growth.[53] To the SPGB there is therefore no permanent crisis, only cyclical periods of economic downturn.

The SPGB and the Increasing Severity of Crises

The SPGB's abandonment of its earlier 'working class underconsumptionist' explanation of crises and its adoption of disproportionality theory as a replacement was generally accepted in the Party, but it had ramifications which were to provoke some controversy. Chief among these was the idea that because capitalism's crises were caused by the "anarchy of production", there could be no discernible pattern to them. No-one could predict with any certainty which industries would over-expand and cause a crisis, or the rapidity and intensity with which sectoral overproduction would spread to other sectors of the economy. One SPGB member who set out to challenge these new prevailing ideas on economic crises was a Party speaker from south London called Terry Lawlor. In 1953 Lawlor had had an article rejected by the *Socialist Standard* Editorial Committee largely on the grounds that it had made reference to the inevitable worsening of wars and economic crises under capitalism. That the Editorial Committee was wary of publishing it was in some ways understandable — the SPGB election address in the 1945 election campaign had predicted a major slump following the war, as had a front-page article in the *Socialist Standard* by Hardy,[54] but the slump had failed to materialise. Lawlor and his supporters, mindful of the Party's earlier position, charged the Editorial Committee with changing the SPGB's view without consultation or Conference vote, and whatever the merits of the actual argument on either side, they were undoubtedly right. Countless articles had previously appeared in the *Standard* referring to capitalism's worsening economic crises, and there had been references in other Party pamphlets and leaflets too. Indeed, as late as 1939 Wilmott had written that "Capitalism's answer to human needs in face of the ever-multiplying productive powers can only be glutted markets, crises and unemployment of ever-increasing severity ... Today the markets are diminishing in relation to this productive expansion."[55] Lawlor's justification for his 'worsening crises' argument also lay in such underconsumptionism, but the question that he raised on the nature of crises was a valid one. Was the tendency of capitalism's crises for them to get worse, stay the same or become less severe?[56] Was it not true that the contradictions of capitalism, such as crises themselves, became more pronounced as the system developed, and that although slumps on their own could never produce socialism, they could at least provide a stimulus to the movement which sought to overthrow the capitalist system?

All that the *Socialist Standard* Editorial Committee were prepared to say was that although crises and slumps were inevitable so long as capitalism lasted, there was no discernible pattern to them, or their frequency and severity. Many members still felt that crises and unemployment would tend to get worse, but the Party had been bitten once before in 1945 and they were wary of any new commitments on the subject. For some time in the 1950s and 60s the Party's official caution appeared justified as world capitalism, even more so in Britain than elsewhere, expanded with only minor and short-lived setbacks. The mass unemployment of the pre-Second World War era did not return until the 1970s, when major downturns in economic activity recurred.[57] When it did return (even during times of relative boom) the SPGB position remained unaltered, while it renewed its attacks on the automatic collapse theories promoted by the Trotskyists and others.

Had the SPGB, in refuting both collapse theory and somewhat mechanical views of ever-worsening slumps inevitably leading to ever-increasing socialist consciousness, gone too far? To a minority of members it certainly appeared that way. To them, the Party had been left with a rather directionless view, based on a theory which argued that capitalism's slumps were entirely unpredictable and lacking identifiable patterns or trends. While it was clearly not the case that every crisis and slump necessarily had to be worse than the previous one in terms of falls in industrial production and investment and increasing numbers of bankruptcies, it was less clear that there was not a general tendency pointing to worsening world slumps over the longer term. Moreover, even if it was generally agreed that capitalism's crises were not exacerbated by underconsumptionist factors — and underconsumptionist type explanations of slumps eventually died out almost completely in the SPGB — this did not mean that other tendencies at work within the capitalist system could not come to have a bearing. For some members, the long-term tendency for the average rate of profit to fall operated as a background factor, prolonging the duration and depth of slumps. The growth of welfare services, ultimately financed by the capitalist class (see Chapter 6) and exercising a further downward pressure on the rate of profit after tax has been seen by others as another important factor shaping capitalism's sporadic development.[58] Similarly — and notwithstanding the theories of Herman Cahn — the massive extension of credit this century has to some noticeably affected the scope and intensity of capitalism's crises and slumps, papering over and delaying economic crises only at the expense of increasing the magnitude of the correction ultimately necessary to restore a semblance of equilibrium, just as Marx had predicted:

> The credit system ... accelerates the material development of the productive forces and the creation of the world market, which it is the historical task of the capitalist mode of production to bring to a certain level of development, as material foundations for the new form of production. At the same time, credit accelerates the violent outbreak of this contradiction, crises, and with these the elements of dissolution of the old mode of production.[59]

To these influences on crises the SPGB has yet to fully and adequately address itself as an organisation. A committee to examine such phenomena and their interaction with capitalism's trade cycle was set up some years after the Lawlor controversy in 1959, though its report, written principally by one member rather than the entire committee, was hurried and inconclusive.[60] In the early 1990s the SPGB set up a similar committee and its initial conclusions demonstrated that it was prepared to go beyond the view that an acceptance of disproportionality as the cause of capitalist slumps must mean there is no pattern to capitalism's economic cycle.[61]

This initial Report also indicated that it is possible that the SPGB will abandon its previously held conviction that capitalism as a mode of production can go on indefinitely until the working class puts an end to it.[62] Indeed, the reason for this was elaborated as long ago as the early 1970s when at least one SPGB internal education document recognised that there are physical limits to capital accumulation.[63] Given a steadily rising organic composition of capital it is mathematically impossible for a rising rate of exploitation to forever offset a declining rate of profit by adding to the entire mass of surplus value. A point would be reached whereby instead of rising sporadically, the mass of profit available for reinvestment in production relative to the total capital would start to spiral downwards leading to falling investment, real wages, tax revenues, and welfare payments with steadily increasing unemployment.[64] Such a situation would by no means lead inevitably to socialism, but possibly instead to a descent into capitalist barbarism — absolute poverty, social crisis and ecological disaster. Though unpalatable to some, an acceptance of this theory with its long-term implications for both capitalism and the response of socialists to its development would certainly not conflict with the Party's conviction that socialism can only be brought about by the action of a conscious working class. Instead it would represent a return to the SPGB's early (and at that time underconsumption-based) recognition of the old social democratic nostrum of 'socialism or barbarism', with its implicit acceptance that socialism is not, as many of the Communists assumed, an inevitable consequence of capitalist disaster.

Neither, it should be noted, would a recognition of the more immediate factors that some contend are working to exacerbate capitalism's periodic crises and slumps commit the SPGB to anything remotely resembling the collapse theories of the Communist Party and others in the 1920s and 30s.[65] The idea that an acceptance of a non-underconsumption based 'worsening crises' scenario might eventually lead to Leninist-type collapse notions is not entirely logical, especially given the SPGB's own elucidation of the factors which always come to bear during a period of slump to ensure that any curtailment of production is only temporary — so long that is, that automation has not brought capitalism to the point at which the total mass of profit has started to decline. Such a fear of being seen to endorse anything that could remotely imply a collapse theory has been, at least in part, a product of the SPGB's desire to distance itself as much as possible from the vanguardism of Leninist groups desperate to seize power on the workers' behalf.

Even if the SPGB's views on economic crises have, in the eyes of some of its own members, grown to be rather short-term and cautious, the Party's role in criticising collapse theory has undoubtedly been most effective and consistent in its insistence that "no crisis of capitalism, however desperate it may be, can ever by itself give us socialism"[66] and in its various criticisms of underconsumptionist economic thought. But from the vantage point of the late twentieth century, a suspicion remains among some of its own members that the SPGB's steadfast opposition to the mechanistic theories of its opponents about socialism arising inevitably from capitalist collapse, has curiously led it to underestimate identifiable tendencies within capitalist development which could yet be among those significant factors raising the popular consciousness it says is required before a social revolution can take place.

Notes

1. *Daily Record*, 22 August 1931.
2. 'Capitalism's Crises' in *Socialist Standard*, February 1932.
3. *Labour Monthly*, August 1921.
4. *The Collapse of Capitalism* by Herman Cahn (Kerr & Co. , Chicago, 1919) pp.9-10.
5. Preface to the English edition of *Capital*, Volume I, by Friedrich Engels, p.113.
6. *Justice*, January 1884.
7. 'Die Wirtschaftlichen Und Politischen Grundlagen Des Klassenkampfes' in *Sozialistische Monatshefte*, February 1901, p.128. Cited by Paul Mattick in *Economic Crisis and Crisis Theory* (Merlin Press, London, 1981) p.80.
8. See 'Will Capitalism Collapse?' in *Socialist Standard* February 1922, April 1927 and 'Capitalism's Crises' in February 1932.
9. *Why Capitalism Will Not Collapse* (SPGB, London, 1932) p.4.
10. *Why Capitalism Will Not Collapse*, p.5.
11. See 'Capitalism's Crises' in *Socialist Standard*, February 1932.
12. *Value, Price and Profit* by Karl Marx (George Allen and Unwin, London, 1951) p.82.
13 *Theories of Surplus Value* by Karl Marx (Lawrence and Wishart, London, 1951) p.373.
14. See 'The Collapse of Capitalism — Attitude of the SPGB' in *Socialist Standard*, September 1934.
15. Editorial Reply to a correspondent in *Socialist Standard*, August 1905.
16. 'Will Capitalism Collapse?' in *Socialist Standard*, April 1927.
17. 'Preface to the First Edition' by Friedrich Engels of *The Poverty of Philosophy* by Karl Marx (Foreign Languages Press, Peking, 1978) p.15.
18. 'Preface to the First Edition' of *The Poverty of Philosophy*, p.6.
19. *The Condition of the Working Class in England* by Friedrich Engels (Panther Books, London, 1984) p.33.
20. 'Preface to the English Edition of Capital', Volume I, Friedrich Engels, pp.112-3.
21. *Reform or Revolution* by Rosa Luxemburg, p.82.
22. *The Accumulation of Capital* by Rosa Luxemburg (Routledge and Kegan Paul, London, 1951) p.347.
23. See 'World Revolution — Another Confused Group' in *Socialist Standard*, August 1980. One of the most convincing critiques of Luxemburg's contentions on the collapse of capitalism was elaborated in German in 1934 by the council communist Anton Pannekoek in his *The Theory of the Collapse of Capitalism*. In many respects Pannekoek took a very similar line in both his political and economic refutations of collapse theory to the SPGB. See *Capital And Class*, Spring 1977 (Conference of Socialist Economists, London).
24. See Ernest Mandel's Introduction to *Capital*, Volume II, p.65.
25. Most notable among the new breed of left communists was the International Communist Current (ICC) who still hold rigidly to the fundamentals of Luxemburg's economic analysis of capitalism. Their views on crises are outlined in *The Decadence of Capitalism* (ICC, London, n.d.).
26. *Social Credit* by Major C. Douglas (Eyre and Spottiswoode, London, 1933) Part Two.

27. See 'The Douglas Scheme' in *Socialist Standard*, May, June and July 1933.

28. See *Post Office Workers, A Trade Union and Social History* by Alan Clinton (George Allen and Unwin, London, 1984) p.392.

29. 'The Douglas Scheme' in *Socialist Standard*, June 1933.

30. *The Nature of Capitalist Crisis* by John Strachey (Victor Gollancz, London, 1935) pp.22-39.

31. 'The Douglas Scheme' in *Socialist Standard*, June 1933.

32. See, for instance, 'Marx's Theory of Crisis and its Critics' by Chris Harman in *International Socialism* 11 (Socialist Workers' Party, London, Winter 1981), *The Revolutionary Road to Communism in Britain, Manifesto of the Revolutionary Communist Group* (Larkin Publications, London, 1984) pp.21-34 and 'The Marxian Theory of Crisis, Capital and the State' by David Yaffe in *Economy and Society*, Volume II, Number Two (London, May 1973).

33. *The Law of Accumulation and Breakdown of the Capitalist System* by Henryk Grossmann (Pluto Press, London, 1992).

34. 'The Falling Rate of Profit' in *Socialist Standard*, June 1960.

35. *Capital*, Volume III, p.339.

36. *Capital*, Volume III, Chapter 14.

37. See 'The Falling Rate of Profit' in *Socialist Standard*, June 1960 and 'The Rate of Profit' in April 1971.

38. *Capital*, Volume III, p.615. Marx was not, in fact, an underconsumptionist, and this statement is a mere aside by Marx in a passage which discusses the interaction between crises, accumulation and capitalism's antagonistic system of income distribution. This quotation was discussed in 'Marx and Underconsumption' in *Socialist Standard*, April 1959.

39. 'The Problem of Unemployment' in *Socialist Standard*, October 1921.

40. *Why Capitalism Will Not Collapse*, p.10.

41. 'Some Theoretical Questions' in *Socialist Standard*, September 1954.

42. *The Theoretical System of Karl Marx* by Louis Boudin (Kerr and Co. , Chicago, 1907) Chapters 7 and 10.

43. 'Notes On Industry' in *Socialist Standard*, April 1933.

44. 'The Collapse of Capitalism — Attitude of the SPGB' in *Socialist Standard*, September 1934.

45. *Capital*, Volume III, pp.486-7.

46. See *A History of Marxian Economics 1883–1929* by M. C. Howard and J. E. King (MacMillan, London and Basingstoke, 1988) pp.168-171.

47. See, for instance, *Unemployment: The Socialist View* (SPGB leaflet, London, 1908).

48. *Theories of Surplus Value*, p.393.

49. *Marxist Economic Theory*, Volume I by Ernest Mandel (Merlin Press, London, 1968) p.354.

50. See 'Crises, Catastrophe and Mr Strachey' in *Socialist Standard*, March 1957.

51. 'Further Reflections on Crises' in *Socialist Standard*, April 1957.

52. See *Productive Labour and Effective Demand* by Sydney H. Coontz (Croom Helm, London, 1965) Chapter 4b.

53. 'Capitalism's Crisis Cycle' in *Socialist Standard*, October 1982.

54. 'The Coming Slump' in *Socialist Standard*, October 1944.

55. 'Why Socialism?' in *Socialist Standard*, August 1939.

56. 'Second Letter From T. Lawlor to the Executive Committee and all Branches of the SPGB' 21 February 1956.

57. See 'Can the Welfare State Survive?' and 'Why Beveridge Re-organised Poverty' in *Socialist Standard*, September and December 1992.

58. Lawlor, having left the SPGB in the mid 1950s, rejoined when the major slump he had predicted would give a new impetus to the socialist movement hove into view.

59. *Capital*, Volume III, p.572.

60. See *Discussion Report on Crises*, SPGB internal document, 1959.

61. See *Report of the 88th SPGB Annual Conference*, Easter 1992.

62. *World Economic Crisis Committee Report* to 89th SPGB Annual Conference, February 1993. This view has since received an airing in the *Socialist Standard*, June 1997.

63. *Guide to Books and Pamphlets on Marxian Economics* (SPGB, London, 1971) p.16.

64. See Ernest Mandel's Introduction to *Capital*, Volume III, pp.87-9.

65. *88th SPGB Conference Report*, and *World Economic Crisis Committee Report*, 1993.

66. *Why Capitalism Will Not Collapse*, p.9.

5. Fascism, Democracy and the Second World War

The SPGB and the Rising Tide of Fascism

By far the most striking aspect of the Socialist Party of Great Britain's response to the rise and spread of European fascism in the 1930s was its obvious dissimilarity to the stance taken by the mainstream left. Often spurred on by notions of capitalist collapse and economic decadence, the Communists of the CPGB, together with the Trotskyists and left communists, were inclined to view fascism as capitalism's final totalitarian political form. Fascism, they thought, was the last political refuge of a capitalist class struggling to hold its system together at a time of acute economic crisis. By smashing the trade union movement, and by using the state to break all democratic political opposition, fascism was able to pursue aggressively imperialistic foreign policies, to restore markets and profit levels for the capitalists, while simultaneously deterring working class demands on the industrial and reform fronts. It legitimised necessary state intervention in the capitalist economy while ensuring that the private property rights of the capitalist class remained intact and unchallenged. John Strachey was one of many prominent British writers putting this view, arguing that the capitalist class supported the introduction of fascism when the crisis of capitalism had become so pronounced that it could no longer tolerate the standard of living achieved by the working class or the presence of organisations seeking to further improve that standard.[1] As such, fascism becomes the form capitalism's political apparatus takes when the underlying structure of the economy has reached a point of decadence and impasse.

Partly because the SPGB never considered capitalism to be at a point of imminent collapse in the 1930s, it did not seek to project fascism in this light.[2] Fascism was not considered to be capitalism's final or, so long as the system itself lasted, permanent political form. Instead, the Party described it in the *Socialist Standard* as no more final or permanent "than the other reform movements that have been used to stave off the inevitable abolition of capitalism".[3] Nor, for that matter, was fascism considered by the SPGB to be essentially a product of a fully developed and well-established capitalist economy and political system. To the SPGB, the rise to power of the Nazi Party in Germany illustrated this particularly well. "National Socialism", the *Socialist Standard* observed in 1939, "marks a stage in the national reconsolidation of German capitalism".[4] Instead of being capitalism's final political form, Nazism in Germany was considered to be a product of a relatively backward and fettered national capitalism, restricted both by Germany's isolated international position after Versailles and by the strong remnants of feudal ideas and practices in a formally democratic state. To the SPGB, it was essentially a movement of bourgeois national unity in Germany "which could bring to reality all the unfulfilled dreams of a century — national centralisation and consolidation, with a view to re-entering the imperialist arena, this time unfettered by any feudal restrictions ... Thus the Nazi movement has been instrumental in consummating the uncompleted bourgeois revolution of 1848, in addition to preparing the ground for an imperialist conflict."[5]

The eventual Nazi rise to power, supported by the industrial section of the German capitalist class and given impetus by their ideas of national capitalist reconstruction and expansion, may in the last analysis have been essentially for the capitalists, but it was not decisively carried out by them. Indeed, as the SPGB ceaselessly pointed out, the Nazis only achieved dominance by enlisting the support of key sections of the working class on the basis of an anti-democratic, nationalist, reform programme. After the failure of the Munich beer hall putsch in 1924, Hitler had recognised the need to win over the mass of the German population to the Nazi programme at a time when most of the German working class voted for parties that supported the Weimar Republic. Moreover, the governments formed by the Social Democrats together with the catholic and centre parties had shown themselves fully capable of using the powers vested in them to put down attempts at minority takeover from both the extreme left and the extreme right wings.

The perceived German humiliation during the First World War and at Versailles, and the mismanagement of the German currency in 1923 which led to hyper-inflation, provided the fundamental basis for the Nazi denunciations of the Weimar Republic and the mainstream democratic political parties which sought to uphold it. But given this foundation of Nazi propaganda, the after-effects of the Wall Street Crash were what, in the SPGB's assessment, gave real impetus to the anti-democratic forces in Germany.[6] The foreign loans and investments which had propped up the German economy throughout the mid to late 1920s ceased, industrial production collapsed and unemployment rose to well over six million. This, together with widespread unease over Germany's international position and the conduct of successive Weimar governments, produced the spread and depth of discontent which Hitler's movement required if it was to mount an effective challenge to the established parties and achieve the eventual abandonment of bourgeois democratic government. The stance and rhetoric of the Nazis was avowedly anti-system, and though not in any way the socialists they proclaimed themselves to be, they were, as the SPGB noted, revolutionary in one sense — as political revolutionaries not social revolutionaries, aiming to seize control of the state machine and fundamentally alter its operation thereafter.[7]

From the SPGB viewpoint, the Nazi rise to power depended crucially on the ability of Hitler to unify an incipient German mistrust of parliamentary democracy with hostility to the parties of the Weimar Republic which had failed to solve the economic crisis and its attendant problems. In this way democracy was equated with austerity and national humiliation, and the slender support for it in Germany was broken, as Hitler knew it had to be. Weak though the real support for parliamentary democracy was, the grip of the democratic parties on the state machine and their control over the armed forces was still such that only a truly mass movement could mount a successful challenge to them. As the SPGB explained:

> Political democracy was born in Germany under most unpromising circumstances and against an unfavourable historical background. Its birth was not the result of a struggle by the workers nor the desire or need of the German capitalist class. It was thrown to the nation by the defeat of 1918 and the temporary impotence of ruling class elements.
>
> Nevertheless, the power of the constitution was such that only a mass movement could break it. The Nazi Party was able to rally those sections of the masses who were the most backward politically and who had not yet shed their dependence on absolutism. Their success was contributed to by the weak and compromising character of German Social Democracy [while] the Communists drew a large section of the working class into opposition to the democratic method.[8]

The lack of maturity of the working class and its mistrust of parliamentary democracy directly contributed to the elevation of Hitler himself to the status of absolute leader. The SPGB argued that "political incoherency" was the real explanation of the Hitler 'leader-cult', with the Nazis themselves having no clear and consistent ideology, attracting support from different sections of society through disparate promises ranging from state capitalist interventionism and the abolition of the gold standard, to the various considerations of race mythology:

> The more backward and confused politically a people are, the stronger is the gravitation towards absolute personal leadership as a unifying force. Conversely, to the extent that the masses become politically enlightened, the need for leadership disappears.[9]

Given the origins and objectives of the Nazis in Germany the SPGB considered them to be, in the last analysis, a party of crisis and war,[10] unable to form a regime of any permanence whose principal task was to prepare Germany for the likely imperialistic conflicts to come, providing a temporary though necessary focus for absolute national unity and international adventurism.

It is worth noting that this view of Nazism was developed by the SPGB entirely independently and without knowledge of the similar, and later much more widely known, interpretation of fascism and Nazism elaborated by the Italian theorist Antonio Gramsci. The SPGB and Gramsci effectively developed analogous, though not identical, analyses of the Italian Fascist and German Nazi movements in parallel.`Gramsci and the SPGB arrived at different conclusions — with Gramsci being prepared to support bourgeois 'democratic' parties in the anti-fascist struggle, but the analyses of the fascist phenomenon they developed had much in common. These analyses were initially undertaken tentatively with regard to Mussolini's Italian takeover (the SPGB's own first analysis of the fascist phenomenon in Italy was an article by Hardy entitled 'Socialists and the Fascisti' in the April 1923 *Socialist Standard*) and then more fully and distinctively in the thirties in response to the rise of German Nazism and the attitudes towards it developed by the Comintern, whose view of fascism as capitalism's final political form was disputed by the SPGB and Gramsci alike. Indeed, on the political 'left', the SPGB and Gramsci were the principal opponents of this view, which was accepted with little critical examination by a great many social democrats, Communists and Trotskyists.

It is also worth remembering that in the 1930s Gramsci was little heard-of as a political theorist outside Italy and his writings did not attract much immediate attention in the English-speaking world. His developed analysis of fascism and Nazism in his *Prison Notebooks* and elsewhere, was not available to the SPGB and other political currents in Britain in the 1930s. If Gramsci was known at all to the Party it would have been in his position as General Secretary of the Italian Communist Party (PCI) from 1924-6 rather than because of his political writings, which only received serious attention from the 1960s onwards with the rise of the so-called 'new left'. Given all this, the SPGB's own analysis of the rise of fascism and Nazism, elaborated above, while certainly not unique, must still rank as original and distinctive enough to warrant an interest it has previously been denied. So indeed, must the original — and controversial — positions it took on the Spanish Civil War and the Second World War.

The Civil War in Spain

When the Spanish Civil War broke out in July 1936 the SPGB was presented with a political dilemma that it had previously managed to avoid in its earlier analysis of the Nazi rise to power in Germany. The Party had affirmed the need for political democracy if the socialist movement was to be successful in its aim of dispossessing the capitalist class of their property rights, claiming that "it has always been recognised by Socialists that it is necessary for the workers to gain the vote, so that they may be able to place themselves democratically in control of the machinery of government."[11] As such the SPGB supported the efforts of workers to secure basic democratic and civil rights not simply for their own sake within capitalism, but so they might be used as a weapon by the working class in the struggle for socialism. Until the 1930s this had never involved giving support to pro-capitalist political organisations. Now the question arose, prompted by the events in Spain, of whether the SPGB should be prepared to give its support to a democratic pro-capitalist government under attack from insurgent reactionary forces intent on abolishing the right of workers to vote together with their rights to organise politically and industrially. This situation had never risen so directly in Fascist Italy or Nazi Germany, where the regimes were both installed with the connivance of sections of the capitalist class and their political representatives, and which were supported by significant numbers of workers.[12] Spain was a rather different matter. There, a democratically elected 'Popular Front' government backed by the majority of the Spanish working class was under threat from an armed revolt led by General Franco aimed at returning Spain to autocratic political rule.

The SPGB had always stated that in the case of an armed revolt against an organised majority of socialists, the socialist revolution would have to be defended by force, as provided for in Clause Six of the Party's Declaration of Principles. In Spain, a similar situation clearly existed with a bourgeois democratic government challenged by a minority of reactionaries. The Party had opposed every other war in its history on the grounds that no working class interests were at stake, but the attitude to be taken by the SPGB in these circumstances was not clear. Some of the interests of the Spanish working class did appear to be at stake, and for one of the few occasions in its political lifetime the SPGB was split on a fundamental issue. A significant portion of the Party membership considered there to be vital democratic interests of the working class in jeopardy and that it made no sense to state that it did not matter to the workers who won the war. This seemed even more evident when the Francoist forces received the backing of the German and Italian dictatorships. With this, many in the Party urged it to back the Spanish republicans in their fight against the spreading forces of fascist totalitarianism.

Those within the Party urging the SPGB to take an overtly pro-republican stand included several Jewish members such as A. E. Jacomb, an SPGB founder member and for some years printer of the *Socialist Standard*, and the prominent Party speaker and writer Adolph Kohn. Robert Reynolds, who wrote theoretical articles in the *Standard* as 'Robertus' also declared in favour of the Republican government.[13] These members of the SPGB were certainly not alone in taking what was for them an unusual stand. The tidal wave of support for the Spanish republicans among the British left led other unlikely groups and individuals to give them their support, including anarcho-communist organisations like the small Anti-Parliamentary Communist Federation and the United Socialist Movement, neither of whom, like the SPGB, were usually well disposed towards elected governments of capitalism.[14]

Wracked by internal division though it was, and despite the urgings of its own pro-republican faction, the official SPGB position was somewhat more circumspect and consistent in its approach to Spain than either of these groups, both of which were later to recant their support for the Popular Front government. The SPGB's written propaganda in this period betrays a marked attempt to steer a steady course between two seemingly incompatible positions

— one definitely pro-republican, the other suspicious of giving any support to a capitalist cause prosecuted by pro-capitalist organisations. The definitive SPGB statement on the Spanish question was drawn up by the then *Socialist Standard* Editorial Committee of Harry Waite, Gilbert McClatchie and Hardy, and published in the May 1937 issue under the heading 'The SPGB and Spain'. In outlining the principles governing the attitude of the SPGB to working class struggles for democracy, the statement began by affirming that the SPGB always took the side of the exploited against the landed and moneyed classes:

> This is true whether the workers concerned are Socialist or not, organised or unorganised, or whether the struggle is a strike or a lock-out, or whether it is concerned with gaining "elbow room" for the working class movement, i.e., the right to organise, to carry on propaganda, to secure the franchise and parliamentary government. These struggles are all the expression of the class struggle and are in the line of development towards Socialism. It is the plain duty of the organised workers in the more advanced countries to support and encourage such struggles, both at home and in the less advanced countries.

But the statement made clear that while individual members of the SPGB could take part in struggles that were not directly for socialism, the SPGB organisationally did not formally ally itself with those who did. The Party only gave material support to other socialists, never to those supportive of capitalism, albeit capitalism in its democratic political form. The statement concluded by saying that whether the Spanish workers were wise in pursuing their costly struggle or not, since they had already decided upon their course of action against the forces of authoritarianism, "Socialists are, of course, on their side", without necessarily agreeing with the precise conduct of the struggle itself. Nowhere did the SPGB state that it supported the Popular Front government. While it supported the efforts of the Spanish workers to pursue democratic political objectives, it would not support the pro-capitalist organisations which they had elected to power. In this way, the SPGB avoided crossing the fine line that existed between being supportive of working class struggles and entering into compromises with reformist groups which, in all other respects, it considered to be thoroughly misguided.[15]

Under the general rubric of 'No Compromise' there were a number of specific reasons why the SPGB would neither support the Spanish Popular Front government or 'Popular Fronts' in other countries, including Britain. First, Popular Fronts could certainly not, in the view of the SPGB, be seriously regarded as potential "saviours of democracy". Popular Front governments, in dealing with the problems associated with capitalism at a time of economic crisis, would be forced to attack the living standards of the working class like any other government of capitalism, alienating the working class still further and driving them directly into the hands of the 'anti-system' parties. Indeed, this was the situation that had developed in Spain before the Civil War, and also later in France, where the Popular Front government led by Blum was forced to renege on its reform programme and cut government expenditure, prompting the *Socialist Standard* to comment that this demonstrated that "putting Labour or Popular Front governments into office merely makes them the prisoners of the capitalist class".[16]

The second main objection raised by the SPGB concerned the political complexion of the Popular Fronts themselves. It was clear that democracy could not be safeguarded by political organisations that did not believe in it and had previously been doing everything within their power to overthrow it. This in effect was the position of the Communists, the Trotskyists, the anarchists, and the syndicalists. To the SPGB, these political currents had done as much to discredit parliament and bourgeois political democracy as the fascists in Spain and elsewhere and they could not be seriously trusted to defend institutions and practices they actually wanted to subvert. The Communist advocates of the Popular Front, who had earlier labelled Labour and social democratic parties as "social fascists", came in for particular criticism for both their conduct in Spain and, in this instance, their advocacy of a Popular Front in Britain:

> They want now to save us from Fascism, and tell us to do it by supporting the Party whose policy when in office was a "Fascist policy". They want to save democracy and fight dictatorship (yet their masters created and glorified dictatorship in Russia), and their method is to have another Labour Government, although they say that the last Labour Government helped to strengthen "the dictatorship of the capitalists". They want to save democracy, although as recently as 1932 they declared it to be a sham.
>
> In short, the Communists are what they have always been, fickle, unscrupulous, superficial in their judgement of working class questions and an unmixed danger to the interests of the working class and the Socialist movement … unwittingly an instrument of reaction, unable to assist in saving democracy in the present, and equally unable to use democracy for the promotion of the Socialist movement.[17]

Beyond their obviously divergent attitudes to parliamentary democracy, there were further divisions between the major constituent elements of a Popular Front that, in the view of the SPGB, would lead it to disaster. This was clearest of all in Spain itself where the social, political and trade union differences seriously weakened, rather than strengthened, the republican resistance to Franco.

The SPGB criticism of the Popular Front tactic was no one-way affair, with the SPGB often being charged with sectarianism by the Communists and ILP. This charge was familiar enough, as was, at root, another which re-emerged during this period: that the experience of the Spanish Popular Front government had entirely discredited the SPGB's revolutionary strategy for democratically taking control of the powers of government and the armed forces. Reactionary elements, it was claimed, would be able to prevent socialists taking effective control of the state machine by organising a military insurrection. In a political swipe at the SPGB, the 'Principles and Tactics' of the Anti-Parliamentary Communist Federation derided the view that revolutionaries could take over Parliament and use it to dispossess the capitalists arguing that "Surely Franco supplies the answer to such a childish notion".[18]

However, the Spanish Civil War and the experiences of authoritarian takeovers in other parts of Europe only served to reinforce the SPGB's view that control of the governmental apparatus and military was essential. Workers' revolts in both Spain and Austria had been easily put down in 1934 and the Spanish Francoist forces only embarked on a struggle against the Popular Front government with the backing of much of the Spanish military and when supported by Italy and Germany. Even then it was without great immediate success.[19] The Nazi takeover in Germany had depended on mass support and the connivance of right-wing politicians, while Mussolini's famous 'March on Rome' was a charade behind which the government and Italian King had already agreed to allow Mussolini into office in an alliance with other, non-Fascist Cabinet Ministers.[20] Whatever the lessons to be learnt from the rise of fascism in Europe and from the Spanish Civil War, for the SPGB the notion that a minority of workers could bypass bourgeois democracy and rise up to overthrow an established government of capitalism was not one of them.

The Causes and Outbreak of the Second World War
As the Spanish conflict wore on, and as the storm clouds of war gathered in other parts of Europe, the analysis of the SPGB centred on the allegedly imperialist nature of the fascist threat. If parliamentary democracy was under attack, this was not considered by the Party to be the main issue at stake — the coming war was, in fundamentals, clearly to be as imperialistic as any other. The SPGB's 1939 May Day address put this point succinctly enough:

> Europe is not on the verge of war for the sake of Nazism and Democracy, but for the sake of a re-division of the spoils of the last great capitalist war.
>
> From a working class point of view, the ideological differences between Chamberlain and Hitler are as nothing to the common cause they both espouse — the capitalist cause. When Hitler declares that German capitalism must export or perish, the representative of British imperialism, Mr Robert Hudson, Secretary for Overseas Trade, answers in the same language of predatory capitalism:-
>
> "We are not going to give up any markets to anyone ... Great Britain is strong enough to fight for markets abroad. Britain is now definitely going to take a greater interest in Eastern Europe. " (Speech in Warsaw, March 21st).[21]

The SPGB contended that the tortuous diplomacy of Chamberlain masked the genuine fear of the British capitalist class that Germany and Italy were set on a course which undermined British economic interests in Europe, North Africa and Western Asia. Chamberlain's foreign policy aims, partially realised in the Munich Agreement of 1938, had been based upon finding agreement with Germany and Italy while weaning France away from its alliance with Russia, making clear that further territorial conquests by the totalitarian states would only be opposed if they threatened British interests.[22] As the SPGB pointed out amid the euphoria of the time, the Munich settlement was destined to have a "very short life indeed"[23] with Hitler demonstrating every intent of pushing the British capitalist class further than they were prepared to go.

When war between Britain and Germany was eventually declared in September 1939, the reaction of the working class in Britain was one of weary resignation rather than fevered patriotism, a far cry indeed from the jingoistic atmosphere which greeted the SPGB in August 1914. The 'war to end all wars' had killed most workers' notions of the supposedly glorious nature of armed conflict and the SPGB was able to state its anti-war position without a great deal of interference, initially both in print and on the outdoor platform. As the Party had expected, its efforts were hampered more by the wartime regulations imposed by the government than any vociferous pro-war sentiment from the working class. Although the activities of its speakers were usually tolerated by the authorities, from July 1940 onwards the *Socialist Standard* did not carry any openly anti-war propaganda because of the Defence Regulations introduced earlier that year, and fearing suppression, apologised to its readers stating "While we deeply regret having to adopt this course, we cannot see any workable alternative to it."[24]

Despite this inconvenience, the SPGB's view of the conflict had already been well aired. Until the Defence Regulations came into force the *Socialist Standard* carried numerous articles attacking the war and the spurious arguments it claimed were being advanced to justify it. The Executive Committee's official statement was printed in the October 1939 issue under the heading 'The Socialist Party of Great Britain and the War', and as the following extract demonstrates, it was prescient indeed:

> The Socialist Party of Great Britain is fully aware of the sufferings of German workers under Nazi rule, and whole-heartedly supports the efforts of workers everywhere to secure democratic rights against the powers of suppression, but the history of the past decades shows the futility of war as a means of safeguarding democracy. After the last Great War described as a war to end war, and as a war to make the world safe for democracy — the retention of capitalism resulted in the building up of terrorisms through the inability of the capitalist States to solve the problems created by the system of private ownership of the means of production and distribution and the competitive scramble for raw materials, markets and control of trade routes ...
> The Socialist Party of Great Britain holds that neither the doctrine of "self-determination" ... nor the German claim for a new carving up of Europe, nor any other policy for settling minority problems and international rivalries within the framework of capitalism, is capable of bringing peace and democracy to the peoples of the world. Another war would be followed by new Treaties forced on the vanquished by the victors, and by preparations for further wars, new dictatorships and terrorism.

The statement ended by repeating the extension of goodwill to workers of all lands made by the Party in 1914.

Other early wartime issues of the *Socialist Standard* spent time analysing the causes of the international conflict and the background to the armaments build up. Charlie Lestor, a travelling orator who had spent many years teaching Marxian socialism in North America before joining the SPGB, wrote a series of articles on this theme, focusing on the reasons behind Hitler's demand for 'Lebensraum' in Eastern and Central Europe. To Lestor and, indeed, other writers and speakers in the SPGB, the crucial factor in the drive towards war had been the breakdown of the international payments system consequent on the world economic crisis of 1929, which in itself had spurred the Nazi rise to power.[25] Because of contracting world trade, Britain had gone off the Gold Standard in 1931, precipitating a new set of trading arrangements between two competing and antagonistic blocs of states. The main bloc of Britain, France, the United States and those countries allied with them, was opposed by the bloc dominated by the totalitarian states of Germany and Italy. Gold was heavily concentrated in the first and most dominant of these blocs, as was access to much of the world's important sources of raw materials and the control of key trade routes.[26]

During the 1930s Germany, Italy and Japan set about challenging allied political and economic hegemony through the adoption of expansionist foreign policies and economic strategies designed to weaken the dominant group. One method used by the totalitarian states to obtain essential raw materials was dumping — selling goods below cost to get much needed currency. Others included the development of bilateral trade agreements and barter. Lestor argued in the *Standard* that such considerations had clearly underpinned the German involvement in Spain during the Civil War, with Germany "seeking a hold on mining areas which would accept a medium in which they could pay — that is, which could be made to take German goods or German services."[27] It was certainly true that Germany and its allies had some success with these aggressive economic policies in Spain, Africa, South America and in Japan's case, South East Asia. But these policies and trade arrangements were soon challenged by the dominant bloc which set about boycotting goods from the totalitarian states while giving credits and other incentives to win over and win back countries attracted by the favourable trading conditions offered by Germany, Italy and Japan. This in turn prompted still more aggressive foreign and economic policies by the Germans in particular, culminating in the Anschluss with Austria and the invasion of Czechoslovakia. War was averted until the German invasion of Poland in September 1939 which proved to be one adventurist act of aggression too many, leading Britain and France to meet force with force.[28]

To the SPGB, the war between Germany and its allies with Britain and France was, then, entirely imperialistic. Ideological considerations simply did not enter into it, and, so far as the SPGB was concerned, it was likely that many of the senior British politicians who were supporting the war in 1939 actually had sympathy with much of the economic and social policy pursued by the Nazis. The SPGB was certainly not alone in thinking this. Its view was shared by other anti-war groups in Britain, notably those anarchists who produced *War Commentary*, without doubt the most outspoken and daring anti-war publication of the time. *War Commentary* declared that the belligerent wing of the Conservative Party was filled with so-called 'anti-Nazis' peddling similarly irrational hatreds:

> The real Tories are not at all anti-Nazi, only anti-German: this is proved by the broadcasts of Sir Robert Vansittart, breathing across the ether the insidious poison of racial hatred: talking of the Germans as Julius Streicher talks of the Jews, Pierre Laval of the English or Oswald Pirow of the Negroes.[29]

Churchill, who posed as the arch enemy of totalitarian government, was viewed in a similar light by the SPGB, seen as more of a shrewd defender of the interests of his class than a crusader against dictatorship. The SPGB pointed out that having initially shown enthusiasm for Franco in Spain, he only turned against him after concluding that "A thoroughly Nazified Spain, retaining its German nucleus, may well be a cause of profound anxiety both to France and Britain."[30] His early praise for both Hitler and Mussolini had been fulsome, referring to the former's attempts to restore German national pride when proclaiming that "If our country were defeated in war I hope we should find a champion as indomitable to lead us back to our rightful place among the nations."[31] Having also praised "the discipline, order, goodwill and smiling faces" of Italy's corporate state after a visit to Rome, the future ally of Joseph Stalin commented:

> If I had been an Italian I would have been entirely with you from the beginning to the end of your victorious struggle against the bestial appetites and passions of Leninism ... your movement has rendered a service to the whole world.[32]

When the ruthlessly anti-democratic regime of Stalinist Russia joined the Allies in the war against the Axis powers in 1941, this was final confirmation to the SPGB that the Second World War was very far indeed from being a war to safeguard parliamentary liberal democracy. It was instead a war to safeguard the interests of threatened sections of the capitalist class, initially in Britain and France, and then in the United States and Russia, and could not therefore be supported by socialists.

Political Democracy and War
The SPGB's opposition to the Second World War, though never in serious doubt, did not go entirely unchallenged from within its own ranks. Having failed in their attempt to persuade the SPGB membership to openly support the efforts of

the Spanish Popular Front forces in Spain, a minority in the Party argued that it should not oppose a war which would be capable of defeating Nazism, even if, as was generally agreed, that was not the express reason why any such a war would actually be fought. In 1938 a group of members around Robert Reynolds put forward the view that as the SPGB's Declaration of Principles made clear that the Party would use force if necessary against undemocratic recalcitrant minorities who refused to accept the will of the socialist majority, so the SPGB could contemplate sanctioning the use of force to safeguard parliamentary democracy and free political rights of organisation. The SPGB, Reynolds claimed, did not actually have a policy towards war in general which meant that it had to oppose every single conflict, only an attitude to specific wars as and when they occurred.[33] This, at least in theory, opened the way for possible SPGB support for war against Nazi Germany.

Reynolds's argument had a clear parallel with the SPGB stance on reforms (see Chapter 1). While opposed to reformism — the advocacy of reform measures — the SPGB did not have a policy of opposing all individual reforms as such, but declared itself prepared to judge each reform which came before the working class on its merits, with possible support dependent on whether the reform at issue was of benefit to the working class or assisted the socialist movement itself. The SPGB, thought Reynolds and his supporters, should judge every war on a similar basis instead of adopting a stance of blanket opposition. This view, logically argued from the standpoint of the Party's Declaration of Principles, gained adherents and even received the narrow backing of one poorly attended SPGB Executive Committee meeting before being overturned when the viewpoint of the bulk of the Party was re-asserted.[34]

After some debate on the matter and more than a little acrimony in the branches and at Party Conference, the SPGB resolved, contrary to Reynolds's view, that it certainly did have a policy on wars, a policy of being firmly against them and a consistent standpoint as to the cause of war in the modern capitalist world. Soon after the Second World War broke out, a statement was drawn up outlining the policy of the Party which was overwhelmingly adopted at the Easter 1940 Party Conference. The statement began by affirming that the SPGB existed solely for the purpose of overthrowing capitalism and achieving socialism, and that it was duty bound to examine any proposed course of action, including war, in relation to three principal considerations, which were:

1. Has the proposed action the purpose of achieving Socialism and will it achieve that result?
2. Has the proposed action the purpose of safeguarding democracy and will it have this result?
3. Has the proposed action the purpose of achieving an improvement in the conditions of the workers, and will it have this result?[35]

With regard to the first consideration, it was clear that none of the protagonists in the Second World War aimed at achieving socialism, or thought this to be the likely result. The second consideration, however, seemed rather more problematical. The Allied forces claimed that their actions were aimed at safeguarding democracy and would have precisely this result. The SPGB's statement was equally sure that it would not:

> The SP now, as throughout its history, holds that this line of argument is fallacious, and that this war, like the war of 1914-18, will not have that result, nor, as far as concerns the prime motives of those who control the Government of Britain and France, is that the purpose of the war.
>
> While we are as anxious as anyone to see all forms of dictatorship destroyed, we hold that war will not secure that object; on the contrary, with the workers of all countries in their existing backward political state, the direct and immediate consequences of war and the sufferings and hatreds accompanying war will weaken and undermine democracy, not strengthen it. This is true even though the defeat of Germany might — as in 1918 — temporarily cause the openly reactionary forces to give up their hold on the machinery of government.[36]

This idea that war against Germany would not safeguard democracy was roundly criticised by the Party rebels. Jacomb, who was expelled for his support for the war, produced two leaflets attacking what he took to be the inconsistencies of this position, arguing that the SPGB's insistence that democracy could not be successfully defended by fighting for it, was elevating the Party to "the mantle of Old Moore".[37] But he neglected to mention that in making the opposite assertion the supporters of the Allied forces were little different, and unlike the SPGB, did not appear to have the experience of history on their side.

A more cogent criticism by Jacomb and Reynolds was that if democracy could not be successfully defended by fighting for it, then the SPGB's revolutionary strategy was seriously flawed. The capitalist class might be able to suspend democracy whenever they were threatened, and there would be nothing the working class could do about it. However, even this argument was not nearly as telling as they imagined, for the SPGB's position was not that democratic forces in charge of the state machine could never defend their democratic authority from insurgents and authoritarians — it was that this could be in no sense guaranteed so long as capitalism lasted, and that the democratic forces were themselves beholden to operate capitalism. Indeed, as the war showed, the victory of the Allies did not safeguard democracy and workers rights in Russia and its Eastern Bloc empire (including East Germany) nor in other states like Spain and Portugal. In Britain, democratic government was suspended during the war, just as the SPGB had earlier predicted it would be:

> One thing is certain. The moment war breaks out democracy will be abolished in all countries participating, and we would, in effect, be defending one Dictatorship against another.[38]

The third consideration in the statement adopted by the SPGB at its 1940 Conference was easily dealt with. Past experience had demonstrated that war did not necessarily result in an improvement in the condition of the workers, and often there was a deterioration, as after the 1914-18 conflict. Indeed, any improvement that did occur would be at a tremendous cost of military and civilian life. After having taken these three considerations into account, the SPGB's statement therefore concluded that neither the Second World War nor the widespread conflicts from China to Abyssinia which had acted as a prelude to it, could be supported by socialists on any of the three grounds advanced — "participation could not be justified either by the hope of achieving Socialism, the safeguarding of democracy, or the improvement in the standard of conditions of the working class".[39]

It must also be noted that the SPGB had its own political independence to consider in this period and was fearful of being subsumed into a leftist 'pro-democracy' movement. The hostility clause in its Declaration of Principles precluded temporary alliances with other political organisations supportive of capitalism, and its belief that it alone constituted the only socialist party in Britain made it especially wary of diluting the socialist content of its political approach. Any alliance with ostensibly 'anti-fascist' groups in Britain would certainly have proved disastrous for the SPGB and would have achieved little — the largest organisation on the left was the Communist Party, which, having initially been in favour of the war, changed course to virulently denounce the war in SPGB-type terms until 1941, only to change course again after the Nazi invasion of Russia and back Churchill.[40]

Some members of the SPGB felt that in being prepared to state that it was on the side of the republican-supporting Spanish workers during the Civil War it had already gone too far in this direction,[41] and it was certainly true that the entry of Germany and Italy into the conflict, turning what was initially a civil war into an international imperialist war, had made the SPGB appear as if it was giving support to one side in an imperialist conflict. However, during the Spanish conflict and the Second World War, the SPGB, despite its minor vacillations, had established an important precedent which was to help guide it in the post-war world, most notably in its later analyses of workers' struggles in totalitarian countries. Fifty years after the outbreak of the Second World War, when faced with the struggle for democracy in the collapsing Eastern Bloc states, the SPGB was guided by the position it had painstakingly developed in the 1930s. In 1990, with the Berlin Wall literally crumbling, the SPGB reaffirmed its political independence together with its principled support for political rights and democratic organisation:

... the Socialist Party of Great Britain wholeheartedly supports the efforts of workers everywhere to secure democratic rights against the powers of suppression. Whilst we avoid any association with parties or political groups seeking to administer capitalism we emphasise that freedom of movement and expression, the freedom to organise in trade unions, to organise politically and to participate in elections, are of great importance to all workers and are vital to the success of the socialist movement.[42]

As during the 1930s, this viewpoint was not a unanimous one, with some SPGB members arguing that the Party could not "wholeheartedly support" the efforts of workers who were supportive of capitalism as well as of liberal democracy.[43] To them, workers opposed to political dictatorship, whether the anti-Leninists of the 1980s or the anti-fascists of the 1930s, were worthy of admiration in the face of severe adversity, but nothing more. This argument, though, was weakened by the fact that the SPGB, while supportive of the efforts of the working class, as a class, to achieve democratic and trade union rights, had never compromised itself by supporting capitalist organisations professing this as their aim. As the experiences of the 1930s and the Second World War proved, this was as much the case in war as at any other time.

Notes

1. *What Are We To Do?* by John Strachey (Left Book Club, London, 1938) p.146.
2. See *Questions of the Day*, 1942, p.87.
3. 'A Few Words on Fascism' in *Socialist Standard*, April 1934.
4. 'The Historical Background of Hitlerism' in *Socialist Standard*, May 1939.
5. *Ibid.*
6. *Questions of the Day*, 1942, p.86.
7. 'Origin and Growth of Nazism' in *Socialist Standard*, September 1943.
8. 'Origin and Growth of Nazism' in *Socialist Standard*, October 1943.
9. *Ibid.*
10. *Ibid.*
11. 'The Civil War in Spain' in *Socialist Standard*, September 1936.
12. For Italy see 'Mussolini and Parliament' in *Socialist Standard*, February 1927, and *Questions of the Day*, 1942, pp.77-80.
13. *The Monument*, pp.98-9.
14. *Anti-Parliamentary Communism*, Chapter 7.
15. 'The SPGB and Spain' in *Socialist Standard*, May 1937.
16. 'Is Democracy Worth While?' in *Socialist Standard*, April 1937.
17. 'The Civil War in Spain' in *Socialist Standard*, September 1936.
18. *Anti-Parliamentary Communism*, p.156.
19. 'The Civil War in Spain' in *Socialist Standard*, September 1936.
20. 'The SPGB and Fascism' in *Socialist Standard*, December 1936.
21. 'May Day and the War Clouds' in *Socialist Standard*, May 1939.
22. *The Socialist Party Exposes Mr Chamberlain and His Labour Critics* (SPGB, London, 1938) p.6.
23. 'The Beginning and End of Czechoslovakia' in *Socialist Standard*, April 1939.
24. 'The *Socialist Standard* in War-Time' in *Socialist Standard*, July 1940.
25. See 'Clashing Interests in the Mediterranean' and 'Germany, the Danube and Rumania' in *Socialist Standard*, May and October 1939.
26. 'Germany, the Danube and Rumania' in *Socialist Standard*, October 1939.
27. 'Clashing Interests in the Mediterranean' in *Socialist Standard*, May 1939.
28. *The Socialist Party and War*, pp.22-3.
29. *War Commentary*, April 1941.
30. See 'Notes By the Way' in *Socialist Standard*, May 1938.
31. *London Evening Standard*, 17 September 1937.
32. *Churchill's War*, Volume I by David Irving (Veritas, Bullsbrook, 1987) pp.20-1.
33. *The Monument*, pp.102-3.
34. *Ibid.*
35. 'Attitude To War' statement adopted at the 36th Annual Conference of the SPGB, Easter 1940.
36. *Ibid.*
37. A. E. Jacomb's *Case Against The Socialist Party*, undated pamphlet issued by A. E. Jacomb, pp.4-5.
38. 'Should We Fight For Democracy?' in *Socialist Standard*, September 1938.
39. SPGB's 'Attitude To War' statement.

40. The reasons for Communist opposition to the war from November 1939 to June 1941 are given in *Why This War?* by R. Palme Dutt (Communist Party, London, 1939). For an explanation of the Communist recantation of this view see the interview with William Gallagher M.P. in the *Daily Telegraph*, 27 June 1941.
41. Criticism by Southend Branch of the 'Attitude to War' and 'Socialists and War' SPGB statements (SPGB internal document, London, November 1943).
42. Resolution passed at 86th Annual Conference of the SPGB, Easter 1990.
43. This perspective has been held by members throughout the Party's history, and for some short periods their view has been the dominant one. This was the case in 1956 when the *Socialist Standard* wrote that the Hungarian revolt was a nationalist and pro-capitalist affair "not worth the spilling of one drop of working class blood". During the early 1980s a group of Party members were for similar reasons unhappy with the SPGB's qualified support for the pro-democracy efforts of workers in Polish Solidarity, and sought, unsuccessfully, to tighten-up the Party's position. By 1991 a group of about two dozen generally older generation SPGB members was expelled from the Party (the greatest number to be so at any one time) for a persistent refusal to abide by SPGB Conference decisions, notably including the 1990 resolution on political democracy. Today, this small group expresses its contempt for capitalist political democracy and the "reformist" stance of the official SPGB in its journal *Socialist Studies*.

6. The Welfare State

The Beveridge Report

As Chapter 1 made clear, the radical reform proposals with which the SPGB had been routinely confronted in its first years of political existence all had their sterling advocates on the political left who claimed that the SPGB was too sectarian to get involved in the actual business of 'practical politics'. During the SPGB's first four decades of political life, parliamentary reform had been enacted, factory legislation approved and state pensions introduced all without the help of the SPGB. The Second World War saw the emergence of a set of reform proposals which, judging by the commitment to reform and the breadth of political opinion of their advocates, clearly dwarfed the others. It was at this time that the welfare reform proposals of Sir William Beveridge emerged, to a largely — though not exclusively — uncritical audience. As will be demonstrated, such criticism as there was came mainly from the SPGB.

The Beveridge Report was the report by the Inter-departmental Committee on Social Insurance and Allied Services, set up by the Minister Without Portfolio in the wartime Cabinet, Arthur Greenwood, in June 1941. Under the chairmanship of Sir William Beveridge it reported back to the House of Commons in November 1942 with its comprehensive proposals for a restructuring of social insurance and welfare provision in Britain. Its terms of reference required it to "undertake, with special reference to the inter-relation of the schemes, a survey of the existing national schemes of social insurance and allied services, including workmen's compensation and to make recommendations".[1] Its various proposals formed the basis for the post-war British 'welfare state', recognised both at the time and since as a milestone in working class history. Reports into social insurance had taken place before, but this claimed to be more comprehensive and more radical in both its guiding principles and recommendations. It stated that:

> organisation of social insurance should be treated as one part only of a comprehensive policy of social progress. Social insurance fully developed may provide income security; it is an attack upon Want. But Want is one of only five giants on the road of reconstruction and in some ways the easiest to attack. The others are Disease, Ignorance, Squalor and Idleness.[2]

In tackling these five evils the Beveridge Report was intended to be much more than another in the series of ad hoc proposals which had previously characterised the development of welfare provision. Most importantly it proposed a national non-contributory health care scheme, the introduction of family allowances and a reorganisation of the entire social security benefits system. It is as such that it has been described as "a turning point in the history of welfare in Britain".[3]

Propaganda in favour of wholesale welfare reform was a feature of the entire Second World War period, echoing Lloyd George's First World War "land fit for heroes to live in" homily. It was recognised that such reform held out the hope of a brighter future after Nazi Germany had been defeated, without which the British working class might not find the necessary resolve to perform its wartime duties. As during the First World War, the 1939-45 conflict also provided a certain legitimisation for large-scale state interventions in the capitalist economy and a spur to planning. In the economic field this led to the ascendancy of interventionist Keynesian economics while in the field of social policy the interventionism of another 'New Liberal' — Beveridge — provided the foundation for the new policy direction of welfarism.

On its publication in late 1942 reaction to the Beveridge Report was almost universally favourable. Organisations from across the political spectrum saw in Beveridge just the kind of salvation needed for war-wracked Britain. This was just as true of Communists as Conservatives. The Communist Party MP Willie Gallacher pronounced on the Beveridge proposals in the House of Commons:

> The trade union movement wants the Beveridge plan, the Co-operative movement wants it, the Labour Party wants it, the Communist Party wants it, and the Liberals and a section of the Tory Party want it. It is clear that the great masses of the people, as represented by these forces, want the plan. Therefore, let the Government give a lead to the people ... and they will be doing something to bring out of this terrible war the hope of salvation for the future of the people of this country.[4]

This was a sentiment widely shared, and virtually the whole of the political left supported Beveridge. However, there were some dissenting voices. For instance, the small but vocal British feminist movement contended that the Beveridge proposals did nothing to alter women's subject status in the household and their dependence on men through the institution of marriage. The strongest criticism of this kind came from the Women's Freedom League and its journal, the *Women's Bulletin*,[5] which argued, contrary to the Beveridge recommendations, that men and women should always be treated as individuals by the state, paying the same insurance contributions and receiving the same benefits. The WFL claimed that the Beveridge plan could not be truly 'national' and comprehensive in character if it treated millions of women as if they were of a lower status than men.

The most rounded political objections to the Beveridge Report came from Marxists outside the Communist Party who claimed that Beveridge was effectively an agent of the capitalist class rather than a benevolent friend of the workers. By far the most sustained critique from this quarter came from the Socialist Party of Great Britain. The SPGB published two pamphlets in 1943 — both largely written by SPGB member Clifford Groves — aimed at dispelling working class illusions about the Report. One was *Beveridge Re-organises Poverty*, the other *Family Allowances: A Socialist Analysis*. While the second pamphlet, to be dealt with below, was very specific in its subject, the first attacked the Report on a number of fronts. It began by stating that Beveridge could be seen as an attempt to buy off the workers during wartime with the hope of something better to come in peace in return for higher productivity:

> these plans have not arisen as a result of a sudden and unexpected outburst of good neighbourliness on the part of the motley crew of politicians, parsons and others who have put them forward, but in order to provide an answer to large numbers of workers, in and out of uniform, who are extremely sceptical as to the outcome of the present war as far as they themselves are concerned. These doubts in their turn tend to put a brake on the workers' productive efforts.[6]

This outlook seemed to find its echo in the Beveridge Report itself which argued that "each individual citizen is more likely to concentrate upon his war effort if he feels that his Government will be ready in time with plans for [a] better world [and] that if these plans are to be ready in time, they must be made now".[7]

In *Beveridge Re-organises Poverty* the SPGB claimed that a major influence on the Beveridge Report was the desire to not only remove obstacles to higher productivity during the war, but to diffuse any possible working class discontent after it. Indeed, this was also the approach taken by the SPGB in its first published reaction to the Report in the *Socialist Standard*, where it was argued that:

> The Report is mistakenly referred to as a measure of insurance for the workers against the evils of capitalism. It would be more accurate to see it as a measure of insurance for the capitalists against the (for them) desperate evil of working class discontent with capitalism. Better far to give something away in time than to risk losing all.[8]

As the SPGB has since pointed out, it felt at the time of the Second World War that the Beveridge Report was to be best judged in the light of the wave of working class discontent which had followed the 1914-8 conflict, which the capitalist class and their representatives feared might be repeated.[9] After the post-First World War social discontent, unemployment benefits had temporarily gone up by over ten per cent, and the SPGB felt something similar might be attempted again. *Beveridge Re-organises Poverty* approvingly quoted Quentin Hogg's dictum to the capitalists that "if you do not give the people social reform, they are going to give you social revolution", and inferred that although social revolution was probably some way off, social discontent and mass strikes certainly were not.

The SPGB also claimed that the general promotion of the Report could not be understood without reference to the way in which the various schemes of poor relief in Britain had previously arisen. With growing industrialisation, labour mobility and the spread of large conurbations, the responsibility for poor relief had gradually moved away from small localities and parishes as employers sought to share out the cost of poor relief with nationally administered schemes. Even so, housing, medical assistance and food for the destitute still rested on a local basis. There was no comprehensive system of poor relief dealing with allied problems, and the system which thus grew up was disparate, unbalanced and in many ways inefficient and expensive. In his Report, Beveridge commented that:

> social insurance and the allied services, as they exist today, are conducted by a complex of disconnected administrative organs, proceeding on different principles, doing invaluable service but at a cost in money and trouble and anomalous treatment of identical problems for which there is no justification ... It is not open to question that, by closer co-ordination, the existing social services could be made at once more beneficial and more intelligible to those whom they serve and more economical in their administration.[10]

In view of this the SPGB argued that Beveridge had performed a "competent piece of work for the capitalists" and had demonstrated how best to solve the complex problem of distributing the barest subsistence to those without regular employment "in accordance with the most modern methods of business efficiency".[11] That unemployed workers should be maintained at subsistence level had a certain justification beyond diffusing any fears of social discontent or beyond the grounds of administrative cost and efficiency. The SPGB claimed on orthodox Marxian lines that it was necessary for the capitalists to keep unemployed workers at a subsistence level during bad times so as to preserve them as efficient wealth producers for when trading conditions improved. Beveridge himself had pointed this out too:

> It is to the interest of the employers as such that the employees should have security, should be properly maintained during the inevitable intervals of unemployment or of sickness, should have the content which helps to make them efficient producers.[12]

For the SPGB then, there were three possible justifications for the Beveridge proposals from the capitalists' point of view: to maintain the morale and efficiency of the workers in wartime, to help allay any social discontent after the war, and to address the problems of poor relief brought about by the changing circumstances of capitalism and the disparate system that had hitherto existed in Britain.

After this assessment of the reasons why the Report occurred when it did, the SPGB sought to consider the merits of the proposals themselves and the benefits or otherwise to be had from them by the working class. The Party accepted that

Beveridge's plan for a rate of benefit of forty shillings a week for a married couple was more than the wartime or pre-war rate, but still considered it a "miserable pittance" for the sick or unemployed and an insult rather than the "hope of salvation" claimed by its supporters for the people of Britain.[13] It contended that:

> a perusal of the Report gives the impression that Beveridge has gone through the administration of poor relief with a fine tooth-comb to remove the possibility that anyone seeking relief shall obtain at any time in his or her life more than a minimum needed for a very bare subsistence, and that this relief shall only be available where it can be shown that it is impossible for the applicants to work in the usual way.[14]

To substantiate this claim, the SPGB cited his criticism of the payment of permanent pensions to widows who could conceivably work, his own citation of an alleged scandal in the 1920s of married women not in search of work claiming unemployment benefit, his contention that blind people should never be given an allowance that could discourage them from working and his assertion that workers often took advantage of the death of relatives to buy new suits or go on jaunts with the proceeds of overly-adequate insurance payments. In addition, the Party also criticised Beveridge's view that it was "dangerous to be in any way lavish to old age" and his recommendation that old age pensions should be framed to encourage "every person who can go on working after reaching pensionable age, to go on working and postpone retirement and the claiming of pension."[15] This, it claimed, gave "a fair indication of his whole approach to the question of poor relief. His aim is to maintain a sufficiently healthy and efficient working population, and when age prevents further work his concern diminishes".[16]

The SPGB argued that while the working class would gain improved rates of benefit and extended medical aid through the Beveridge proposals, this was at least partially offset by the factors outlined above together with the increased contributions required for the scheme. But in the last analysis, the SPGB's economic critique of the Beveridge plan was underpinned by its Marxian class standpoint, and Beveridge had ignored the class issue completely:

> The outstanding problem of our age is the poverty of the working class. It is not the result of unemployment or of illness, or of industrial accident, or of inadequate powers of wealth production. It exists side by side with great wealth and affects the employed as well as the unemployed worker. It is the result of the private ownership by the capitalist class of society's means of producing and distributing wealth ... why should the workers allow themselves to be side-tracked by inquiries into poverty which start off by excluding the major factor in the case?[17]

Indeed, Beveridge spoke only of abolishing "want", which the SPGB took to mean "the condition into which the workers fall when their wages stop, not the condition in which they always are because they are carrying the capitalist class on their backs",[18] making clear the difference between absolute and relative poverty neglected by Beveridge himself.

Nevertheless, the SPGB conceded in late 1942 that in terms of holding out the hope of benefits to come for the workers — and because of its propaganda value against Nazism — the Report could be justifiably described as "an instant success for the Government". But it predicted that it would be a shallow victory, with the scheme being dependent on the faulty assumption that it would in all probability cost the state little, with unemployment permanently and substantially reduced after the war.[19] Though this gloomy prophesy took longer to be fulfilled than the SPGB expected, fulfilled it eventually was with the eventual return of mass unemployment and the development of the associated problems of welfare state finance in the 1970s and beyond.

Family Allowances

Perhaps the proposal in the Beveridge Report which received widest acclamation was his recommendation to introduce non-contributory family allowances at the average rate of eight shillings per week.[20] The movement for family allowances had received fairly widespread support in working class political circles from the early 1920s onwards and until Beveridge its greatest initial success came when the Samuel Commission (of which Beveridge was a member), set up to examine the problems of the British coal industry, recommended the introduction of children's allowances for mining families.[21] Much of the campaigning for family allowances was undertaken by the predominantly bourgeois Family Endowment Society, under the leadership of Eleanor Rathbone, but support came from across the left. The Independent Labour Party, the most notable partisan of family allowances, adopted family endowments as part of its 'living wage' proposals in the mid 1920s.[22] The ILP claimed that family allowances recognised the individual rights of women and children while at the same time had the economic benefit of raising working class purchasing power, and in so doing revitalising demand and offsetting slump.[23]

In 1927 the Labour Party and TUC set up a joint committee to look into the living wage and family allowances issues, which did not finally report until June 1930 after much discussion and argument. The Majority Report favoured cash allowances but a small though significant section of the trade union movement was unenthusiastic. In September 1930 the TUC General Council rejected family allowances and the subject largely disappeared from the left-wing political agenda after the collapse of the 1929-31 Labour Government. It was only to emerge once more after lengthy campaigning by Eleanor Rathbone and others during the Second World War when it was seen in a rather more enthusiastic light by politicians together with a Treasury under pressure to adopt a concerted wartime economic plan covering wages, prices, profits and taxation.[24] The appointment of Beveridge to head the commission investigating the social security system and allied services was itself a victory for the family allowances movement — Beveridge had been an early member of the Family Endowment Society and was on its Council for many years.

While support for family allowances came from various quarters, during the war the left saw it as another opportunity to make interventionist economic headway and extend the boundaries of the allegedly 'socialistic' state. In contrast the SPGB opposed family allowances vigorously, both before the war and during it. The Party's pamphlet *Family Allowances: A Socialist Analysis*, published in 1943, was particularly virulent in its attack on this new 'reform' and those who advocated it. Explaining why the SPGB did not advocate family allowances or any other reform of capitalism, it stated:

> It does not necessarily follow that reforms can never be of any benefit to the workers, although it is true to say that reforms cannot abolish the major evils of Capitalism, nor will they generally be introduced to deal with some of the minor evils except when their introduction is necessary to ensure the continued smooth running of the capitalist system. There are, however, some proposals for social reform which may be harmful in themselves, and perhaps the most obnoxious of all are those which on the surface appear philanthropic, but which in effect work towards a lowering of the already low standard of living of the working class. We may place in this category the schemes that have been put forward from time to time for Family Allowances.[25]

The SPGB contended that the introduction of family allowances would work towards a lowering of working class standards of living. As Clarke, Cochrane and Smart have noted, the SPGB dismissed them as "little more than an attempt to reduce the earnings of individual workers and increase employers' profits".[26] The reasoning behind this view lay, again, in Marxian economics. Following Marx, the SPGB claimed that wages fluctuated around the value of the commodity labour power. Wages had to be enough to ensure not only the training and existence of the worker him or herself, but future generations of wage workers as well. From this assumption it went on to comment:

> It is quite logical therefore from a capitalist point of view to raise objection to a condition which in a large number of cases provides wages "adequate" to maintain children for those who in fact possess no children. If the actual statistics of population are examined it will be found that the number of workers without families to support greatly exceeds those with families ... Here then from an employer's point of view is an anomaly that should be adjusted.[27]

The pamphlet explained how, in the last census at which the relevant figures were available, 60.6 per cent of male persons over twenty were single or married without dependent children, 16 per cent had one dependent child, 10.5 per cent had two dependent children, and 12.9 per cent had three or more. From this the SPGB deduced that the capitalist was "paying what is for him a fair market price for a commodity and in at least sixty cases out of a hundred being cheated on the scales!"[28] So while family allowances were being presented as a great philanthropic gesture on behalf of the ruling class, and were generally accepted as such by large sections of the political left, the SPGB deduced that they were really nothing of the sort:

> It might at first sight appear paradoxical to claim that a saving in the total national wage bill can be effected by additional payments being made to certain sections of the workers, but in the long run such a saving will result from the introduction of Family Allowances. As soon as the cost (or perhaps more truly the "alleged" cost) of rearing some or all of the workers' children is considered by the employers to have been provided for outside of wages, the tendency will assert itself for wages to sink to a new level based on the cost of maintaining a worker and his wife, or a worker, his wife and one child as the case may be.[29]

Despite the relative simplicity of this argument, there was much to support it. Conservative M.P. Leo Amery had claimed during the war that:

> If a system of Family Allowances were introduced now it would not only relieve the existing hard cases, but would afford a logical basis upon which a stand could be made against all further wage increases, except to the extent that they are justified by a rise in the cost of living.[30]

Beveridge was one of many advocates of family allowances who contended that they would indeed serve to facilitate real wage cuts, and possibly curb trade union militancy. On the Samuel Commission he argued that real wage cuts were essential to restore the profitability of the British coal industry and that a scheme of family allowances would be the best, and most humane way, to achieve this. In 1940 he stated that "We cannot in this war afford luxuries of any kind, and it is a luxury to provide people with incomes for non-existent children".[31] Indeed, Beveridge convinced Eleanor Rathbone that her movement would get nowhere if it insisted on seeing family allowances purely as a supplement to income rather than an effective transfer from some employees to others.[32]

The SPGB claimed that experience from abroad supported its analysis about the deleterious effects of family allowances on wage levels. It noted that where family allowances had been introduced in other countries it had generally been at a time of rising prices — and in 1943 prices were rising at the start of the great British inflation, putting the onus on trade unionists to resist real wage cuts. This fight was made more difficult by the introduction of endowments. In Germany, Holland, France, Belgium and other European states, family allowances had been introduced during the inflation period of the 1914-18 conflict. As early as 1931 the SPGB was able to quote economists in these countries who stated that their real intention was to facilitate wage cuts. The Dutch economist De Walle, for instance, had announced that "whenever central and municipal authorities have introduced family allowances it has been with a view to making economies in their wages bills."[33] The SPGB also quoted Australian journals to show how the family allowance system put into effect in New South Wales had noticeably cut real wages and effectively handed increased profits to the capitalists. As it pointed out, even supporters of the Australian Labour Party admitted that "The New South Wales scheme, instead of redistributing wealth, actually meant a reshuffling of wages between single and married men",[34] and one commented that:

> It is now common knowledge that if the NSW basic wage had been increased in accordance with the increase in the cost of living, the increase would have been 12s. per week, or approximately an addition to the wages bill of the State of something like £13,000,000. Under the Family Endowment Act the employers' contributions amount to £3,000,000 per annum, equal ... to an increase of 3s. per week in the basic wage.
>
> It is plain that, because of the adoption of Child Endowment, the employers of New South Wales have been made a present of something like £10,000,000 per annum, which they would have to pay if the basic wage had been computed on the old basis. Industry can hardly be said to be unduly penalised when, as a matter of fact, the employers are actually saving £10,000,000 per annum because of the change in the method of computing wages".[35]

The British ILP complained that the family allowance scheme advocated by them — the type of state scheme put forward by Beveridge — would not have the adverse effects of the other employer-based schemes. They thought that a state rather than employer-based system would act specifically as a supplement to wages. But the SPGB pointed out that whether the scheme was state or employer-based had been of no real consequence in practice — wherever family allowances had been introduced, real wages had, other things being equal, tended to fall. Indeed, New South Wales itself adopted a state-based system which ended with the same results as elsewhere.[36]

From this the SPGB argued that the trade unions should not be ruled by their political affiliations and should not therefore campaign for family allowances. Instead, their role was to defend the working class over wages and conditions of employment rather than give in to momentary, and often false, inducements. Their primary task was to ensure that the working class got all it could within capitalism:

> Trade Unions should direct their energies to obtaining general rises in wages for all sections rather than accept the very doubtful advantages of Family Allowances and then vainly attempt to resist the normal law of Capitalism for wages to gravitate to the new subsistence level.
>
> We do not accept the view that the capitalists cannot afford general wage increases. This plea has been put forward on nearly every occasion when the working class have sought to improve their conditions or resist the encroachments of their employers ... In spite of whatever advances the workers may have made, the wealth of the capitalists increases and continues to increase.[37]

Thus the SPGB's rejection of family allowances was almost entirely economic, and it had little if anything to say on the payment of family allowances specifically to women, one of the key proposals put forward by Eleanor Rathbone and welcomed, then and certainly since, by much of the feminist movement. It can be argued with some justification that the SPGB did not pay enough attention to this social — rather than purely economic — argument for family allowances, but so far as the SPGB's argument against family allowances went, there were definite grounds to support it, and also its related view about the external pressures of capitalism on the development, and nature of, the welfare state.[38] All told, the Party contended with force that the Beveridge proposals could be seen as an attempt not to improve the lot of the workers by seriously encroaching into the profits of the capitalists, but as a redistribution of poverty amongst the workers themselves — "They will level the workers' position as a whole, reducing the more favourably placed to a lower level and putting the worst placed on a less evil level. This is not a 'new world' of hope but a redistribution of misery".[39] That this was the primary intention of the reform was spelt out most clearly of all by Beveridge himself:

> ... correct distribution does not mean what it has often been taken to mean in the past — distribution between the different agents in production, between land, capital and labour. Better distribution of purchasing power is required among wage earners themselves, as between times of earning and not earning, and between times of heavy family responsibilities and of light or no family responsibilities.[40]

The State and Taxation
Though the SPGB denounced most of Beveridge's proposals as an attempt to redistribute poverty among the working class, this has not been the only significant aspect of its economic analysis of the welfare state. Welfare services in Britain, as in other countries, came to be financed out of general taxation as well as Beveridge's National Insurance scheme. Indeed, the proportion of welfare spending financed from general taxation has generally been about ninety per cent.[41] Throughout its political lifetime the SPGB has had a particularly distinctive set of arguments about taxation and in the post-war era it has begun to marry them with its analysis of the welfare state.

Its arguments on taxes and welfare have been fundamentally linked to the question of who pays for the welfare state and the functioning of the state machine in general. From the first issue of the *Socialist Standard* onwards, when Jack Fitzgerald wrote an article entitled 'The Bogey of the Taxes',[42] the SPGB's position on taxation has always been clear. It has contended that taxation is a burden on the propertied class and is therefore of no real concern to the workers. It claims that struggles over which sections of the propertied class should pay the brunt of the taxation needed to finance the offices and services of the state dominate capitalist politics. With universal suffrage and the increased number of taxpayers among the working class, these struggles eventually come to infect the consciousness of the workers:

> Right through the history of taxation the spectacle has been seen of one section of the propertied class trying to shift the burden of taxation on to another section, and the question in many minds is ... 'Can they shift it on to the working class?' We answer no! The working class does not own property. They exist alone by selling their energy (their power to labour) to the employing class, the owners of the means of production.[43]

This argument derives from the Marxian theory of wages which postulates that the wages and salaries of the working class represent the cost of production of the workers themselves. Wages take into account the skills and time spent in education by the workers and the cost of raising their families. Under capitalism human labour power becomes a commodity with both a use value to the capitalists and also a value in exchange, priced in the form of wages and salaries. This value of labour power, expressed as wages, is not a hypothetical sum but a real amount received for the purpose of reproducing labour power. If extra nominal payments have to be made, for, say, income tax, nominal wages will have to gravitate upwards if the real value of labour power is to be realised. The ultimate burden of the tax then falls on profit and not wages. Long before the SPGB and Marx, this had been recognised both by Adam Smith[44] and English MP and economist David Ricardo, who stated this view from the standpoint of his own particular theory of value:

> Taxes on wages will raise wages, and therefore will diminish the rate of the profits of stock ... A tax on wages is wholly a tax on profits; a tax on necessaries is partly a tax on profits and partly a tax on rich consumers. The ultimate effects which result from such taxes, then, are precisely the same as those which result from a direct tax on profits.[45]

Marx and Engels were both certain that even if taxes were nominally paid by workers, the ultimate burden for them rested on the capitalists. Marx commented:

> The level of wages expressed, not in terms of money, but in terms of the means of subsistence necessary to the working man, that is the level of real, not of nominal wages, depends on the relationship between demand and supply. An alteration in the mode of taxation might cause a momentary disturbance, but will not change anything in the long run.[46]

Following from this:

> If all taxes which bear on the working class were abolished root and branch, the necessary consequence would be the reduction of wages by the whole amount of tax which goes into them. Either the employers profit would rise as a direct consequence by the same quantity, or else no more than an alteration in the form of tax-collecting would have taken place. Instead of the present system, whereby

the capitalist also advances, as part of the wage, the taxes which the worker has to pay, he [the capitalist] would no longer pay them in this roundabout way, but directly to the state.[47]

Engels had similarly written of the burden of taxation that "The state and municipal taxes, as far as they affect the capitalist class, are paid from it [surplus value] as are the rent of the landlords, etc. On it rests the whole existing social system."[48]

Throughout its existence the SPGB has sought to explain in its propaganda how taxes come to be a burden on the capitalists and not the workers, even when the workers pay them directly to the state. In doing so, it has conceded that such a situation does not come about automatically once a tax has been levied or increased, but only through the operation of a general economic tendency. Most importantly, its analysis is not based on the example of an extra charge placed on an individual worker. The extra tax or charge has to be sufficiently widespread to enter into the average cost of production of labour power. When it does there will then be pressure for nominal wages to rise so that the extra tax can be paid in a similar manner to which there is pressure for wages to increase when there has been a general rise in prices.[49]

The situation with indirect taxes like VAT and excise duties is similar. If some prices rise because of taxes there will be general pressure for the price of labour power to rise to take account of this, and the SPGB has pointed out that in the post-war era wages have risen faster than prices far more often than not. However, according to the SPGB, prices do not always rise because of indirect tax increases — often they do not rise at all because prices can only move so much as the market allows them to:

It is a widely held assumption that tax alterations are bound to affect prices, but the facts show that this is not the case ... At one time the market may allow a manufacturer to recoup a tax increase by putting up his price — or perhaps even to overcompensate by putting the price up by more than the rise in tax. At another time selling conditions may not allow such an increase and the manufacturer will have to yield up some more of his profit to the government.[50]

Often manufacturers and retailers attempt to 'pass on' tax rises to the consumer but find that the market will not bear the new price. Excise duties are invariably levied on firms in a monopoly position or where markets are dominated by cartels, so that the government can cream off 'excess' profits. The SPGB has therefore contended that once all these factors are taken into consideration, there is no reason to suggest that the burden of indirect taxes falls on the workers either. Instead, the chief factors determining the workers' standard of living under capitalism are the effectiveness of trade union action and the state of capitalism's trade cycle,[51] leading the SPGB to state that "struggling to raise wages is in line with working class interests, campaigning over taxation is not".[52]

Because of what amounts to its near-unique position in modern politics on the nature of taxation,[53] the SPGB has been able to claim that the cost of maintaining the entire state machine through taxes falls exclusively on the capitalists. This is as much true of welfare expenditure as it is of warfare expenditure.[54] But this analysis has presented the SPGB with a problem. If the welfare state is primarily financed through taxation — which is in the last analysis a burden on the capitalists — does the welfare state represent a clear gain for the working class, beyond the improvements, always accepted by the SPGB, on the previous welfare arrangements? If this can be demonstrated, the SPGB's anti-reformist arguments in relation to the welfare state and its advocates would be seriously undermined.

The SPGB has approached this problem in a variety of ways. The first has been to attempt to either ignore or seek to diminish the amount of capitalist profit used to finance the welfare state. This was the Party's initial approach, which tended to focus on the payments made by the working class through the National Insurance system. In 1950, for instance, the *Socialist Standard* felt able to assert that "as far as the health services are concerned, the working class are just getting what they pay for",[55] thus ignoring the massive contribution from surplus value in the form of taxation. As late as the 1970s the then *Socialist Standard* Editorial Committee appeared reluctant to acknowledge the relatively large contributions of the capitalists to the welfare state on the grounds that "If it were true that the NHS was paid for wholly by the employers, its arrival would have meant an automatic gain in wages by the majority of workers — since voluntary contributions schemes were superseded, and they no longer had to pay for health necessities. [In reality] this did not happen."[56] Objection was raised to this Editorial view by members of the Party itself. One, Adam Buick, claimed that "if the welfare state is financed out of surplus value (as it is)" then:

> to the extent that the increased welfare benefits decrease the cost of reproducing labour power then the tendency would be for wages to fall (or, in the current era of chronic inflation, to rise less quickly than inflation) so that, in the end, the working class would be no better off at all; they would still only get enough to reproduce their labour power, as can only be the case under capitalism.[57]

The implication of this was clear — if it was not for the arrival of the NHS and other welfare services, the wages of the working class would have had to rise by a much greater extent than they actually did. This view, while acknowledging the role of surplus value, did not present the welfare state as a reformist 'gain' for the working class. Rather, it advanced the perspective mooted in *Beveridge Re-organises Poverty* that the welfare state was virtually a necessity brought about by the actual development of capitalism. This point had sometimes been made in articles in the *Socialist Standard*:

> … there is nothing to be gained by seeing the welfare services as something which they are not. They do not give the worker something for nothing. They are not free handouts.

Reforms — social, economic and political — are necessary all the time to keep the capitalist system running smoothly. They do not represent a challenge to the system or a concession from the system, rather they are demanded by the system.[58]

In this view the welfare state was primarily financed by the capitalists, but they had relatively little choice in the matter if they wished to keep their system running smoothly and efficiently. In short, the welfare state was a necessary 'expense' of production.

Out of this analysis arose an idea which gained widespread acceptance in the SPGB from the 1980s onwards when the welfare state as it had evolved post-1945 came under assault from successive governments. This was the view of the welfare state as an expense of production which the capitalist class were out of necessity forever seeking to keep as low as possible. At times of high unemployment this involved cutbacks in benefit levels (most obviously the break between benefits and earnings) and relative cuts in NHS expenditure. The SPGB argued that with the advent of three million unemployed, it was not in the capitalist state's interest to spend increasing amounts on health care if such a huge army of unused labour existed. An article in the *Socialist Standard* on 'The Health Service Under Attack' asserted that from the capitalists' viewpoint "it is uneconomic to spend money on the health care of 'non-producers' such as the unemployed or the elderly".[59] But the SPGB's most challenging analysis increasingly centred on the difficulty of the capitalist class — in Britain and also abroad — to adequately finance all state expenditures, especially the huge amounts spent on the welfare state, out of taxation and borrowing. As government expenditures as a proportion of GNP rose to well over 40 per cent, especially during times of recession, an almost intolerable burden was being placed on the private sector — usually the only (and invariably the dominant) profit-making sector of the economy. Marxist economist Paul Mattick had outlined the basis for this analysis in the following terms:

The private sector of the economy must be taxed for current government needs and for the costs of the national debt. A larger part of its profits are taken by taxes and a correspondingly smaller part can be capitalised ... Instead of being capitalised, an increasing part of the social profit dissipates in additional government spending ... How much can the government tax and borrow? Obviously not the whole of national income. Yet the non-profit sectors of the economy have constantly risen in all capitalist nations ... If this trend continues, there must come a time when the non-profit sector outweighs the profitable sector and therewith endangers the latter's existence. There must then be a limit to the expansion of the non-profitable part of the economy.[60]

This perspective led the SPGB to question whether the post-1945 welfare state and its component parts like universal benefits could survive for a further prolonged period,[61] and to suggest that, although initially sound in principle, it may have evolved into a rather costly aberration from the capitalist 'norm' represented by the more austere pre-Beveridge years.

While the capitalist class and their political representatives have not seen this problem in the Marxian terms laid out by the SPGB, they have certainly come to see non-profitable expenditures as a great burden on the capitalist economy which need to be reduced to more 'manageable' levels. As the Conservative Chancellor Norman Lamont emphasised, the commitment of governments has clearly become "to reduce the proportion of the nation's wealth pre-empted by the public sector".[62] The SPGB has felt driven to comment that:

> The need to keep health and social security expenditure in check does not therefore come about because of the blind malice and hatred of politicians but because of the need to keep the amount of profit taken off the capitalists as low as possible. The spectre of a declining rate of profit after tax — restricting future investment in the profit-making sectors of the economy — is not something the capitalist class are simply going to sit back and accept. This was demonstrated by the rise of so-called 'Thatcherism' in Britain and other industrialised countries in the 1980s, whose overt mission (not altogether successfully carried out) was to reduce borrowing and the proportion of the capitalists' accumulated wealth taken through tax.[63]

So as the SPGB initially expected, the future well-being of the welfare state came to be threatened by the forces of profit and capital accumulation. These were the same forces which set it in motion but which have since found its continued growth in a stagnating economy with widespread unemployment a difficulty almost too great to bear. Some of its features, most notably family allowances, may well have represented a "redistribution of poverty" as the SPGB claimed in 1943, but the main challenge to its existence came not from the disgruntled working class but from a system which has found it far more costly and burdensome than that initially anticipated by either its protagonists or opponents, Beveridge himself certainly included. The SPGB's analysis of "better far to give away a little now save risk losing all" had been turned on its head as that which seemed all too necessary during the Second World War and afterwards was to seem excessive once the full employment and sustained growth the welfare state depended on for its continued expansion had been removed. The SPGB had always contended that the hope of permanently reduced unemployment after the war was a dangerous assumption on which to base a welfare system, and in that, at least, its fears certainly proved well founded and today give a partial justification for its refusal to become embroiled in the original Beveridge bandwagon promoted with such enthusiasm by the reformers on the political left.

Notes

1. *The Beveridge Report* (HMSO, London, 1942) p.5.
2. *The Beveridge Report*, p.6.
3. *Ideologies of Welfare* by John Clarke, Allan Cochrane & Carol Smart (Hutchinson, London, 1987) p.86.
4. *Parliamentary Debates*, 17 February 1943, column 1880.
5. *Ideologies of Welfare*, p.107.
6. *Beveridge Re-organises Poverty*, (SPGB, London, 1943) p.6.
7. *The Beveridge Report*, p.171.
8. 'Some Socialist Points on the Beveridge Report' in *Socialist Standard*, December 1942.
9. 'Why Beveridge Re-organised Poverty' in *Socialist Standard*, December 1992.
10. *The Beveridge Report*, p.6.
11. *Beveridge Re-organises Poverty*, p.11.
12. *The Beveridge Report*, p.109.
13. *Beveridge Re-organises Poverty*, p.15.
14. *Beveridge Re-organises Poverty*, p.16.
15. See *The Beveridge Report*, p.96.
16. *Ibid.*
17. 'Some Socialist Points on the Beveridge Report' in *Socialist Standard*, December 1942.
18. *Ibid.*
19. *Ibid.*
20. *The Beveridge Report*, p.158.
21. *Report of the Royal Commission on the Coal Industry*, (HMSO, London, 1926) pp.160-3.
22. *The Movement For Family Allowances 1918-45* by John MacNicol (Heinemenn, London, 1980) p.139.
23. *New Leader*, 22 May 1925.
24. *The Movement For Family Allowances 1918-45*, p.170.
25. *Family Allowances: A Socialist Analysis* (SPGB, London, 1943) pp.4-5.
26. *Ideologies of Welfare*, p.111.
27. *Family Allowances: A Socialist Analysis*, p.8.
28. *Ibid.*
29. *Family Allowances: A Socialist Analysis*, pp.8-9.
30. Letter to *The Times*, 14 January 1940.
31. *The Times*, 12 January 1940.
32. See *The Movement For Family Allowances 1918-45*, p.33.
33. 'Why Socialists Oppose Family Allowances' in *Socialist Standard*, February 1931.
34. *Ibid.*
35. *Family Allowances: A Socialist Analysis*, p.10.
36. 'Why Socialists Oppose Family Allowances' in *Socialist Standard*, February 1931.
37. *Family Allowances: A Socialist Analysis*, pp.12-3.
38. For this see *Ideologies of Welfare*, p.108 and p.114.
39. *Beveridge Re-organises Poverty*, p.20.

40. *The Beveridge Report*, p.167.
41. *Paying For Welfare* by Harold Glennerster (Basil Blackwell, Oxford, 1985) p.127.
42. 'The Bogey of the Taxes' in *Socialist Standard*, September 1904.
43. 'Rates and Taxes - Do They Fall Upon the Working Class?' in *Socialist Standard*, March 1912.
44. *The Wealth of Nations* by Adam Smith (Black, Edinburgh, 1843) pp.390-2.
45. *The Principles of Political Economy and Taxation* by David Ricardo (J. M. Dent and Sons, London, n.d.) p.140.
46. *Collected Works of Karl Marx and Friedrich Engels*, Volume VI (Lawrence and Wishart, London, 1976) p.225.
47. *Collected Works of Karl Marx and Friedrich Engels*, Volume VI, p.329.
48. *Engels on Capital* (Lawrence and Wishart, London, 1937) p.6
49. This is discussed with specific relation to the Poll Tax in answer to a correspondent in the *Socialist Standard*, August 1989.
50. 'The Budget' in *Socialist Standard*, May 1964.
51. *Election '87* (SPGB, London, 1987) p.8.
52. 'Income Tax and the Wage Struggle' in *Socialist Standard*, November 1963.
53. This position was also held by the SLP, and still is by the British SLP's American parent. For the SLP position on taxation as laid down by De Leon himself see *Who Pays the Taxes?* by Daniel De Leon (Socialist Labour Press, Glasgow, 1912).
54. For an SPGB analysis of the burden of war expenditures see, for instance, 'Who Pays For the War?' and 'The Finance of War' in *Socialist Standard* November 1916 and September 1959.
55. 'The Welfare State' in *Socialist Standard*, June 1950.
56. Correspondence in *Socialist Standard*, December 1976.
57. Ibid.
58. 'The Welfare State' in *Socialist Standard*, April 1965.
59. 'Health Service Under Attack' in *Socialist Standard*, March 1985.
60. *Marx and Keynes* by Paul Mattick (Merlin Press, London, 1980) pp.162-3.
61. See 'Can the Welfare State Survive?' in *Socialist Standard*, September 1992 and *The Market System Must Go - Why Reformism Doesn`t Work* (SPGB, London, 1997), Chapter 9. See also SPGB 88th Annual Conference Report.
62. *Daily Telegraph*, 24 July 1992.
63. 'Why Beveridge Re-organised Poverty' in *Socialist Standard*, December 1992.

7. Keynes and Inflation

Keynes — the Saviour of Capitalism?

The severity of the world slump of the 1930s led to a fundamental questioning and re-assessment of previously well established economic theories. While many on the left turned towards Marx and the various (and sometimes conflicting) ideas propagated by those economists in the Marxian school for an explanation of the prolonged falls in production, shrinking world trade and massive unemployment of the time, the only bourgeois economist to attract widespread attention and emerge from this period with an enhanced reputation was John Maynard Keynes.

As the economy dipped in the 1920s and 30s, so did the reputations of the more orthodox economists — men such as Marshall, Pigou and Edgeworth,[1] who had all thought a major world slump unlikely. To these economists — dubbed the 'classical school' by Keynes[2] — 'Say's Law' that every seller brings a buyer to market largely held true.[3] Unemployment in the capitalist economy was considered by them to be an essentially transient phenomenon, caused principally by either temporary and isolated overproductions in certain spheres of industry or by wage inflexibility promoted by trade union power. Any long-term unemployment, they thought, could be eradicated through adjustments to real wages.[4]

That unemployment in Britain had never gone below ten per cent of the insured work force[5] in the 1920s despite periodically falling real wages and lulls in trade union militancy, served to undermine the basis of these classical economic theories before the post-1929 slump discredited them almost entirely. By the 1930s a new theory was effectively needed within the realms of bourgeois economics which could both explain, and provide a remedy for, mass unemployment while rejecting the dangerous analysis of the Marxians. It was into this gap that Keynes successfully manoeuvred, developing in *The General Theory of Employment, Interest and Money* an economic doctrine which challenged the conventional wisdom of the 'classical school' without formally recognising the contributions made to economic thought by the "illogical" and "obsolete" Marx.[6]

Much differentiated the approach of Keynes to that of Marx and his latter-day followers in organisations like the SPGB, though one common factor did unite them in opposition to the classical school. This was their rejection of Say's Law of Markets, considered at the time to be the most radical aspect of Keynes's new theoretical system. The supposed revelatory discovery of Keynes was that capitalism did not naturally tend towards an equilibrium point of full employment because every seller did not necessarily bring a buyer to market. In certain circumstances individuals and enterprises could choose to save or hoard their wealth instead of spending it. Due to this hoarding of profits — what Keynes called "liquidity preference" — there could be periods of insufficient market demand for both consumer and producer goods.

Keynes contended that flights towards "liquidity preference" were in turn partly explicable in terms of what he described as the "propensity to consume", which would tend to decline as incomes rose.[7] As capitalism expanded, providing for rising incomes particularly at the top of the income scale, people would choose to spend proportionately less of their incomes on consumer goods, causing contractions in market demand. Therefore, to the extent that capitalism provided for the further accumulation of capital out of profits, and proceeded to concentrate more and more wealth into fewer hands, it would tend in the long run not towards full employment but unemployment and stagnation. Keynes observed:

> Thus our argument leads towards the conclusion that in contemporary conditions the growth of wealth, so far from being dependent on the abstinence of the rich, as is commonly supposed, is more likely to be impeded by it.[8]

This view placed Keynes well and truly in the camp of underconsumptionism.[9] Hoarding — and in some instances saving too — constituted subtractions from purchasing power, and so production in capitalism, he claimed, would tend to outstrip aggregate market demand for consumer goods, with this leading to a falling marginal efficiency of capital, a contraction in the producer goods sector, economic crisis and slump.

The elaboration of these ideas in the 1930s against the previously received wisdom of Say's Law was a revelation to Keynes's supporters and those desperate to understand the causes of mass unemployment. It was not, however, nearly such a revelation to those who, like the SPGB, had troubled to study Marx's economic writings. For a full seventy years before Keynes, Marx — principally in *Capital* — had already elaborated a theory which had removed the foundations on which the classical and neo-classical schools of economic thought had been built. To Marx, the "comical" Say had propounded an idiocy, and the classical economists were no better for having accepted it:

> Nothing could be more foolish than the dogma that because every sale is a purchase, and every purchase a sale, the circulation of commodities necessarily implies an equilibrium between sales and purchases. If this means that the number of actual sales accomplished is equal to the number of purchases, it is a flat tautology. But its real intention is to show that every seller brings his own buyer to market with him ... But no one directly needs to purchase because they have just sold.[10]

Marx argued that if the interval between sale and purchase becomes too pronounced, a dislocation results in the circulation of commodities and accumulation of capital which finds expression in an economic crisis.

Despite Marx and Keynes's common rejection of Say's Law it did not lead them to the same conclusions. Marx's conclusion was that capitalism could not be prevented from periodically lurching into economic crisis and stagnation. Keynes thought that given the correct stimuli it could, and that, moreover, he had discovered the basis for governmental action to avert future slumps. Keynes's solution to the problems posed by capitalist development sprang directly from his theoretical analysis of the problems themselves. As capitalism tended towards stagnation caused by an insufficient aggregate monetary demand, measures would have to be taken to increase demand, reduce the preference for liquidity and stimulate production. In this way Keynes maintained that governments could take positive action to ensure permanent 'full employment' and sustained growth.

To increase the level of investment in the economy, Keynes argued that governments could actively intervene and undertake to provide the investment that private industry was unwilling or unable to make. If necessary, this meant running large budget deficits. Once the state had intervened to provide investment, the 'multiplier' effect, first introduced into bourgeois economic theory by R. F. Kahn,[11] would ensure a disproportionately large expansion in national income.[12] To increase consumption, a restructuring of the tax system was required, ensuring that those on high incomes and with a low propensity to consume were taxed to a far greater extent than those on low incomes with a high propensity to consume. Lastly, consumption and investment could both be stimulated by a more relaxed monetary policy than that previously advocated by the neo-classical school, reducing the preference for liquidity and any tendency towards hoarding.

This Keynesian prescription for capitalism's ills came to be taken up, at least in theory, by all the main political parties in Britain. It was first enunciated in government as the basis for economic policy in the 1944 *White Paper on Employment Policy*, issued by the wartime coalition, where the National government accepted as one of its "primary aims and responsibilities" the "maintenance of a high and stable level of employment after the war".[13] A more adventurous rendition was elaborated soon after by the Labour Party in their document *Full Employment and Finance Policy* which stated that when a slump threatened:

> we should at once increase expenditure, both on consumption and on development — i.e. both on consumer goods and capital goods. We should give people more money and not less to spend. If need be we should borrow to cover government expenditure. We need not aim at balancing the budget year by year.[14]

From the Second World War onwards, the Socialist Party of Great Britain, in utilising the theoretical framework handed to it by Marx and the early Marxians (see Chapter 4), did not hold out much hope for this newly adopted Keynesian policy. While Keynes had recognised some of the contradictions of capitalism — such as the crucial antagonism between capital accumulation and consumption — and also identified many of the problems associated with the system's development, including the tendential fall in the rate of profit (or "marginal efficiency of capital" as he called it), he had certainly not found a way of correcting capitalism's in-built tendency towards stagnation and slump. The SPGB predicted that if the post-war Labour government attempted to put Keynes's theories into practice it would "not succeed in avoiding unemployment and crises".[15] It argued in a *Socialist Standard* editorial entitled 'Lord Keynes: Economist of Capitalism in Decline' that capitalism was fundamentally based on an antagonistic system of income distribution and that at a time of economic crisis, any attempts to effectively increase the purchasing power of the working class, as Keynes advocated, would squeeze profits, further sap the confidence of the capitalists and delay recovery in much of the private sector:

> Capitalism depends for its relatively smooth functioning on the capitalists' confidence in their prospect of selling their goods at a profit. By the time bad trade threatens the capitalists will already be apprehensive and the proposed government policy would sap their confidence still more. It is one thing to propose to increase the workers' purchasing power, but the capitalists (including the Government itself in State industries) are at all times forced by competition to seek to reduce the purchasing power of the working class in relation to the mass of goods produced for the market.[16]

This argument clearly rested on the analysis of Marx in relation to the difficulties associated with surplus value production on the one hand, and surplus value realisation on the markets on the other:

> The conditions for immediate exploitation and for the realisation of that exploitation are not identical. Not only are they separate in time and space, they are also separate in theory. The former is restricted only by the society's productive forces, the latter by the proportionality between the different branches of production and by the society's power of consumption.[17]

Because of this, the requirements for reducing overproduction of commodities for the market — primarily the encouragement of expenditure and consumption — were in direct spatial conflict with the requirements of capital for investment and accumulation.

For a period in the 1950s and 60s, when the economy in Britain, if not elsewhere, went through a prolonged boom, the SPGB's prediction seemed to have been proved wrong. The Keynesian economist Michael Stewart opined that "Whatever the qualifications, the basic fact is that with the acceptance of the *General Theory*, the days of uncontrollable mass unemployment in advanced industrial countries are over".[18] However, true though it was that unemployment in Britain fell to abnormally low levels, the SPGB contended that the application of Keynesian economic theory had not been responsible for it, as even some of Keynes's supporters recognised.[19] Indeed, Keynes's recommendations, though adopted in theory, did not perhaps — at least until the 1970s — make a colossal practical impact, with economic policy in Britain more being governed by the bastardised Keynesianism of 'stop-go' with the overriding concern of framing fiscal policy in response to Balance of Payments movements. Unemployment had risen to over 900,000 in 1959, but there was no major slump to avert because of Britain's relatively advantageous trading position immediately after the war.

The SPGB's explanation of the 'long boom' attributed by some to Keynesian policy, was elaborated by Hardy in the Party's 1959 economic crises committee report, by Party speakers and in the *Socialist Standard*, most clearly of all in response to an enquiry by Terry Lawlor, who had left the Party over a disagreement about inevitably worsening economic crises (see Chapter 4). The SPGB re-affirmed that Britain's relatively prosperous economic condition could not last, and that Britain would be eventually beset by the kind of slumps that had occurred in most other industrialised countries, including the US and Germany, since 1945. It stated that the wartime destruction meant that Britain had been able to emerge from the war ahead of many of its chief competitors, becoming a market leader in car and aircraft manufacture, man-made fibres, electricity, electrical engineering, television, chemicals, oil, armaments manufacture and nuclear power.[20] The SPGB contended that this advantageous position could not inexorably continue and that the big test for the Keynesians would come with the return of the classic Marxist crisis cycle in Britain.[21] The *Standard's* Editorial Committee argued that the competitive drive to accumulate capital would bring about economic crises caused by disproportionate sectoral expansion and there would be nothing that governments could do about it:

> The Keynesians claim that the Government can, when it likes, stimulate capital investment and consumption and at other times damp down over-expansion. When the present motor car boom slackens off as it inevitably will, what can the government do if the world market for cars is temporarily saturated, except wait for demand to recover? Theoretically, the government could have prevented the industry from expanding so rapidly — and left the market to be filled with the cars of other producers — but the car manufacturers, the trade unions and Tory and Opposition MP's would all have protested.[22]

Nor, according to the SPGB, was it possible for states to simply tax the hoarded profits of enterprises or borrow from the private sector of industry to ensure increased investment and demand during a slump. While the state itself could provide a stimulus by acting in this manner, this could only be at the expense of the non-state sector where the bulk of profits are accrued and re-invested. With state expenditure increasing and jobs being created, most of the private sector would find its ability to re-invest in production reduced, thereby promoting further cutbacks. The SPGB argued that the experience of the neo-Keynesian New Deal 'showpiece' in America had been along these lines, with massive increases in state expenditure coming at the expense of the expenditure of the private sector, leading overall to only minimal decreases in unemployment. In the United States unemployment fell from 24.1 per cent in 1932 to 19.1 per cent in 1938, while in Britain unemployment fell from 22.1 per cent to 13.5 per cent, despite the application of an entirely different economic policy, which at the time had been derided by Keynes.[23]

The most concerted application of Keynesian economic policy in Britain during a slump was eventually to come in 1974-5 when the new Labour government under Wilson and Healey increased real state expenditure, ran large budget deficits and restructured taxation in the hope of redistributing income towards those with a higher marginal propensity to consume. Large additional sums were used to help stimulate industry, and, in particular, the crisis-stricken housing sector, but unemployment rose from about 600,000 in 1974 to over 1,600,000 by 1977 and the index of take home pay fell from 105 in July 1974 to 97 by July 1977.[24] Just as the SPGB had expected it would, this seemed to confirm the failure of Keynesian policy when put to a serious practical test. Indeed, in the case of the Labour government, it proved so disastrous as to bring about widespread policy reversals, and the abandonment of the entire 'pump-priming' Keynesian approach.

The SPGB pronounced that the Keynesian method was clearly incapable of providing full employment and sustained growth, and that this was as true of the bastardised Keynesianism of the 1950s and 60s as it was of the more full-blooded Keynesianism resorted to by the Labour government in the 1970s. But according to the SPGB, the Keynesian approach was more fatally flawed than even this suggested. For not only had Keynesianism failed both in Britain and abroad to realise its principal policy objectives of sustained growth and full employment, it had succeeded in creating an additional problem for capitalism in Britain in the post-war period — persistent rises in the price level.

The Marxian Theory of Inflation

Prices in Britain rose to such an extent that by 1999 the general price level was approximately thirty times higher than it had been at the onset of the Second World War five decades earlier,[25] and prices had risen every single year. Never before had there been such a lengthy and sustained period of general price rises in Britain. From the 1950s onwards the SPGB developed the view that these price rises (which were mirrored to varying degrees in other countries) were not the result of normal capitalist economic development. The SPGB noted that in the earlier history of capitalism, price movements tended to be cyclical, with prices rising in booms only to fall again in slumps.[26] At the start of a boom, competition between capitalists for raw materials and other products tended to put an upward pressure on prices which was reversed in slumps when the holders of commodities, faced with lower demand, were prepared to turn them into money at reduced prices. The price level at the start of the First World War in 1914 had been virtually the same as a century earlier, having risen during periods of expansion and fallen back under the influence of economic downturns. As *The Economist* has since demonstrated, prices in both Britain and America fell slightly more years than they rose, and the longest unbroken period of rising prices in either country lasted only six years.[27] In the seventeenth, eighteenth and nineteenth centuries the general price level in Britain had remained broadly stable in the long run, usually fluctuating year on year due to variations in agricultural output and because of the influence of the trade cycle.[28]

It was clear to the SPGB by the mid-1950s that the post-war boom in Britain could not solely account for the large-scale increase in the general price level that had started at around the beginning of the 1939-45 conflict. By 1957, for instance, the price level was already over three times its pre-war level and was continuing ever upwards.[29] Some additional factor other than the boom was obviously at work. The explanation advanced by the SPGB to account for this extraordinary rise in prices focused on this new factor. The SPGB contended that following Keynes's advice on adopting a looser monetary policy, governments had not thought it necessary to watch and control the creation of currency for use in the economy:

> Continually since 1939 it has been the policy of successive governments, National, Labour and Tory, to inflate the currency; that is, to increase the amount of notes and coins in circulation far beyond the amount that would have been sufficient to keep up with the growth of production, trade and population. The note issue in 1938 was under £600 million, it reached £1,400 million in 1945, and it is now over £2,000 million.[30]

This monetary explanation of the post-war price rises in Britain and other countries was based on what the SPGB, under the influence of its most prodigious writers and speakers on economics, took to be the Marxian theory of inflation, derived principally from Marx's labour theory of value.

Marx had dealt with the nature of money and inflation in Chapter 3 of Volume I of *Capital* and in his *Critique of Political Economy* — to the SPGB's satisfaction — and its analysis of inflation as a peculiarly monetary phenomenon, applied and developed throughout the post-war era, cannot be understood without reference to Marx's own writings on money. To Marx, money arose out of commodity exchange when one commodity emerged as a universally acceptable medium of exchange. To fulfil this role it had to have a value in its own right, the amount of socially necessary labour time required to produce it from start to finish under average conditions of production. Various commodities could function as money, but the precious metals gold and silver were generally found to be the most convenient. Marx argued that when one commodity, like gold, emerged as the money-commodity, other commodities acquired a price which expressed how much of the money-commodity they would exchange for. From this, an underlying value relationship could be said to exist between the money-commodity and other commodities, and that if the value of the money-commodity altered for some reason then this would affect all other prices. A fall in the value of gold would mean that the general price level would rise because, with the values of other commodities remaining the same, they would be the value equivalents of a greater amount of gold. Marx argued therefore that an inverse relationship existed between the value of the money-commodity and the general price level.[31]

Apart from such changes in the value of the money-commodity, Marx contended that the general price level could persistently rise for another reason if the money-commodity itself circulates. In Marx's day, a pound was the conventional name for about one quarter of an ounce of gold. If the government debased the coinage by issuing gold coins stamped 'one pound' but weighing only one eighth of an ounce of gold, prices would double as market forces would change the word 'pound' from being the conventional name of one quarter of an ounce of gold to being the conventional name of one eighth of an ounce. Though the underlying value relationship between the money-commodity and other commodities would remain the same, the price-names of the other commodities would change and their prices would rise because of this currency debasement, a phenomenon which occurred as late as the eighteenth century.

Having analysed the relationship between the money-commodity and other commodities, Marx examined the factors determining the amount of the money-commodity actually needed to circulate in the economy at any one time. In opposition to the Quantity Theory of Money put forward by Hume and Ricardo, Marx argued that with a circulating money-commodity like gold:

> If the velocity of circulation is given, then the quantity of the means of circulation is simply determined by the prices of commodities. Prices are thus high or low not because more or less money is in circulation, but there is more or less money in circulation because prices are high or low.[32]

This law held true even if gold coins were replaced as a circulating medium by coins of less precious metal or even by virtually worthless pieces of paper so long as these were backed by the money commodity, gold, and were convertible into it at a fixed rate, e.g. one quarter of an ounce of gold for one pound sterling. However, if the notes and coins circulating in the economy performing the function of the money-commodity were not convertible, then the situation was drastically changed. In the case of such an inconvertible currency, the pieces of paper issued by the state and given forced circulation become merely tokens for real money (gold) and so their purchasing power is determined solely by their quantity in relation to the amount of gold they are supposed to represent. In this situation the Quantity Theory of Money becomes relevant:

A law peculiar to the circulation of paper money can only spring up from the proportion in which that paper money represents gold. In simple terms the law referred to is as follows: the issue of paper money must be restricted to the quantity of gold (or silver) which would actually be in circulation, and which is represented symbolically by the paper money ... If the paper money exceeds its proper limit, i.e. the amount of gold coins of the same denomination which could have been in circulation, then, quite apart from the danger of becoming universally discredited, it will still represent within the world of commodities only that quantity of gold which is fixed by its immanent laws. No greater quantity is capable of being represented. If the quantity of paper money represents twice the amount of gold available, then in practice £1 will be the money-name not of one quarter of an ounce of gold, but one eighth of an ounce. The effect is the same as if an alteration had taken place in the function of gold as the standard of prices. The values previously expressed by the price of £1 would now be expressed by the price of £2.[33]

So the effect of issuing an excess of inconvertible paper currency over and above the amount of gold coin necessary to circulate in the economy was therefore, according to Marx, the same as debasing the currency, leading to rising prices. This theory demonstrated that the total amount of needed currency in the economy represents a total mass of value, and therefore a total weight in gold, so that if the total of gold is replaced by inconvertible currency, the total face-value of this paper 'token' money must not be greater than the total value of gold that would be otherwise required to circulate. If the inconvertible currency is issued in excess of this, as the SPGB contended was the case in post-war Britain, prices will go up.[34]

By way of explanation, the SPGB occasionally outlined what happens in practice in the capitalist economy when there is an overissue of inconvertible currency. Prices tend to rise in response to buyers of commodities offering larger amounts of money "in the same way that prices of accommodation and other things rise in holiday resorts in the summer season when holidaymakers come in large numbers".[35] In effect, there results an artificial bloating of monetary demand for commodities which does not arise out of an increased real demand based on value added in production. This bloating of monetary demand proves only temporary with prices quickly rising in response to it.

Following Marx, the SPGB contended that if currency inflation is to be avoided under conditions of inconvertibility, the total amount of token money (representative of a total weight of gold) needed to circulate must be roughly equal to the number of transactions carried out in the economy multiplied by total prices, the product of which is divided by the velocity of circulation of the token money.[36] This is expressed algebraically as M=TP/V.

It can be deduced from this analysis that the SPGB has used the term 'inflation' in a rather different way to most post-war economists, for whom rising prices and inflation have been entirely synonymous. The SPGB has effectively gone back to the pre-Keynesian usage of the term in arguing that 'inflation' is currency inflation — the depreciation in the value of a currency, not simply rises in the Retail Price Index. So far as the SPGB has been concerned, the RPI could rise without any inflation at all during a boom and still register falls in a heavy slump if there was only a very moderate currency inflation. It has pointed out that in reality, however, prices have continued to rise in slumps as well as booms in the post-war period because the depreciation of the currency undertaken by successive governments has more than outweighed any cyclical downward pressure on prices caused by the downturns in economic activity which returned in Britain from the late 1960s onwards.[37]

The SPGB has claimed that the history of British capitalism provides startling confirmation of its views on inflation and rising prices. It has expended much time on outlining its arguments on inflation (at least in part because it considers them to be a confirmation of the validity of the labour theory of value) and they are invariably backed up by a copious amount of statistics. The SPGB has contended that there have been three main periods of currency inflation in Britain — during the Napoleonic Wars, then during the First World War and just after, and lastly in the period from the onset of the Second World War to the present day. After the Napoleonic Wars inflation was halted when Britain went on to the Gold Standard. Under this convertible money system, the note issue was controlled so that beyond a low fixed limit the Bank of England could not issue additional notes without adding an equivalent amount of gold to its reserves.

It is the situation after the 1914-8 war which probably provides the most useful illustration of the SPGB's case. In 1914 Britain went off the Gold Standard and abandoned convertibility so that it could pay for much needed raw materials and other imports with gold. This paved the way for an inflation of the currency which was only halted in 1920 after the publication of the Cunliffe Report on the monetary system. Following the recommendations of the Report, the Coalition government under Lloyd George set a ceiling on the note issue and embarked upon a deliberate policy of currency deflation, taking about £66 million of notes out of circulation.[38] This, coupled with the effects of the 1920-1 world slump, reduced the price level by about thirty per cent.[39]

After rejoining the Gold Standard in 1925 (in a slightly different form) Britain was to eventually abandon it again in the midst of the Great Depression. When the economy gradually recovered during the 1930s after the slump, both prices and the amount of currency in circulation rose slowly until the onset of the Second World War. At this point — as in 1914 — inflation spectacularly took off. Indeed, from 1940-3 the amount of notes and coins in circulation almost doubled from £560 million to £1,030 million despite the war itself being a time of economic retrenchment.[40] Prices soon began to rise, but as the SPGB noted, a crucial difference emerged at the end of the Second World War compared to the 1914-8 conflict. This time, inflation was not deliberately halted by the monetary authorities, and prices continued to rise.

Precise reasons why inflation was not halted after the war are dealt with in the last section of this chapter, but according to the SPGB the key underlying factor lay in the changed attitudes of governments and the monetary authorities towards the note issue. Keynes, whose influence in such circles was probably greater than that of any other single economist, had taught that it was no longer necessary for governments to "watch and control the creation of currency".[41] Monetary policy was generally thought by Keynes to be a relatively impotent economic policy weapon[42] and currency was viewed as being a factor of, at best, secondary importance. From the Second World War onwards, notes and coins in circulation were certainly not viewed as a major determinant of the price level.

While it has been mentioned that not all of Keynes's views and recommendations came to be immediately taken up in Britain, his outlook certainly influenced the attitude of both the Bank of England and the Treasury towards monetary policy. Some years after his death, Keynes's viewpoint was notably enshrined in the post-war Radcliffe Report by the Committee on the Working of the Monetary System. The authors of the Report stated that "the authorities have explained to us in evidence that they do not regard the supply of bank notes as being the only, nor nowadays the only important supply of money."[43] Notes and coins were described as being "the small change of the monetary system" without any particular importance. As a vestige of the earlier real control of the note issue, the power of the note issuing authorities was formerly limited by the Currency and Bank Notes Act of 1954, but this allowed the Treasury and Bank of England to increase the note issue above a ceiling of £1,575 million so long as the Treasury presented a Statutory Order extending the excess issue before Parliament every two years. This order has to date only been challenged once, in 1962.

The main theoretical reason for the Keynesian inspired downgrading of the note issue as only "the small change of the monetary system" will be discussed in the next section, but its importance has been such that to the SPGB it has been a prime factor in opening the door to the massive, unhalted, post-war inflation of the currency. Despite the increased use of means of payment like cheque books and credit cards which slow down the velocity of circulation of notes and coin, and — other things being equal — reduce the amount of currency needed to circulate in the economy, the note issue since the Second World War has soared well beyond any warranted increase caused by expanding production and trade. As the *Socialist Standard* put it in 1990:

> The amount of currency in circulation with the public in 1938 was £442 million. It is now more than thirty times as much, at £14,388 million, and is still steadily increasing. The bath has been slopping over for fifty years and one dotty thing the Labour and Tory plumbers have been agreed about is that they need not turn off the tap.[44]

Monetarism and the 'Bank Deposit Theory of Prices'

Notwithstanding the SPGB's own monetary-based approach, the Keynesian-inspired view that monetary policy was of minor importance as a policy instrument did not command total support among the bourgeois parties and economists, certainly not after the late 1960s. At this time a new school of bourgeois economic thought, loosely labelled 'monetarism', emerged by way of challenge to the varieties of Keynesianism dominating orthodox economic theory, in a similar way to which Keynesianism itself had arisen as a challenge to the neo-classical orthodoxy of the pre-1930s period. But if the mass unemployment of the 1930s had provided the intellectual stimulus for the switch towards Keynes and his followers, the unparalleled rise in prices in the post-war era became the principal justification for the swing away from it pursued by leading monetarists like Milton Friedman. To Friedman, the lax monetary policy inspired by Keynes had been the principal cause of the post-war rise in prices. He wrote that "Inflation is always and everywhere a monetary phenomenon — in the sense that it is and can be produced only by a more rapid increase in the quantity of money than in output."[45] The SPGB was quick to point out that this seemed to be an attempt to restate the view, held by economists as diverse as Marx, and — in his earlier days, Keynes himself — that an excess issue of an inconvertible paper currency causes proportionate rises in the general price level.[46] As was soon to become clear, however, it was no such thing. Friedman and the vast majority of the monetarists, who were opposed to the labour theory of value and any arguments based on it, did not use the term 'money supply' in the same way as Marx and the SPGB. They were not referring specifically to notes and coins in circulation, the token and inconvertible representatives of the money-commodity, gold, but to bank deposits and other 'near-liquid' assets as well. This demonstrated to the SPGB that the monetarists' break with Keynes was not nearly so profound as they had claimed. Indeed, they had accepted one of the major justifications advanced by Keynes and the Keynesians for the view that currency was the almost irrelevant "small change of the monetary system". This was the claim that bank deposits function as money and constitute the great bulk of the 'money supply'.

The monetarists essentially took up a new version of the Quantity Theory of Money. In doing so they did not claim that an excess issue of paper currency could never cause inflation, only that the 'money supply' should include bank deposits instead of just currency. They argued that bank deposits were of major significance as a cause of rising prices because of the alleged ability of the banks to 'create' credit, and hence new deposits, from a given initial deposit base. This supposed power of the banks, at the heart of the monetarists' claims, was not discovered by the monetarists themselves, having been originally mooted and discussed by economists in the nineteenth century before being taken up the Keynesians and others. The monetarists, however, gave it a greater importance by linking it firmly with inflation (Keynes had initially done this also, in his *Tract on Monetary Reform*, before downgrading its importance again in the *General Theory*.) To the monetarists — who had much in common with the early economic outlook of Keynes — bank deposit creation increased purchasing power in the economy and pushed up prices in the same way as an excess currency issue.

To understand why, and how, the SPGB rejected this monetarist bank-deposit based analysis of inflation, described by Hardy for the SPGB as a "fallacy",[47] it is clearly necessary to examine the 'credit creationist' viewpoint which underpinned it. The view that banks could create vast multiples of credit and hence new bank deposits from a given initial deposit base had been a contentious issue in bourgeois economics since the days of John Gray (who argued in favour of it) and John Stuart Mill (who argued against).[48] The contention arose out of the views of two schools of economic thought with completely different conceptions of the nature of banks and banking, and indeed, the origins of purchasing power itself. Those opposed to credit creationist ideas like Mill held banks to be mere intermediaries in the financial process. To them, depositors made purchasing power available to banks by depositing sums of money, which the banks could then, in large part, make available to others by transferring it to them as loans. The credit creationists held the contrary view that banks were not intermediaries but active agents creating, rather than redistributing, purchasing power.

The most crude of the credit creationists — and possibly the best known — was Major Douglas, leader of the Social Credit movement in Britain. He not only held that new money could be created by "the stroke of the bankers pen"[49] but argued that this power of the banks could be harnessed so as to ensure the continual purchase of all the commodities produced by society, thereby averting slumps, which, he contended, arose from an otherwise chronic lack of purchasing power within capitalism (see Chapter 4). Most of Major Douglas's ideas on capitalism, slumps and purchasing power were dismissed by bourgeois economists, but his view that banks could actually create rather than redistribute purchasing power received eventual recognition in 1931 and was thereafter to find its way into standard economics textbooks. In that year, the MacMillan Committee on Finance and Industry issued its Report, which gave an official endorsement to creationist theory.

The MacMillan Report, in large part drafted by John Maynard Keynes, argued that banks really could create purchasing power. Its argument in support of this contention rested on a series of assumptions which the SPGB, and others, found completely untenable. It posited a simplified model of a banking system where only one bank existed, and in which a depositor had placed £1,000 in cash.[50] Operating with a ten per cent cash reserve, the bank lent out £900 of this money which was then withdrawn from the bank by cheque before coming back to the same bank as a new deposit. Because of this, the total deposits in the bank had risen to £1,900, consisting of the original £1,000 and the later cheque deposit of

£900. Against this liability the bank had cash of £1,000 and loans to customers of £900 on the asset side of its balance sheet. The MacMillan Report argued that this lending process could be repeated nine more times, assuming a ten per cent cash ratio. When these transactions had been completed, the bank's books would eventually show £10,000 of deposits balanced by £1,000 cash and £9,000 in loans owed by borrowers. From a £1,000 cash deposit base, £9,000 of deposits had therefore been 'created'.[51]

The way in which the MacMillan Committee thus 'proved' that banks could create credit has been variously described by the SPGB as "a masterpiece of rigged argument"[52] and "Alice in Wonderland economics".[53] Others, when the controversy was at its height, were equally dismissive, including at least four of the thirteen-strong Committee who remained opposed to the majority viewpoint. Professor Edwin Cannan of the London School of Economics, a quantity theorist and the most notable of the bourgeois economists who repudiated credit creationist arguments during the 1920s and 30s (and who was inexplicably never asked to join the Committee) described the credit creationists as the "mystical school of banking theorists", a phrase which won him the respect of the SPGB.[54]

Like Cannan, the SPGB contended that the "mystical school" which had influenced the MacMillan Report had based their arguments on a model of banking which was very far removed from actual banking practice, and it backed up its case with attacks on the theoretical deficiencies of the creationist view with quotations from the large numbers of practising bankers who entirely repudiated it. Both at the time of the adoption of creationism by the MacMillan Committee in the 1930s, and then during the time of the rise to prominence of the monetarists in the post-war era, the SPGB sought to expose the artificial assumptions which underpinned the arguments of the creationists. These included the assumption of a banking system with only one bank, and most crucially of all, the assumption that none of the borrowers ever withdrew money except by cheques which could only be deposited with the same bank. Although the MacMillan Committee and those who repeated their argument had assumed a ten per cent cash reserve, they illogically assumed that this cash reserve was never called upon by depositors. Their analysis took it for granted that the initial £1,000 cash deposit remained entirely unchanged throughout the whole series of transactions, an entirely unrealistic proposition by any standard. As the SPGB pointed out, the real world of capitalism was a lot more complex than the Committee's simple model assumed:

> This line of reasoning which isolates from a continuous in-and-out flow of deposits and withdrawals of cheques and cash, one single deposit of cash, is fallacious. If it were valid it could be applied in reverse; that is, the Committee could have isolated a single withdrawal of £1,000 cash and treated it as a permanent reduction by £1,000 of the amount of cash left in the bank. It only needed one of the ten borrowers of £900 to take it out in cash to destroy the

whole of the Committee's case. It appears to have been a belated recognition of this fallacy that later led J. M. Keynes to put a view contrary to that of the Report he had signed.[55]

Indeed, in Keynes's most influential work, his *General Theory*, published five years after the MacMillan Report, he effectively abandoned the theory which he had helped gain credence:

> ... no one can save without acquiring an asset, whether it be cash or a debt or capital goods, and no one can acquire an asset which he did not previously possess, unless either an asset of equal value is newly produced or someone else parts with an asset of that value which he previously had ... The notion that the creation of credit by the banking system allows investment to take place to which 'no genuine saving' corresponds can only be the result of isolating one of the consequences of the increased bank-credit to the exclusion of others.[56]

This is precisely what the SPGB argued that the MacMillan Committee had done.[57] The Party also observed that if the Committee was correct in its assertions, banks would be able to make extraordinary rates of profit, many times higher than those enjoyed by other enterprises quite unable to use more than their own capital and reserves plus any borrowings. In 1935 the *Socialist Standard*, in attacking the *Daily Herald* for putting credit creationist views, challenged its editor to explain how it was that the *Herald's* owners, Odham's Press Ltd, made profits at nearly double the rate of the Midland Bank "if the latter has the advantage of creating credit, which earns profits, out of nothing and at no cost?"[58]

Though most of the left-wing groups and self-styled Marxists were swept along by the credit creationists,[59] the list of authorities quoted by the SPGB in its opposition to the "mystical school" was impressive. Foremost in their contention that banks were mere 'intermediaries' in the financial process were many of the leading bankers themselves. For instance, in 1934, Mr F. L. Bland, a director of Barclay's Bank, had stated in his inaugural address as President to the Institute of Bankers that banks were little more than the channels through which aggregated saved sums of money flowed before being directed to their ultimate destination. He described the notion that banks could create wealth with the stroke of a pen as a "popular illusion" which "needed definite contradiction".[60] Another notable opponent of creationist ideas was Walter Leaf, for many years chairman of the Westminster Bank, who wrote:

> The banks can lend no more than they can borrow — in fact not nearly so much. If anyone in the deposit banking system can be called a 'creator of credit' it is the depositors; for the banks are strictly limited in their lending operations by the amount which the depositors think fit to leave with them.[61]

As the SPGB indicated, Walter Leaf's viewpoint was supported by numerous other bankers, both in Britain and abroad.[62]

It was also supported by several leading economists who thought the idea that banks could create wealth ridiculous.[63] Of particular relevance to the Marxian SPGB, the notion that banks could lend out no more than had been deposited with them had been the position taken by Marx himself decades earlier:

> [the bankers] appear as middlemen between the real lender of money capital and its borrower. To put it in general terms, the business of banking consists ... in concentrating money capital for loan in large masses in the bank's hands, so that, instead of the individual lender of money, it is the bankers as representatives of all lenders of money who confront the industrial and commercial capitalists ... A bank represents on the one hand the centralisation of money capital, of the lenders, and on the other hand the centralisation of the borrowers. It makes its profit in general by borrowing at lower rates than those at which it lends.[64]

Marx demonstrated how such banking profit could not arise mystically, out of nowhere, but only as a portion of surplus value, the product of working class exploitation. Indeed, here lay the crux of the Marxian argument against credit creation deployed by the SPGB. Seen from the standpoint of Marx — and the SPGB — the creationist view was essentially a negation of the labour theory of value. The acceptance of such a notion would mean that, in Marxian terms, purchasing power could arise from the process of circulation rather than just from the process of wealth production,[65] and that conflicted with virtually everything Marxians understood about economics. The SPGB approach, not surprisingly, was to brand credit creationist ideas as another form of currency crankism.

While the labour theory of value bequeathed by Marx provided the foundations for the SPGB opposition to creationism, the ultimate test of any economic theory for the SPGB always lay in its application to the real world of capitalism, and on virtually all counts the case against credit creationism was overwhelming. It was clear that the necessary consequences of the alleged ability of the banks to create credit simply did not exist in reality. The banks' own statements proved that in practice they could only lend out less than what had been deposited with them, rather than many times as much.[66] The banks did not make massive rates of profit, as some of the creationists had initially expected, and banks — especially during the 1930s and 1970s when creationist ideas, ironically, had their greatest vogue — proved that they could go bankrupt just like any other capitalist enterprise. Furthermore, if banks could actually create purchasing power, rather than redistribute it, then prices would indeed persistently rise, as the monetarists were to claim. Yet during most decades before the Second World War, this simply did not happen.

When the monetarists emerged as the most powerful advocates of the view which linked credit, bank deposits and rising prices, their views on the nature of the 'money supply' led them to argue that if governments were determined to bear down on inflation it would be necessary for them to try and control the rate at which new bank deposits, and hence purchasing power, grew. This approach to inflation, dubbed the "bank deposit theory of prices" by Edwin Cannan long before the term 'monetarism' had ever been coined,[67] eventually became official government policy in Britain and elsewhere in the late 1970s and 80s. The various monetary targets adopted by both Labour and Conservative governments in this period were almost all primarily made up of various kinds of bank deposits. The SPGB predicted — on both theoretical grounds and past empirical performance — that none of them would prove to be a reliable guide to rises in the Retail Price Index[68] and argued that the reason why the Retail Price Index was rising so quickly at the time had nothing to do with the expansion of bank deposits.

According to the Marxian analysis of the SPGB, not only was credit creation a demonstrable myth but bank deposits were not money, simply being a record of what banks owed their depositors, or, from the depositors' viewpoint, being assets that could be turned into money at varying degrees of notice. So, for that matter, were houses, cars, household goods and most other commodities, none of which had the characteristics, discussed earlier, of an inconvertible paper currency. Only an excess of inconvertible currency, the SPGB claimed, could inject purchasing power into the economy that had not arisen from the production process. The idea that an expansion in bank deposits was inflationary arose directly from the flawed creationist perspective. There could therefore be no theoretical justification for regarding bank deposits as a determinant of the price level.

The SPGB pointed out that on an empirical basis past history had demonstrated that there was no direct relationship between the level of bank deposits and the general level of prices. Between 1921 and 1933 prices in Britain fell by over forty per cent, and they continued falling whether the total of bank deposits in the economy was rising, stationary or declining. Indeed, between 1926 and 1933 the level of bank deposits rose by seventeen per cent while at the same time prices went down by nineteen per cent.[69] When monetarism was beginning to make its big impact in Britain the SPGB was able to show how the price level had risen by twelve per cent between 1968 and 1970 even though the level of bank deposits had fallen.

The SPGB not only contended that the level of bank deposits in the economy was irrelevant but that it was very doubtful, in any case, that it could be controlled.[70] In the 1980s the Party felt its analysis to have been finally justified when the alleged link between the RPI and the 'money supply' figures composed primarily of bank deposits was so obviously misplaced that the Conservative government was forced to abandon this hitherto central aspect of its anti-inflationary strategy.

Wages, Borrowing and Interest Rates

As well as the "bank deposit theory of prices", the SPGB had to respond in the post-war era to the various claims of reformist organisations who blamed inflation on the greed of the working class, the recklessness of profiteers or the incompetence of a particular capitalist government. One of the most widespread and persistent of these alternative explanations for the massive rise of prices in Britain, particularly among Keynesians, has been the view that it has been caused by the excessive wage claims of the working class. The SPGB has devoted attention to this theory not only because it believes it be wholly wrong, but because of its political implications for the ability of the working class to defend its living standards under capitalism.

The claim that high wage increases, or wage increases above and beyond increases in productivity, cause rising prices is an old one and was prevalent long before Keynesian economists put their particular 'cost-push' and 'demand-pull' variants of it. Much of the thrust of Marx's Address to the General International Congress of the International Working Men's Association of 1865 (published as *Value, Price and Profit*) was aimed at discrediting this view. In his Address Marx ridiculed Citizen Weston's proposition that "The prices of commodities are determined or regulated by wages"[71] just as Ricardo had ridiculed the same idea fifty years before him.[72]

The SPGB, like Marx and Ricardo, also ridiculed it and saw it as a fundamentally anti-working class proposition, a theory that was ideally suited to the self-interest and purposes of the capitalist class. Recognising that exchange-value equals price at the level of the whole economy, it argued that the values of commodities are not determined by the amount of wages paid to the workers who produce them but by the amount of socially necessary labour time required for their production, the difference between the two being surplus value. If wages were to go up, this would be at the expense of the surplus value accruing to the capitalists. Like most of the classical economists, the SPGB disputed the view that the capitalists could always raise prices to compensate for any wage increases incurred.[73] It acknowledged that an increase in wages would tend to raise the demand for many of the goods bought primarily by the working class and push those prices up, but argued that this would be offset by the declining demand of the capitalists for commodities including raw materials and machinery, as well as luxury goods. There would be no general increase of demand in the economy leading to rises in the general price level, merely a disturbance and rearrangement of the prices of commodities caused by an altered wages/profits relationship.

Though this was the position of Marx, it has certainly not been the position of most 'Marxist' organisations in post-war Britain. Despite its serious implications for trade unionism, the idea that wage increases are the principal cause of inflation has been held by a large number of self-styled Marxist organisations, including the International Socialists/Socialist Workers Party, which has stated that wage increases "must have some effect on prices ... Quite simply, business raises its prices when increases in costs threaten its profit margins".[74] In contrast, the SPGB has contended that enterprises can only sell their products at prices the market can bear.[75]

The SPGB has utilised the available empirical evidence to support its claim that wage increases do not cause persistent price increases and has argued that simply because wage increases go hand in hand with price rises does not mean that the former necessarily causes the latter. Indeed, it has often quoted Enoch Powell in support of its view that in the matter of inflation, trade unionists are the sinned against rather than the sinners.[76] It has pointed out that large increases in real wages can occur, and have occurred, without any significant effect on the price level. As Hardy has commented in the *Socialist Standard*, the age-old 'wage increases as a cause of inflation view':

> ... is easily shown to be fallacious. While the price level in 1914 was almost exactly the same as in 1850, average money wages rose by ninety per cent in that period. And in the years 1870 to 1914, while wages went up by forty-two per cent, prices actually fell by ten per cent. What was happening in those years was that fast growing membership and improved organisation helped the unions to share in the small annual growth of output per worker and also to make inroads into profits.[77]

While Keynesianism resurrected this 'high wages' explanation of inflation from an earlier era, the Keynesian school has since sought to promote other explanations of inflation that are largely its own. Notable among these is the idea — developed by discontented Keynesians and then later adopted by the monetarists — that large-scale government borrowing to finance budget deficits is the cause of inflation. The 'cure' for inflation according to this theory must therefore be a budget surplus, an anti-inflation strategy advocated by some, including Harold Wilson, during the 1950s. The SPGB has sought to demonstrate that at no time in British post-war history has this strategy of running a budget surplus to curb rising prices worked. Its most contemporary exponent was the Conservative Chancellor Nigel Lawson, who ran four consecutive years of budget surpluses in the late 1980s, without the anticipated results. The SPGB commented at the time that even though the budget surplus ran to £14 billion, the RPI surged into double figures.[78] It also noted that the *Financial Times* was driven to comment that the Chancellor "has done exactly what the doctrine told him to. Indeed, he has overfulfilled the plan and has been repaying the National Debt. Yet here we have inflation moving up ... "[79] The SPGB argued that budget deficits could not be the cause of inflation, and that budget surpluses certainly were not the cure. There was no mystery about this, as budget deficits financed by borrowing did not inject any additional purchasing power into the economy, merely serving to re-arrange it. The additional government expenditure did not arise out of nothing but arose because investors (particularly capitalists and institutions like pension funds) were prepared by lend the government funds if the rates of return were favourable enough by buying government bonds and securities, instead of lending to private industry. This argument applied equally to injections of international finance from outside the domestic economy. This can only be attracted on the basis of high interest rates and lucrative yields on government bonds, both of which are likely to 'crowd out' investment in the private sector.

In recent years, the SPGB has had to respond to another widespread contention about the cause of inflation, sometimes linked to the 'bank deposit theory of prices'. This is that inflation is caused by low interest rates and that the solution to price rises is to tighten monetary policy and put interest rates up again. Its opposition to multiple deposit creation (and contraction) aside, the SPGB has disputed this particular theory on a number of other grounds. Though it accepts the truism that an increase in interest rates means that borrowers have higher interest payments, reducing the amount they can otherwise spend and thus, other things being equal, having a 'dampening' effect on the economy, it has pointed out that this commonly put view only takes one side of the transaction into consideration:

> The effect of higher interest rates being paid by borrowers is, of course, that they have less to spend on other things, but this is exactly balanced by the lenders' income being increased. The combined purchasing power of lenders and borrowers is exactly the same as it was before interest rates went up.[80]

Increased interest rates alter the conditions through which borrowers and lenders trade but do not, of themselves, significantly alter the total amount of purchasing power in the economy as a whole. There is therefore no overall 'dampening' effect on the economy. While consumers may have less to spend, investors have more.

The SPGB has suggested that the relationship between interest rates and rising prices is very different from that put forward by those who view high interest rates as a cure for price rises. The relationship, it has argued, is almost exactly the opposite of that suggested by this theory. It is that when prices are rising, an upward pressure is put on interest rates. Interest rates are the price of borrowing money capital, and are affected by inflation like other prices. The lenders of capital need high interest rates when prices are rising in order to protect their assets which would otherwise be eroded by inflation. Lenders have to be principally concerned with the rate of interest they get after rising prices are taken into account — the 'real' rate of interest.[81] So instead of the price level being partly dependent on interest rates, it is the other way around, with interest rates being in part dependent on the rate at which prices are rising.

When interest rates are high, this by no means indicates that overall spending in the economy will then be curbed and that the rate of price rises is going to slow down. This, the SPGB has claimed, was clearly demonstrated during the 1980s when the base interest rate rose from 8.5 per cent in December 1987 to 15 per cent by October 1989. Despite the base rate rise, the volume of consumer spending, taking price rises into account, continued to increase. So, indeed, did prices themselves, the RPI doubling its annual rate of increase from 3.7 per cent to over 7 per cent.[82]

The SPGB has noted that at other times increases in the RPI can slow down when interest rates are high but it has contended that this is never simply because of the level of interest rates. The RPI began to slow during 1990–2 but this, it has argued, was because of the capitalist crisis of overproduction and subsequent economic contraction, of which high interest rates were an exacerbatory symptom rather than the underlying cause. The prelude to this economic crisis was one of the reasons why interest rates had originally risen, rates having been driven up by increased demand for money capital as the boom reached its peak and economic crisis neared. In support of this analysis the SPGB has quoted Marx on the relationship between interest rates and the trade cycle to the effect that "a low rate of interest corresponds to periods of prosperity or high profit, a rise in interest comes between prosperity and its collapse, while maximum interest up to extreme usury corresponds to a period of crisis".[83] This process can be distorted for a while, as it was in Britain and other European countries during the late 1980s and early 1990s by to the perceived need to keep central bank base rates high to defend over-valued exchange rates. The SPGB has affirmed, however, that interest rates cannot be sustained at levels which do not reflect the market demand for money capital for long[84] and that even if they could be, this would, of itself, have little appreciable influence on the overall price level.

Why Inflation?

The explanation of inflation advanced by the SPGB, and the arguments that it has used to refute alternative explanations, have generally been clear and consistent. One aspect of the SPGB's analysis of inflation has been rather less so, with some writers and speakers putting emphasis on factors others ignore or dispute. This lack of clarity has arisen not out of the question of what causes inflation, but out of *why* it is that successive governments push an excess issue of inconvertible currency into circulation, thereby causing prices to rise. Some in the SPGB have viewed currency inflation as arising simply out of the aforementioned ignorance of monetary authorities who no longer deem it necessary to control the creation of currency, which is, supposedly, only the 'small change' of the monetary system. Others have gone further and have seen the persistent excess note issue in countries like Britain as something more than this — in short, as a deliberate policy. A particular form of this latter view, sometimes found in the *Socialist Standard*, is that governments, ignorant of all the consequences of their actions, deliberately inflate the currency to supplement their revenue:

> Governments everywhere have resorted to inflationary currency policies because this is an easy way of raising money to finance their spending — and of

course government spending has grown immensely this century ... the first Keynesian budget [in Britain] was that of 1940, when inflation was ... deliberately adopted as a way of financing the war. This policy was continued after the war to finance other government spending, including that on social reform measures (education, health service, social security benefits).[85]

In blatant contradiction of this view, writers in the *Socialist Standard* have also variously argued that "It is a mistake to think that the British government's interest in inflation is to provide revenue by printing notes"[86] and that "Inflation cannot be described as a deliberate revenue-raising exercise by those elements in the government who control the currency issue".[87] The reason for this discrepancy in the SPGB's analysis is actually quite simple. The view that governments deliberately inflate the currency to, at least in part, raise additional revenue has generally been put during times when governments have appeared to do precisely this. This argument was aired most frequently in the Party during the 1970s when the expansion of the note issue, in percentage terms, was particularly large. On other occasions, such as at times in the 1980s, the increase in the note issue has not been nearly so drastic and therefore has not leant itself so easily to the 'revenue-raising' argument.

During such periods, some SPGB speakers and writers have instead focused on other reasons for the continuation of inflation such as the fact that inflation generally favours the borrowers of money capital, like the industrial section of the capitalist class, who are able to pay back their loans in depreciated currency. Apart from the obvious truth that governments are not entirely beholden to the interests of the industrial section of the capitalist class at the expense of finance capital, this argument suffers from its implication that governments do recognise the link between the note issue and rising prices and act accordingly to secure a steady rise in the price level. The SPGB is otherwise clear that they recognise no such thing, and therefore it is difficult to apply this argument logically. The claim that governments inflate the currency because they themselves are major borrowers and can pay back investors in government bonds in depreciated currency suffers for the same reason.

There are some in the SPGB who have moved so far away from the 'revenue-raising' argument that they have stated that the government has no policy on currency inflation at all.[88] They have claimed in opposition to the 'revenue-raising' view that the Treasury and the Bank of England only passively make currency available in response to the demands of the banking system.[89] In this sense, the only policy they have regarding the note issue is that they deliberately have no policy on it, acting simply to meet the needs of the Bank's customers. Though there is undoubtedly an element of truth in this argument there are also a number of reasonable objections to it as the sole explanation of why governments have inflated the currency. One is that it entirely overlooks the fact that the Bank of England's biggest customer of all is the government itself. Another objection is that this argument alone cannot account for the periods of economic slump — such as the early 1980s and early 1990s — when the amount of currency in circulation has continued to increase despite falling retail sales, production and growth. These have been periods when the demand from the Bank's customers, the government apart, has pointed to a declining rather than increasing note issue.

A rather more compelling (and widely held) view among SPGB members has linked the persistent post-war inflation more firmly with the influence of Keynesian economic thought on successive governments and the desire to ensure high levels of employment and growth. Starting from the premise that governments do not generally consider an excess note issue to be inflationary, this argument proceeds on the basis that governments have been prepared to issue currency to stimulate investment, lending by the banks, production and trade. Keynes frequently argued that falling prices and bank lending were bad for business,[90] and during the slump of the 1930s many economists and pro-capitalist newspapers called for a policy of currency inflation for precisely this reason.[91] As an SPGB education bulletin from the early 1970s put it, the main reason for inflation is therefore "the widespread acceptance of the erroneous belief that inflation is a means of maintaining 'full employment'".[92] This theory has the advantage that it can account for the continual inflation experienced since the Second World War, even during slumps.

It is possible, however, that no one explanation of the post-war currency inflation is correct when viewed in isolation. There are probably elements of truth in both the view that the Treasury and Bank of England inflate the currency in part because of a "passive" willingness to meet the needs of the banking system, and in the view that they also issue currency as an intended stimulus to demand. These two arguments are, indeed, complementary rather than contradictory. In acknowledging this, it is also possible to recognise at least the periodic validity of the contention that governments inflate the currency as a revenue-raising exercise. For even though it may be the case that the amount of revenue raised for the government through inflation is often small, there have certainly been times — as the SPGB acknowledged in the 1970s — when the amount raised through inflation has been significant. It is also true that even on those occasions when the amount raised in this way has been trivial, governments and the monetary authorities have still shown an awareness of the way in which government revenue benefits from increases in the currency issue. The Radcliffe Report of 1959 demonstrated this when it commented that:

> An increase in the fiduciary note issue [notes not backed by gold] ... generates an influx of funds into the Exchequer, since when the fiduciary note issue is increased the proceeds are invested with the Exchequer by the Issue Department of the Bank of England ... the increases in the fiduciary issue which have taken place in fact contributed £700 million towards meeting the authorities' financing problems during the period 1951–2 to 1957–8.[93]

The Exchequer directly benefits from this process because while the increase in the note issue is likely to cause rising prices and hence higher government expenditure, this is offset by increased revenue from taxation.[94] The increase in the note issue therefore represents a real increase in government revenue.

As some in the SPGB contend, the revenue-raising argument certainly cannot be dismissed entirely. When the modern inflationary process began during the Second World War it was given impetus by the government following Keynes's advice that it could at that time safely finance part of its budget deficit via an increase in the note issue.[95] Furthermore, when the Labour government of 1974–9 embarked on its 'reflationary' programme to reduce unemployment and restore economic growth a substantial proportion of the real increase in government expenditure was financed via the printing press.[96] In the first eighteen months, increases in the fiduciary issue accounted for over £1,200 million of additional government revenue.[97] Similar strategies, having similar consequences, have since been adopted by governments in other countries, notably Mitterrand's 'Socialist' government in France in 1981–2. It would follow from this that the SPGB's earlier suggestion that governments inflate the currency in part to augment their revenue, does at least have some periodic evidence to support it.

Any differences in the SPGB over this comparatively minor question of why governments have continued to push an excess of currency into circulation have, however, been dwarfed by the clarity and consistency of the SPGB's main contentions on the subject. Its utilisation of Marxian economics to explain how and why prices have risen enormously since the onset of the Second World War, and to debunk the non-Marxian explanations which have infected the labour and trade union movement, has been a particularly distinctive feature of its economic analysis of capitalism in the post-1945 period. While recognising that Keynes himself was not generally a crude inflationist who may well have been appalled at many of the actions taken in his name, the SPGB's principal — and most damning — contention has been that Keynesian economic theory, in the variety of ways discussed, has laid the basis not for full employment and growth but for an unprecedented inflation of the currency in Britain and other countries which has resulted in persistently rising prices. To the SPGB, therefore, government attempts to solve the various social and economic problems engendered by capitalism through the 'more money' approach have merely succeeded in creating a new problem — inflation — which has refused to go away despite the later, and rather belated, attentions, of the Keynesians and monetarists alike.

Notes

1. Alfred Marshall, founder of the Cambridge school of bourgeois economics, Arthur Pigou, successor to Marshall at Cambridge, tutor to Keynes and pioneer of 'welfare economics', and Francis Edgeworth, Oxford economist.
2. *The General Theory of Employment, Interest and Money* by John Maynard Keynes (MacMillan, London, 1936) p.3.
3. Say's Law of Markets was named after the early nineteenth century economist Jean-Baptiste Say, who held that general overproduction for the market was impossible because of the reciprocal nature of commodity exchange. His concept underpinned much of classical economic thinking.
4. *Unemployment* by Arthur Pigou (Home University Library, London, 1913) p.51.
5. *Industry and Empire* by Eric Hobsbawm (Penguin, Harmondsworth, 1986) pp.208–9.
6. *Laissez Faire and Communism* by John Maynard Keynes (St Martin's Press, New York, 1926) p.48.
7. *The General Theory of Employment, Interest and Money*, Chapters 8-10.
8. *The General Theory of Employment, Interest and Money*, p.373.
9. See *Socialist Standard*, May 1979.
10. *Capital*, Volume I, pp.208-9.
11. See 'The Relation of Home Investment to Employment' by Richard F. Kahn in the *Economic Journal*, June 1931, pp.173-98.
12. See *The General Theory of Employment, Interest and Money*, pp.113-34.
13. *White Paper on Employment Policy* (HMSO, London, May 1944) p.16.
14. For Labour's conversion to Keynesian economics see the Labour Party *Report on Full Employment and Financial Policy* adopted at its Annual Conference, 1944.
15. 'Lord Keynes: Economist of Capitalism in Decline' in *Socialist Standard*, June 1946.
16. *Ibid.*
17. *Capital*, Volume III, p.352.
18. *Keynes and After* by Michael Stewart (Penguin, London, 1967) p.299.
19. See, for instance, the review of *Keynes and After* in *The Times*, 22 January 1968.
20. Editorial reply to correspondent in *Socialist Standard*, October 1964.
21. *Ibid.*
22. *Ibid.*
23. See article on 'The Economic Crisis — The Marxian Explanation' by E. Hardy in *The World Socialist*, Number One, (SPGB, London, April 1984) pp.24-6. A similar argument was advanced in the SPGB's 1959 *Discussion Report on Crises*, pp.16-18. Marxist theoretician Paul Mattick developed another version of this view of the relationship between private and state investment in an article in the November-December 1955 *Western Socialist*, journal of the World Socialist Party of the United States, and companion party of the SPGB. Parts of this early article were later used in Mattick's book *Marx and Keynes*.
24. *The British Economic Disaster* by Andrew Glyn and John Harrison (Pluto Press, London, 1980) p.117.
25 Calculated from statistics supplied by the Central Statistical Office in its Annual Abstract of Statistics.

26. Editorial reply to a correspondent in *Socialist Standard*, August 1957.
27. See *The Economist*, 22 February 1992.
28. *Ibid.*
29. 'The Mystery of Rising Prices' in *Socialist Standard*, June 1957.
30. *Ibid.*
31. *Capital*, Volume I, p.193.
32. *A Contribution To A Critique of Political Economy* by Karl Marx (Lawrence and Wishart, London, 1971) p.105.
33. *Capital*, Volume I, pp.224-5.
34. *Marxian Economics* (SPGB, London, 1978) p.16.
35. *The Marxian Theory of Inflation* (SPGB Education Bulletin, London, 1974) p.3.
36. 'The Evolution of Money — From Barter to Inflation' in *Socialist Standard*, February 1980.
37. See, for example, 'Thatcher's New Clothes' in *Socialist Standard*, December 1989.
38. 'Inflation and Prices' in *Socialist Standard*, September 1965.
39. 'Four Fallacies About Inflation' in *Socialist Standard*, August 1989.
40. *International Financial Statistics*, Volume I, Number One (International Monetary Fund, Washington, 1948) p.126.
41. *Marxian Economics*, p.17.
42. *Keynes and After*, p.147.
43. *Radcliffe Report — Working of the Monetary System* (HMSO, London, 1959) p.118.
44. 'Inflation: the Endless Farce' in *Socialist Standard*, April 1990.
45. *The Times*, 15 September 1970.
46. 'From Marx To Milton Friedman' in *Socialist Standard*, November 1970.
47. See 'Was Marx A Monetarist?' in *Socialist Standard*, January 1983.
48. See 'Can Banks Create Credit?' in *Socialist Standard*, July 1971.
49. *The Monopoly of Credit* by Major C. Douglas (Eyre and Spottiswoode, London, 1931) p.17.
50. *Report of The MacMillan Committee into Finance and Industry* (HMSO, London, 1931) p.34.
51. This basic explanation of the alleged ability of banks to 'create' credit is repeated in many modern economics textbooks. See, as a notable example, *An Introduction To Positive Economics* by R. G. Lipsey (Weidenfeld and Nicholson, London, 1983) Chapter 38. A less extravagant and more sophisticated version, based on a multi-bank model, is put in *Economics* by Paul Samuelson (McGraw-Hill, New York, 1980) Chapter 16. However, Samuelson does not prove that the banking system as a whole can create credit, only that currency circulates — for this see *Socialist Standard*, July 1990.
52. 'Inflation: the Endless Farce' in *Socialist Standard*, April 1990.
53. 'Militant Confusion About Inflation' in *Socialist Standard*, January 1981.
54. See *An Economist's Protest* by Edwin Cannan (P. S. King and Son, Westminster, 1927) p.256. The SPGB's admiration for much of Cannan's views on monetary economics was reciprocated by Cannan who in the 1930s praised a series of articles in the *Socialist Standard* dealing with the myth of credit creation. Cannan, in fact, is the only lifelong supporter of capitalism ever to have received an official

obituary in the *Socialist Standard* (June 1935). The *Standard* justified its action on the grounds that "as an economist, he was of more than usual significance in the development of economic thought".

55. 'Can Banks Create Credit?' in *Socialist Standard*, July 1971.
56. *The General Theory of Employment, Interest and Money*, pp.81-2.
57. 'Can Banks Create Credit?' in *Socialist Standard*, July 1971.
58. 'A Book For Students of Currency Problems' in *Socialist Standard*, April 1935.
59. This has remained true throughout the entire post-Second World War period. Virtually all Leninist groups have explicitly or implicitly supported credit creationism, and many have used this as added justification for their attacks on the banking and financial sections of the capitalist class. An SPGB critique of the Militant Tendency's use of creationist theory for this purpose is to be found in the *Socialist Standard*, January 1981.
60. *The Times*, 15 November 1934.
61. *Banking* by Walter Leaf (Home University Library, London, 1926) p.102.
62. 'A Book For Students of Currency Problems' in *Socialist Standard*, April 1935.
63. See *An Economist's Protest*, pp.256-7.
64. *Capital*, Volume III, p.528.
65. See 'Banks and Credit' in *Socialist Standard*, February 1975.
66. See 'Inflation: the Endless Farce' in *Socialist Standard*, April 1990. To take a statistic at random, for the financial year 1983 the National Westminster Bank declared the amount of money lodged with it to be £55.2 billion and the money lent out £45.2 billion.
67. *Modern Currency and the Regulation of its Value* by Edwin Cannan (P. S. King and Son, Westminster, 1931) p.88.
68. 'Can Banks Create Credit?' in *Socialist Standard*, July 1971.
69. *Ibid.* See also the an editorial reply to a correspondent in *Socialist Standard*, December 1933.
70. 'Was Marx A Monetarist?' in *Socialist Standard*, January 1983.
71. *Value, Price and Profit*, pp.37-41.
72. *The Principles of Political Economy*, pp.60-2.
73. Editorial Reply to a correspondent in *Socialist Standard*, October 1933.
74. *Socialist Worker*, 4 August 1973.
75. For practical examples see 'Why Prices Go Up' in *Socialist Standard* February, 1964.
76. *The Times*, 20 November 1970.
77. 'Four Fallacies About Inflation' in *Socialist Standard*, August 1989.
78. *Ibid.*
79. *Financial Times*, 11 January 1989.
80. 'Four Fallacies About Inflation' in *Socialist Standard*, August 1989.
81. 'Labour's Futile Policy' in *Socialist Standard*, June 1991.
82. Editorial reply to a correspondent in *Socialist Standard*, July 1990.
83. *Capital*, Volume III, p.482.
84. 'Labour's Futile Policy' in *Socialist Standard*, June 1991.
85. 'From Barter To Inflation' in *Socialist Standard*, March 1980.

86. 'Inflation: the Endless Farce' in *Socialist Standard*, April 1990.

87. Editorial reply to a correspondent in *Socialist Standard*, August 1990.

88. Letter to the author from E. Hardy dated 20 November 1990.

89. *Ibid.*

90. *John Maynard Keynes — The Economist As Saviour* by Robert Skidelsky (MacMillan, London, 1992) p.149.

91. See, for instance, *Sunday Express*, 15 May 1932.

92. *The Marxian Theory of Inflation*, p.4.

93. *Radcliffe Report — Working of the Monetary System*, p.34.

94. There is some evidence to suggest that necessarily increased government expenditure occasioned by rising prices is more than offset by increased revenue from taxation as taxpayers tend to be pushed into higher tax brackets. For a discussion of this particular consequence of inflation see 'Inflation, Taxation, Indexation' by Milton Friedman in *Inflation — Causes, Consequences, Cures*, various authors (Institute of Economic Affairs, London, 1974) pp.73-81.

95. *How To Pay For The War* by John Maynard Keynes (MacMillan, London, 1941) p.63 and pp.197–8.

96. A description of the indirect method used in Britain to augment government revenue via an increased note issue is given in *The Marxian Theory of Inflation*, pp.9-11.

97. See *Bank of England Quarterly Bulletin*, Second Quarter, 1976.

8. Socialist Planning

The Marxian Conception of Socialist Planning

As was briefly stated in Chapter 1, the SPGB inherited a view of socialist society that had been developed by Marx, Engels, Morris and others in the early Marxian tradition. From its foundation the SPGB was convinced that socialism would, of necessity, be a system of society based on common ownership of the means of production and distribution, democratic control, and production solely for use. There would be no money or financial system and the producers in socialist society would not exchange their products. The SPGB, like Marx and Engels, proposed the "communistic abolition of buying and selling"[1] with direct access to consumption goods and services. However, just like Marx and Engels, the SPGB was rarely specific about the details of socialist society beyond those features of capitalism that would be absent from it, such as commodity production, money, private property, wage labour and capital. Absent too from socialism would be the 'anarchy of production' inherent to the market economy, a phenomenon to be abolished by the establishment of a planned system where the vicissitudes of the market would be superseded by conscious social control. From Marx and Engels again the SPGB inherited the view that crises, slumps and other failures of the market could only be abolished by this system of society-wide planning. As Engels had written of the socialist revolution:

> With the seizing of the means of production by society production of commodities is done away with and, simultaneously, the mastery of the product over the producer. Anarchy in social production is replaced by plan-conforming conscious organisation.[2]

Marx and Engels had viewed planned production as an essential feature of socialist or communist society from their conversion to communism in the 1840s. Such was the importance with which Marx viewed planning that he contended that communism would be the beginning of real human history because for the first time humankind would not be at the mercy of blind historical and economic forces. In communism, people would be able to consciously regulate their interaction with the natural world and would thereby live in a truly human society, one compatible with human nature:

> Freedom, in this sphere, can consist only in this, that socialised man, the associated producers, govern the human metabolism with nature in a rational way, bringing it under their collective control instead of being dominated by it

as a blind power; accomplishing it with the least expenditure of energy and in conditions most worthy and appropriate for their human nature.[3]

Marx was well aware that achieving this would be a huge organisational task. Matching the various wants of communist society would entail massive, detailed planning and (non monetary) accounting. In Volume III of *Capital* Marx commented that although exchange value would be abolished in communism along with the commodity and its fetishistic character, "the determination of value still prevails in the sense that the regulation of labour-time and the distribution of social labour among various production groups becomes more essential than ever, as well as the keeping of accounts on this."[4] Marx claimed that calculations would be required to determine how much labour time would be needed to produce particular items of wealth. In using the specific example of long-term projects, he commented that accounting would be vital, though without the use of a common economic unit such as money:

> The matter would be simply reduced to the fact that the society must reckon in advance how much labour, means of production and means of subsistence it can spend, without dislocation, on branches of industry which, like the building of railways for instance, supply neither means of production nor means of subsistence, nor any kind of useful effect for a long period, a year or more, though they certainly do withdraw labour, means of production and means of subsistence from the total annual product.[5]

In socialism/communism calculations would also be necessary in order to estimate the real demand for both consumption and production goods. An overall plan would then have to be formulated so as to allocate labour-time and other resources to the branches of production in the correct magnitudes. For this reason Marx commented in the *Grundrisse* that "economy of time, along with the planned distribution of labour time among the various branches of production, remains the first economic law on the basis of communal production."[6] Any miscalculations of labour-time allocation could be corrected in the next plan, as for example with overproduction of certain goods, where the anarchic element leading to economic crisis would be removed by planning itself.[7]

The true extent of the colossal overall planning envisaged by Marx can be seen from those works, principally *The Critique of the Gotha Programme* and Volume III of *Capital*, where he lists the vital functions of communism with major claims on the total product of society. These necessary functions would have to be planned and resources deducted from that part of the social product intended for general consumption. Marx contended that these claims on the social product would include replacing the means of production used up in producing wealth, expanding the means of production so as to provide for a larger social product and the provision of a small surplus to provide against natural disasters, accidents and miscalculations. In addition it would be necessary to provide resources for social consumption such as schools and hospitals, and also resources for social administration not connected with production.[8]

The importance attached to planning in socialism by Marx was mirrored in the writings of Engels, who was if anything even more enthusiastic than his colleague. Engels's short pamphlet *Principles of Communism* contains no less than three separate remarks about the need for society-wide conscious planning and his major work *Anti-Duhring* is similarly replete with references to it. On occasions Engels even gave the impression that he was more sanguine about the prospects for complex and intricate planning than was Marx, arguing that overall planning was little problem as "Society can simply calculate how many hours of labour are contained in a steam engine, a bushel of wheat of the last harvest, or a hundred square yards of cloth of a certain quality".[9]

Such was Engels's apparent identification of socialism/communism with the planning of production that he felt able to write that even the appearance of monopolistic cartels in capitalism prepared the way for socialism because of the extension of planning that their emergence involved. In that part of *Anti-Duhring* republished as *Socialism: Utopian and Scientific*, he claimed that while the capitalist mode of production was inherently anarchic, it contained within itself the exact opposite of anarchy — the planning of production within each enterprise. In capitalism's evolution towards socialism, the area of planning became larger, first with joint-stock companies, then with trusts and finally with nationalisation.[10] Eventually, he contended that the overall planlessness of capitalist production is fully overturned with the attainment of state control by the proletariat, followed by the conversion of the statified means of production into common property. The anarchy of production is then properly dispensed with and a society based on the harmony of a "single vast plan" created:

> Only a society which makes it possible for its productive forces to dovetail harmoniously into each other on the basis of one single vast plan can allow industry to be distributed over the whole country in the way best adapted to its own development, and to the maintenance and development of the other elements of production.[11]

Despite Engels's striking rhetoric about this "single vast plan" (by which he may have meant the overall combination and interconnection of various plans of production) there are aspects of the writings of both Marx and Engels which suggest that their conception of socialist planning was not as centralised as might actually be thought. One clue to this is that Engels, for instance, did not hold that the anarchy of production would diminish as capitalism developed and became centralised, but that it would be exacerbated. In *Socialism: Utopian and Scientific* he wrote that as capitalism had progressed "this anarchy grew to greater height".[12] This was because for Marx and Engels the anarchy of capitalist production was inexorably linked with economic crises, which Engels in particular held would grow worse; certainly, no amount of centralisation and planning could overcome them. As Engels made clear in his comments about the merits and demerits of nationalisation, central planning of itself was insufficient so long as the unstable hand of monetary exchange and market disequilibrium existed to push society towards economic crisis. Though planning was essential to post-capitalist society, the existence of, say, a single administrative body in each industry was not of itself socialistic. Indeed, there is nothing to suggest that either Marx or Engels considered that the centralisation that had developed throughout the history of capitalism would be a continuous process carried over into socialism. Many of their writings suggest precisely the opposite.

Marx's early philosophical writings reveal an outlook about socialism completely at variance with the requirements of a "single vast plan". In such a centralised, planned environment it would be impossible to "hunt in the morning, fish in the afternoon, rear cattle in the evening, criticise after dinner ... without ever becoming hunter, fisherman, shepherd or critic."[13] Clearly, the alienation of labour from man's human essence could not be overcome in such a system and it is impossible to harmonise central planning in communism with the famous words of the *Communist Manifesto* that "the free development of each is the condition for the free development of all."[14]

None of this counter-evidence against Marx and Engels's penchant for centralised planning prevented most of Marx's followers from adopting a model of central planning for socialism on the lines of Engels's single society-wide plan. Indeed, in the Second International, the major working class political parties did exactly this, being influenced by leading Marxist theoreticians and advocates of central planning like Engels himself, Kautsky and Bebel. The writers and parties of the Second International period often elevated central planning into a socialist totem, just as their Bolshevik rivals later did. Plekhanov's Second Draft Program for the Russian Social-Democrats referred to capitalism's replacement by "a new system of social production according to a previously drawn-up plan".[15] August Bebel was no less clear in his classic *Woman and Socialism* text which was more explicit about the nature of socialism than most works of the time, and which was widely read in working class organisations, including the SPGB. Bebel spoke of a central planning authority comprising "an executive board of managers" responsible for the allocation of labour time and for all other necessary calculations such as the itemisation of stocks of goods and factors of production. This included estimating the extent of social demand.[16]

Ideas of central (or total) planning in socialism influenced the strand of social democracy from which the SPGB emerged in 1904, though like Hyndman's SDF, the SPGB had little specific to say about the nature of socialist planning in its early years beyond assertions that it would overcome the anarchy of capitalist production — the same platitude invariably given by other working class parties at the time — and the confident prediction that issues in capitalism such as working hours and conditions would become "trifling matters" for the socialist commonwealth.[17] The Party always pointed out that speculations as to the nature of socialism by individual writers in the *Socialist Standard* were just that. Its only real concession to detail came via its opposition to industrial unionism and syndicalism where common ownership appeared to be sacrificed on the altar of sectional control (see Chapter 1).

There can be little dispute that the views of the SPGB about socialist planning were influenced in fairly large measure by the arguments of Engels and others on the need for a central allocative plan of production. Nevertheless, the full commitment of the SPGB to Engels-type central planning is undermined at least in part by the SPGB's early publication (in 1907) of Morris's *Art, Labour and Socialism* and by the general, if not entirely uniform, veneration given by Party members to Morris's other works like *News From Nowhere*, which painted a picture of socialist society far removed from the one suggested by Engels. This outlook was in turn reflected in articles in the *Socialist Standard* like 'Socialism and Work' from October 1910, which eulogised the craftsmanship and "security of life" of the middle ages. But if the SPGB's commitment to central planning was by no means total, it never once in the *Socialist Standard* or any of its pamphlets gave an indication that it thought Marx and Engels were mistaken in some of their statements on this matter and that central planning was not an essential feature of socialism.

This commitment to socialist central planning naturally characterised the wing of social democracy which manifested itself in Leninism and its variants.[18] Of particular relevance is that a number of groups and parties from this sector holding to the non-market vision of socialism promoted by the SPGB were to follow the 'central planning' conception of socialism with more clarity and enthusiasm than the SPGB ever did. This strand of Marxian thought was probably taken to its apogee by the political current in Italy which became known as the 'Bordigists', followers of Gramsci's rival Amadeo Bordiga, an avowed left communist. Bordiga advanced a semi-Leninist theory whereby the socialist political party, the advanced guard and 'political brain' of the working class, would transform itself with the abolition of capitalism into the social and administrative brain of the centrally-planned new society:

When the international class war has been won and states have died out, the party, which is born with the proletarian class and its doctrine, will not die out. In this distant time perhaps it will no longer be called a party, but it will live as the single organ, the 'brain' of a society freed from class forces.[19]

The SPGB, of course, holding that as all political parties were but the expression of class interests, maintained that there would be no political parties of any kind in the classless society.

It is likely that it was the Russian experience which focused the SPGB's attention more precisely on what sort of planning socialism would practically entail. In the 1930s the forced industrialisation and central control of Stalin's Five Year plans had already come under sustained attack from anti-Communists in the West, and the SPGB was understandably sensitive to the charge of 'over-centralisation' laid against bureaucratic Stalinism in particular, and socialists generally. As a result, by far the Party's most authoritative pre-World War Two statement on socialist planning came in the late 1930s in response to a letter from an enquirer to the *Socialist Standard* who asked whether the socialist arrangements envisaged by the SPGB would be based on 'Central Government'. The reply revealed a major shift on the position implied — if not explicitly stated — by Engels, and outlined above. For the first time the reply made clear that so far as the SPGB was concerned, centralisation would not necessarily be a major feature of the socialist future, where decision-making would be devolved wherever possible:

> The workers will simply carry on with the operation of industry, transport and administration with the elimination of its capitalist features. Changes will be introduced in an orderly fashion, as agreed by the workers themselves in co-operation with their fellows in other lands. The basis of industrial organisation and administration will start from the arrangements existing under capitalism at the time of the transformation, and this will present no difficulties because the Socialist movement will already be thoroughly international both in outlook and practical organisation. As far as the machinery of organisation and administration is concerned, it will be local, regional, national and international, evolving out of existing forms. Railway organisation, for example, would naturally follow the land areas served by the railway systems, but would need to be co-ordinated with local road services, international air services and steamship routes. Postal services would (as now) require both local, national and international organisation. Administration would follow similar forms, doubtless with the utmost variety of modifications to meet both local needs in the different continents.[20]

Thus the SPGB here showed itself willing to unambiguously depart for the first time from the commitment to central planning which had hitherto dominated socialist thinking about post-capitalist society. But this still did not go as far as some in the Party wanted it to. By the early 1950s a dispute arose in the SPGB over the nature of the future society with a vociferous group around Tony Turner, one of the Party's greatest orators, convinced that only a *News From Nowhere* type, non-industrial, and highly-decentralised society was worth struggling for — where freedom of the individual could reign as portrayed in Marx's *German Ideology*.[21] The ideas of these members reflected the feeling that large-scale industry, increasing automation and the centralised control instituted by the post-war Labour government were leading to a steady de-humanisation of capitalist society. Largely because of its anti-industrial bias, this view made no real headway and many of its advocates left the Party altogether, but from this point detailed critiques of the SPGB's object became more frequent. Opponents and some members alike wanted the SPGB to be far more specific about its notion of what life in socialism would actually be like, how it would differ from capitalism, and ultimately, what role planning and central control would have in socialist society.

Its most persistent critics on this issue from outside the Party were to emerge in the form of the anti-planning free marketeers of the libertarian right. During their period of ascendancy in the 1970s and 80s they were to use an argument against the SPGB which forced it to reconsider its conception of the socialist future much further than it had previously. This was an argument primarily developed in the first quarter of the twentieth century and directed at the centralist type of socialist vision promoted by the parties and theorists of the Second International. It came to be known as the 'economic calculation' argument.

Economic Calculation

'Economic calculation' developed from the writings of a number of bourgeois economists who were generally unsatisfied with the 'human nature' based analysis that had tended to characterise most nineteenth century assaults on socialism by anti-socialist writers and academics. Steele has pointed out[22] that the genesis of the economic calculation argument can be traced back to Adam Smith, but it was first expressed in a recognisable form in 1854 by H. H. Gossen who claimed that socialist planning would run into difficulties because "Only under private property can the measure be found for placing a value on goods. Therefore [non-market] socialists would find that they had taken upon themselves a task to which they were not adequate."[23] He implied that without money and markets it would be impossible to calculate whether one good was 'worth' more than another and whether the production of any particular good was efficient in terms of the costs used up, and opportunities foregone, in producing it. Steele has shown that developments on this line of thinking were made by Friedrich von Wieser — an originator of the marginal utility theory — and then most notably by the Dutch economist Nikolaas G. Pierson and the Austrian School theorist Ludwig von Mises. In 1902 Pierson heard Kautsky lecture on the nature of social revolution at Delft and in reply wrote a paper entitled 'The Problem of Value in the Socialist Community' where he elaborated the idea that a socialist society would be unable to calculate the net amount of income available for consumption:

> What is to be regarded as income, and what therefore comes into question when considering the division? Naturally only net income; but the income of the socialist State will also be gross income. Raw materials will be required for the goods which it manufactures, and in the course of manufacture fuel and other things will be consumed and machines and tools may be wholly or partly worn out. The livestock which has been reared will have consumed fodder. In order to calculate its net income the communist society would therefore have to subtract all this from gross product. But we cannot subtract cotton, coal and the depreciation of machines from yarns and textiles, we cannot subtract fodder

from beast. We can only subtract the value of one from the value of the other. Thus without evaluation or estimation the communist State is unable to decide what net income is available for division.[24]

Like many socialists, Pierson pictured socialism as being under the domination of one single plan, and although accounting would clearly be essential, he claimed in effect that socialism would have the in-built difficulty of being unable to calculate the amount of exchange value in existence at the end of a year compared with at the beginning and so be unable to establish the net addition to society's annual product. Pierson concluded that because of this deficiency allocation of factors of production would be seriously hindered, markets would eventually have to emerge for scarce resources and soon factors of production would have to be evaluated in terms of prices. He confidently went on to claim that because of this "The phenomenon of value can no more be suppressed than the force of gravity. What is scarce and useful has value ... to annihilate value is beyond the power of man."[25]

In his 1920 work 'Economic Calculation in the Socialist Commonwealth' Ludwig von Mises assimilated the problem identified by Pierson and advanced it considerably in the first really clear and rounded exposition of the economic calculation argument. Mises claimed that not only should society as a whole know its net income but that it is vital that individual units of production should know theirs as well. Calculation of this sort, Mises argued, would be impossible in socialism. He concluded that not only would net income be impossible to calculate without prices and money but that a society without exchange and markets would be incapable of performing a whole series of calculations that are necessary in any advanced social organisation. Foremost among these, Mises argued, would be the ability to allocate resources — particularly factors of production — as efficiently as possible. Owing to its inability to reduce all the factors of production to a common denominator, socialism would have no mechanism for deciding through the medium of the plan whether it would be more efficient to use one resource or another in the manufacture of a product, or indeed whether that product should be manufactured at all. To demonstrate his point, Mises gave this example:

> Picture the building of a new railroad. Should it be built at all, and if so, which out of a number of conceivable roads should be built? In a competitive and monetary economy, this question would be answered by monetary calculation. The new road will render less expensive the transport of some goods, and it may be possible to calculate whether this reduction of expense transcends that involved in the building and upkeep of the next line ... It is not possible to attain the desired end merely by counterbalancing the various physical expenses and physical savings. Where one cannot express hours of labour, iron, coal, all kinds of building material, machines and other things necessary for the construction and upkeep of the railroad in a common unit it is not possible to make calculations at all.[26]

Like Pierson, Mises claimed that if society were to dispense with money, a system of economic calculation would be rendered impossible. Socialism "would involve operations the value of which could neither be predicted beforehand nor ascertained after they had taken place. Everything would be a leap in the dark. Socialism is the renunciation of rational economy".[27] Instead of relying on a calculation of economic value, socialism would have to depend on "vague estimates" to guide its plans. It would more than likely give rise to a serious misallocation of resources — initially plans would have to be constantly revised, but this would prove so burdensome and imprecise that factor markets would eventually emerge to make economic calculation possible once more so that efficient allocation of resources could take place.

When this line of argument was taken up against the SPGB in the 1970s and 80s by libertarian free marketeers,[28] they claimed that the SPGB was the last organisation in existence which refused to acknowledge the validity of economic calculation, and that in advocating a marketless future without money or prices, the SPGB constituted the "last Socialist Party".[29] Because of the SPGB's purist Marxian position on the abolition of money and partly because some members of the Libertarian Alliance had started their political lives in the SPGB, the Party in this period endured a disproportionate amount of criticism from the Libertarian Alliance and others affirming the necessity of economic calculation and the impossibility of planning in socialism without it.

One of the SPGB's fiercest and most persistent critics was David Ramsay Steele, a Party member who had left under the spell of the economic calculation argument in the early 1970s. Steele debated the SPGB on what he termed the practical impossibility of socialism and employed Misian arguments to counter the SPGB's assertions about the nature of the socialist future.[30] Following Mises, Steele claimed that decision-makers in any advanced industrial society need to compare millions of different factors according to a common unit. For example, if a consumer good X could be made with either A+2B or 2A+B (where A+B are both factors such as kilowatt-hours of electricity, gallons of oil or tons of steel) then a choice has to be made about the relative efficiency between two technically possible methods of production. This would involve ascertaining which one used up the least resources and therefore left the most over for other uses. Unless a calculation is made to find out which of the two factors is worth more, a sensible choice cannot be made.[31]

Steele and the libertarians claimed that if prices were to be abolished, or if there was an effective government freeze on prices, there could be no mechanism for deciding which resources should be used and when. As a result, "industrial production would likely collapse within a few months, and mass starvation would appear within a year or two", though the appearance of black markets would tend to mitigate the damage.[32] Steele argued that this would happen with the socialist abolition of markets and money as actual market prices are, or strongly tend towards, the unique prices which bring the available stocks of a resource and the implemented uses of that resource into balance.[33] If the price of a resource rises, producers become less inclined to use it because they view use of that resource as more costly. If the price of a resource falls the converse happens and producers become more likely to use it. But without markets and money, according to Steele, there could be no matching up of demand with supply. This situation would quickly lead to some resources being piled up as stocks grew far in excess of what was necessary, with other resources not being produced in nearly enough quantity.

If all resources were superabundant — which libertarians took to mean that the use of a resource no longer curtailed any other possible use for it — then the economic calculation argument would necessarily fall, as Steele acknowledged.[34] In such a circumstance no comparison of costs would be necessary or desirable. But the supporters of the free market argued that this situation was unlikely ever to come about. It would effectively mean that, in a market economy, all prices had fallen to zero. This has not happened, nor does it show any likelihood of happening precisely, they have claimed, because resources are scarce and have competing uses.

So, for the Libertarian Alliance, the economic calculation argument stood as the best refutation of SPGB-style socialism. Socialism would be unable to efficiently allocate resources, particularly factors of production, without the use of money. But with the continued use of money and prices, there would be no socialism at all — as the SPGB would be the first to acknowledge — so either way the SPGB's socialist vision was practically impossible. The challenge to the SPGB seemed to be to come up with a system incorporating another unit of cost instead of money and prices that worked to efficiently allocate scarce resources via a plan. Two main suggestions had been advanced by those interested in the problem from Marx's day onwards. These suggestions — labour time accounting, and the attribution of factor valuations by solving millions of simultaneous equations, were not, as will be seen, suitable for the SPGB's purposes. So far as it became the task of the SPGB to undermine the basis of the economic calculation argument and thus prove the Marxian vision of socialism possible after all, some fresh thinking was needed.

The SPGB and Socialist Planning

At an early stage in the debate over economic calculation some members of the SPGB conceded that the Party's conception of the socialist future needed refinement. In particular, the Party's Guildford branch, which had organised a series of verbal debates with notable free marketeers in the late 1970s and early 80s, sought to turn the Party's attention to its conception of socialist planning. In a circular entitled 'Is "central planning" compatible with socialism?' Guildford accepted that the SPGB needed to move completely away from the implication that socialist production could be co-ordinated via a series of a priori plans, including a plan at the global level. Given the complexity of the calculations seemingly necessary in socialism, Guildford branch claimed that the very idea of such plans should be dismissed out of hand:

> ... a world plan if it is a plan at all is, by its very nature, inflexible, each component of the plan relating to every other in a specific pre-determined way. It postulates definite targets that must be rigorously adhered to as each target depends for its accomplishment upon the successful accomplishment of other targets (e.g. X tons of steel require Y tons of coal). It cannot brook variation or initiative or local autonomy if it is to remain intact. If variation occurs the plan must change with consequences that will feed through the entire economy and compel continuous recalculation. But variation happens all the time despite the "best laid plans of mice and men" and will happen all the time in socialism. Consequently the formation of a World Plan will be a pointless and meaningless exercise. Were it to be insisted upon it would make a mockery of free access and voluntary co-operation; the former would be perverted into an insidious rationing, the latter into a form of administrative coercion.[35]

Guildford acknowledged that a single world centre would be obliged to solve an immense matrix of millions of simultaneous equations of supply and demand covering the whole economy, a task they derided as "out of the question" for a complex economy. Any form of central planning would also, they contended, be at variance with the proposed democratic nature of socialism, with its emphasis on local control and the fullest access to information. A centrally planned system based on the simultaneous equation model, then, was clearly unsatisfactory.

The option of comparing costs through labour-time accounting, implicitly supported by a small number of SPGB members, and the favoured choice of Marx and Engels, was fraught with other difficulties. Chief among these was the problem pointed out by Mises in 1920, that:

> ... Such a manner of regulating distribution would be unworkable, since labour is not a uniform and homogeneous quantity ... Hence, it becomes utterly impossible in any socialist community to posit a connection between the significance to the community of any type of labour and the apportionment of the yield of the communal process of production.[36]

If an attempt was made to overcome this problem by declaring all labour to be of equal worth there would still be the difficulty of calculating the amount of labour contained in the production of each article of wealth, and of the allocation of consumer goods without adopting a universal accounting equivalent such as labour-money. With labour-money, the Marxian law of value would still apply, measuring the relative 'efficiency' of labour inputs, and labour-money tokens could easily come to circulate,[37] quickly undermining the basis of socialism as a non-exchange society. As noted in Chapter 1, the SPGB had always been opposed to the labour-voucher system proposed by Marx and the SLP as unnecessary in socialism and probably unworkable, for similar reasons.[38]

Guildford branch and other members engaged in polemics with the free marketeers in journals like *Free Life* and the *Libertarian Student* suggested that instead of some common unit of account like labour hours, socialism could dispense with 'common unit' cost accounting altogether. Indeed, herein lay the first part of what was to be their solution to the economic calculation argument — calculation via the medium of a common unit of cost could be replaced completely by 'natural calculation', or calculation in kind:

> ... it is perfectly possible to calculate 'costs' without resorting to prices and this is done all the time today: how much energy does this process consume per unit of output compared with another; which strain of wheat yields greater output; does this product use up more of a particular resource spread over the lifetime of the product than a comparable product, is the productivity of workers sorting mail by hand more or less than in the case of automatic sorting, taking into account the labour embodied in the machinery used.[39]

Calculation in kind had been advanced for use in socialism in the 1920s by the German Social Democrat Otto Neurath,[40] and had later been supported by Amadeo Bordiga.[41] Like them, members of the SPGB claimed that there would not need to be any economic calculation in socialism at all — calculation, in fact, would be technical rather than economic. They rejected the view that economic calculation was an indispensable tool of any advanced society, and claimed that it was a necessary function of the market economy only. This was because "The real function of economic calculation in the market system is not to facilitate the practical, technical organisation of production; it is ultimately about calculating the exploitation of labour"[42] through ascertaining which method of production procures the greatest monetary profit. With the ending of exploitation, there would be no need for common-unit cost accounting to decide which productive methods were more 'efficient' in these terms.

The SPGB's rejection of economic calculation was essentially underpinned by the belief that socialism would not be a society where absolute scarcity of resources reigned. From its earliest years the SPGB had disputed the first principle of bourgeois economics forming the basis of the free marketeers' case — that resources are scarce while wants are limitless. The Party contended that human wants were not and could not be limitless, and that this definition of scarcity was so wide as to be meaningless, varying greatly from the accepted usage of the term. For instance, just because there was an opportunity cost involved in using a resource did not necessarily mean that that resource was scarce, as the libertarians claimed. The SPGB argued instead that scarcity and abundance could only be understood as relative terms, relative that is, to needs. In an article attacking the notion of scarcity entitled 'The Fallacy of Economics', Adam Buick of the SPGB clearly set out the strategy of the Party in its attempts to undermine the economic calculation argument via this route. Socialists, he said:

> reject [bourgeois] economics as a pseudo-scientific ideology constructed on the

basis of an erroneous first principle. If we can show that the first principle is wrong and that needs are not in fact infinite, then the theoretical construct of economics will begin to collapse and to look more like an apology for existing capitalist society than a so-called "law of nature".

Human 'needs, desires and wants' are perhaps difficult to measure, and are perhaps immense ... but they are not 'infinite' in the literal sense that economics posits. Once this point has been conceded, then the possibility of resources being sufficient to meet needs must be admitted ... [then] we move away from the realm of unreasonable definitions (such as 'scarcity' being the absence of infinite resources) into the realm of verifiable facts (are, or are not, resources sufficient to meet needs?).[43]

If, as the SPGB and capitalism's own specialist food and health organisations claimed, world resources were enough to meet needs,[44] then bourgeois economics stood refuted and the main problem of production and distribution was changed from being that of having competing uses for scarce resources to that of deciding what methods to employ to use abundant or sufficient resources to meet non-competing uses. Though calculations and choices would still have to be made there would no longer be any reason to employ a common unit of cost accounting such as money. Nor would there be any useful purpose served by trying to calculate aggregate sums such as net income, as Pierson had claimed. Instead, socialism could simply set up statistical clearing-houses at a local, regional and global level to collate information about the production of physical quantities of goods, and make this information available for the use of decision-makers and productive units. Such information could include reference to factors such as labour-hours expended in production, materials used up, as well as social and environmental considerations.

In his 1920 article Mises conceded that such a socialist society operating a system of calculation in kind would be able to decide on what it wanted — its problem would instead be to decide how to achieve this in a rational way:

It will be evident, even in a socialist society, that 1,000 hectolitres of wine are better than 800, and it is not difficult to decide whether it desires 1,000 hectolitres of wine rather than 500 litres of oil. There is no need for any system of calculation to establish this fact: the deciding element is· the will of the economic subjects involved. But once this decision has been taken, the real task of rational economic direction only commences, i.e. economically, to place the means at the service of the end. That can only be done with some kind of economic calculation ... Calculation in natura, in an economy without exchange, can embrace consumption goods.only; it completely fails when it comes to deal with goods of a higher order. And as soon as one gives up the concept of a freely established monetary price for goods of a higher order, rational production becomes impossible.[45]

According to Mises, a socialist system of calculation in kind would not be able to solve problems of investment and of the development, and use, of producer goods. How to efficiently plan the production of goods was the principal problem socialist society would face. And as has been seen, calculation of investment via central planning, for reasons accepted by the SPGB, represented no solution.

Confronted with this, members of the SPGB set about examining the new technologies available in capitalism and out of them began to gradually develop a new concept of socialist planning to complement calculation in kind — a system of self-regulating stock control, unheard of and unthinkable in the days of Marx and Engels. This system, which became widely accepted in the SPGB by the mid 1980s, was based on the type of operation already used by retail outlets in capitalism, initially by supermarkets and other large stores linked to their suppliers by computers. The Party claimed that stock control in socialism, dealing solely in physical quantities, would be able to replace the market mechanism completely. Responsive stock control itself would provide the signals required by all units of production — including producer goods industries — regarding quantities of output, that were otherwise provided by prices:

> Production for use ... would operate in direct response to need. These would arise in local communities expressed as required quantities such as grammes, kilos, tonnes, litres, metres, cubic metres etc. , of various materials and quantities of goods. These would then be communicated as required elements of productive activity, as a technical sequence, to different scales of social production according to necessity.
>
> Each particular part of production would be responding to the material requirements communicated to it through the connected ideas of social production. It would be self-regulating, because each element of production would be self-adjusting to the communication of these material requirements. Each part of production would know its position. If requirements are low in relation to a build-up of stock, then this would be an automatic indication to a production unit that its production should be reduced. If requirements are high in relation to stock then this would be an automatic indication that its production should be increased.[46]

In this system real social (rather than monetary) demand would arise in local communities through individual consumers exercising their right of free access to consumer goods and services according to their self-defined needs, constrained only by what could be made available. There would be no need for an a priori allocative plan.[47] This would apply with relation to producer goods, also. The demand for producer goods would arise via the network of consumption outlets signalling their needs to units of consumer production which through the stock control mechanism would in turn provide the appropriate signals for the suppliers of production goods. Where particular factors of production were scarce or difficult to obtain for some reason, this would constitute a signal to economise on the use of that factor and to turn to more readily available substitutes. Any overproduction of goods would be in relation to real needs not market demand, and could be adjusted without the threat of slump. Via this stock control system, the production of producer goods would not be decreed in a hit or miss fashion by an allocative plan, but would essentially be demand-led.

The SPGB claimed that in socialism, there would be no overall plan, as such, needed, only the regulating hand of the stock control mechanism, aided by calculation in kind. Furthermore, because this system incorporated an element of feedback it would permit decision-makers to alter their decisions in the light of changing circumstances, unlike a priori planning. So-called 'investment decisions' would not be a particular problem as stock control provided all the signals and information necessary as to resource allocation and depletion. As a result, economic calculation was not the truly devastating assault on the workability of socialism that the free-marketeers imagined it was.

Organising Production for Use
In response to demands from its members, the SPGB set up a committee in 1982 to "prepare a report on positive statements which the Party can make on the organisation of production for use".[48] This Report, which spawned a pamphlet called *Socialism As A Practical Alternative*, sought to provide a clearer picture of the socialist future envisaged by the SPGB, without setting out a blueprint. The Report examined how socialist production could be organised in a democratic manner, and looked at some of the advantages of production for use compared with production for profit. It also attempted to anticipate some of the principal difficulties socialism would face in its early years, particularly the problem of world hunger.

Just as production in socialism would respond to individual needs via a regulated and responsive, polycentric system of production for use, so the Report held that democracy in socialism would follow this pattern. There would be no all-powerful central planning authority taking decisions for the supposed benefit of the rest of the community. Decision-making (rather like the demand for goods) would arise from the bottom-up rather than being made hierarchically and decreed to be implemented downwards.

Due to the importance of continuity, the Report claimed that the three main spheres of decision making — local, regional and global — would be based on a development of the institutions of capitalism, namely local councils, national governments, and a world council formed out of the United Nations organisation. The Report argued that the system of local, regional and world democracy outlined in the February 1939 *Socialist Standard* was the best democratic mechanism for socialism. This is not surprising, as this method of decision-making — based on the principle of delegated function — was also the method used in practice by the SPGB internally. As in the Party itself, this was conceived as a buffer against central control:

If we are to avert any possibility of centralised control, where decisions are made centrally, flow outwards, and are imposed upon the wider community, we must adopt the principle of 'delegated function' which is the working basis of the Party's constitution.

This principle of delegated function has served the Party well; it allows decisions to be made by majorities within the basic unit of organisation. Once these decisions are made they flow throughout the organisation for implementation according to the system of delegated function. With this procedure, decisions flow in a practical way from the majority. In the case of the Party, the basic unit of organisation is the Branch. In Socialism it would be the local community.[49]

In practice this system would work as follows. Socialism would, for instance, want to increase the world's food supply. This would require a world decision, but the proposal for it — as with all proposals — would commence at the local level. If successful there it would advance to the regional agenda for a regional decision, and, if successful regionally, would finally progress on to the world agenda where it could become a world policy decision. With the status of a world policy decision, the proposal would then be passed for implementation to the relevant world specialist body attached to the world council. In the case of food production, the SPGB has suggested that this would be the United Nations Food And Agricultural Organisation (FAO).[50] Such specialist bodies, aided by a network of statistical information systems, would themselves be in operation at a local, regional and world level and it would be up to local communities to implement their recommendations.

The SPGB has suggested that specialist bodies like the FAO could assist the implementation of democratic decisions in a wide variety of fields. Indeed, it has identified other specialist organisations in capitalism which could be converted to use by socialism including, among others, the World Health Organisation, the United Nations Education, Scientific and Cultural Organisation, the International Telecommunications Union and the International Civil Aviation Organisation.[51] Through its use of such bodies a scrupulously democratic society, like SPGB-style socialism, would be able to call on expert opinion and have full access to information in all policy areas. Though the basic unit of organisation in socialism would be the local community, socialism would not be an insular system as there would be every facility for world contact through the operation of specialist bodies and projects as well as through the working of information systems which could provide a 'window on the world'.

In addition to this outlining of possible democratic structures for use in socialism, the SPGB's 'Production For Use' Report sought to claim that such a democratically operated and socially regulated system of society would have a large number of intrinsic advantages compared with capitalism. Not only would socialism be more democratic, but problems such as say, sufficient food production, would have a much greater chance of solution primarily because society would be able to vastly increase the number of people available for useful production.

The Report claimed that first, the ranks of the unemployed would be able to do useful work in socialism denied them in the capitalist system, thereby reducing wastage and increasing the numbers of those engaged in production. Second, the large number of workers under capitalism employed in work necessary only for the maintenance of the capitalist system itself could be transferred to socially useful tasks. The Report stated that capitalism involves a huge amount of labour that is not intrinsically useful including large numbers in the armed forces and the armaments industries, much of the state bureaucracy, and perhaps most significantly of all, the entire financial apparatus of capitalism, with its accountants, ticket collectors, cashiers, bank clerks, and tax officers.[52] Because of this, capitalism is for the SPGB really a system based on wastage and inefficiency, despite the 'efficiency' its supporters claim on its behalf. Even many of the occupations that seem socially useful under capitalism would in fact be redundant in socialism according to the SPGB, thereby increasing the numbers of those available for really useful production. The Report claimed that, for example:

> ... statisticians, systems analysts and computer programmers present themselves as being apparently useful functions, and undoubtedly Socialism would require these skills, but under capitalism many such workers are running entirely useless processes. One use of information systems by companies is to monitor the cash values of their stocks in relation to continuing inflation. This is not only a complete waste of the skills of the operators, but is a waste of the hardware equipment involved.
>
> Teachers present themselves as being useful, but this depends upon what they are teaching. For example, teachers of accountancy, the law, business studies, etc., are obviously useless.
>
> Printers might present themselves as being useful. Again, this is a skill which Socialism would require, but most of the paperwork and the millions of documents concerning invoicing, taxation, the law, insurance, etc., which involve printing, is entirely useless.[53]

The Report also contended that the misused equipment involved in such printing, banking and computer programming contains a mass of labour time which spreads itself throughout the entire structure of production, involving manufacturing, transport, mining and energy, as well as the misuse of natural materials. As such, the true extent of 'wasted' labour under capitalism is large enough to be difficult to estimate accurately. However, the SPGB had for many years claimed that socialism could at least double the number of people available for the production of socially useful goods and services, and the Report claimed that this remained a reasonable assertion.

Additionally, the SPGB argued that production could be increased in socialism by devices other than those intended to expand the useful workforce. These devices would most obviously involve greater use of existing production methods. Socialism would be unencumbered by three main factors that have kept the rate of productivity in capitalism down. First, the Party claimed that competition in capitalism often leads to situations where firms have to write off their investments in equipment and scrap existing means of production, thereby wasting equipment embodying useful labour that has not been fully utilised. Second, capitalism's economic slumps detract from the overall productivity of labour by making workers redundant and means of production idle. Finally, class conflict in capitalist society leads to a position where workers operate restrictive practices, often seeking to resist the introduction of more productive machinery. Socialism would not be affected by any of these factors.[54] In its pamphlet *Socialism As A Practical Alternative*, the Party claimed that socialist society would therefore be able to vastly increase the productiveness of labour, although it acknowledged that rises in productivity would be offset by some changed work practices such as moves away from the reliance in capitalism on techniques which reduce workers to becoming mere appendages of machines. Indeed, though the SPGB did not go so far as to acknowledge it directly, gains in productivity could be more than offset by this:

> ... socialism would be unlikely to use methods like conveyer belt systems which reduce workers to mechanical functions as a way of maximising output. This cannot satisfy the need for work as a fulfilling activity. Socialism would be unlikely to follow the example of capitalism in energy production where a cheap and competitive way of converting fossil fuels into electricity causes massive release of pollutants into the atmosphere ... Massive inputs of fertilisers may be a necessary part of the competitive production of food in capitalism but socialism would be unlikely to want to saturate the land with harmful chemicals. The confinement of animals in the dark and in cramped spaces may be part of the most 'labour efficient' method of converting cereal inputs into meat products, but socialism would surely not carry this on.[55]

Clearly, there would be a trade-off in socialism between increasing overall production and the use of potentially harmful methods of production. The SPGB has itself commented that "there is a vital need to achieve a non-destructive balance between productive activity and protection of the total environment."[56] It is clear that tensions between increasing production and protecting the "total environment" would be most noticeable in the early years of socialism when a rapid expansion of production of goods and services would be required to meet the needs of the world's population.

In the 'Production For Use' Report, the SPGB argued that socialist production could be split into four identifiable phases.[57] The initial phase of socialism — the one most obviously faced with the environmental and technical difficulties bequeathed by capitalism — would be characterised by attempts to rapidly increase output of goods and services, particularly in the spheres of agriculture and health care, and to get to a state of minimum sufficiency. Once this had been achieved, the second phase would concentrate on the development of durable goods, and in particular, fixed means of production. This would provide the basis for the spread of automation and labour-saving devices throughout the productive network, helping to eliminate those occupations considered undesirable for humans to undertake. The third phase would correspond with a fall in total production with enough fixed means of production being available and the supply of durable goods of all kinds being sufficient. The SPGB has characterised the consequent, fourth phase, as "zero growth", with stable levels of production for stable levels of consumption, assuming there are no population explosions or that the means of production is not subject to constant innovation. This fourth phase would be a "steady-state economy",[58] utilising non-polluting technology wherever possible, where production would be principally geared to meeting current needs and to replacing and repairing the stock of means of production, in a sustainable relationship with the rest of nature:

> ... socialism will not go on with the increased production of goods and services for the sake of it. This would be a self-imposed treadmill. We would not follow the example of capitalism where life's objectives are focused on the acquisition and consumption of material things.[59]

Instead, after providing for a situation where there was sufficient decent food, clothing, housing and entertainment foe everyone, socialism would concentrate on building a society free from the assumption that more happiness comes with ever-increasing consumption.

From the 1970s onwards the SPGB has tended to respond to the political advances of the ecological movement by attempting to acquire the 'green' mantle for itself, with slogans such as "One Green World" frequently evident in its political propaganda.[60] In doing so its principal contention has been that in order to provide for the needs of society in an ecologically acceptable manner, members of society have to be in a position to be able to control society's productive forces and direct their purposes — and this can only happen in a system of production for use free from both the market and bureaucratic centralism.[61] This has clearly reflected a change in the Party's approach from mere anti-capitalism to a more positive and focused attempt to publicise the practical nature of its political goal, and the positive move towards highlighting the alleged ecological benefits of socialism has been a product of this.

The catalyst for this change was undoubtedly the arguments directed at the SPGB's conception of socialism by the supporters of free-market capitalism, particularly over socialist planning and economic calculation. These arguments effectively forced the SPGB to examine the nature of socialist organisation in more depth and to challenge a number of its own, sometimes untenable, received assumptions about the socialist future. This in turn has helped supplement its anti-capitalism with a more positive approach. The extent to which this approach is in need of further refinement is discussed in the conclusion.

In defending itself from political attack the SPGB has been virtually alone amongst socialist parties in Britain in making practical proposals for the organisation of non-market socialism, and in addition has made an important contribution to challenging the anti-socialist arguments of the libertarian right-wing. Other self-styled socialist organisations have rarely ventured into this territory, being content to employ the well-worn rhetoric about 'socialist planning' used earlier in the century by the parties and theoreticians of the Second International they have otherwise vilified.[62] The SPGB, however, has at least been prepared to demonstrate that the tag of 'dogmatic Marxists' that has often been applied to it is in some respects far from the truth. In advancing its own conception of how socialism could democratically organise a system of production solely for use without the market, the SPGB has made developments in a sector of socialist thought usually neglected entirely by socialists.

Notes

1. 'Manifesto of the Communist Party' in *Marx and Engels: Basic Writings*, p.64.
2. *Anti-Duhring* by Friedrich Engels (Lawrence and Wishart, London, 1954) p.392.
3. *Capital*, Volume III, p.959.
4. *Capital*, Volume III, p.991.
5. *Capital*, Volume II, p.390.
6. *Grundrisse* by Karl Marx (Penguin, Harmondsworth, 1973) p.173.
7. *Capital*, Volume II, pp.544-5.
8. See 'Critique of the Gotha Program' in *Marx and Engels: Basic Writings*, pp.157-8.
9. *Anti-Duhring*, pp.429-30.
10. 'Socialism: Utopian and Scientific' in *Marx and Engels: Basic Writings*, pp.142-4.
11. *Anti-Duhring*, p.411.
12. 'Socialism: Utopian and Scientific' in *Marx and Engels: Basic Writings*, p.137.
13. 'The German Ideology' by Karl Marx in *Marx and Engels: Basic Writings*, p.295.
14. 'Manifesto of the Communist Party' in *Marx and Engels: Basic Writings*, p.70.
15. *Selected Philosophical Works*, Volume I, by Georgii Plekhanov, (Lawrence and Wishart, London, 1961) p.358.
16. *Woman and Socialism* by August Bebel (Socialist Literature Company, New York, 1910) p.371.
17. 'The Political Organisation of the Working Class' in *Socialist Standard*, March 1905.
18. This is amply demonstrated in *From Marx to Mises: Post-Capitalist Society and the Challenge of Economic Calculation* by David Ramsay Steele (Open Court, Illinois, 1992) pp.65-9.
19. See 'Bordigism' by Adam Buick in *Non-Market Socialism*, p.136.
20. Editorial reply to a correspondent in *Socialist Standard*, February 1939.
21. See 'What Socialism Will Be Like', internal SPGB circular by A. Turner, May 1952.
22. From *Marx to Mises*, p.73.
23. *The Laws of Human Relations, and the Rules of Human Action Derived Therefrom* by H. H. Gossen (MIT Press, Cambridge, Ma., 1983) p.15.
24. 'The Problem of Value in the Socialist Community' by Nikolaas Pierson in *Collectivist Economic Planning* ed. by F. A. Hayek (A. M. Kelly, Clifton, 1975) p.70.
25. 'The Problem of Value in the Socialist Community' in *Collectivist Economic Planning*, p.75.
26. 'Economic Calculation in the Socialist Commonwealth' by Ludwig von Mises in *Collectivist Economic Planning*, pp.108-9.
27. The Libertarian Alliance was founded as a non-party propagandist organisation dedicated to the free market, individual liberty and opposition to statism in all its forms. For a brief summary of its aims and positions see the leaflet *Introducing the Libertarian Alliance* (Libertarian Alliance, London, n.d.)
28. *Socialism: An Economic And Sociological Analysis* by Ludwig von Mises (Yale Univerity Press, New Haven, 1951) p.122.
29. See, for instance, *Libertarian Student* (Alliance of Libertarian Student Organisations, London, April 1986.)
30. Steele debated the SPGB on several occasions, but perhaps most notably against Hardy on 9 September 1979. A tape recording of this debate, entitled 'Socialism

versus the Free Market' is available from the SPGB. Also of interest is the review of Steele`s book on the economic calculation argument in the *Socialist Standard*, June 1993 and the letter of response from Steele with an Editorial Committee reply in the *Standard* of April, 1994.

31. Open letter by David Ramsey Steele to Guildford Branch of the SPGB, 27 July 1982.
32. *Libertarian Student*, Volume III, Number One, n.d.
33. One member of the SPGB, Robin Cox, refuted this argument on the grounds that supporters of capitalism have no way of knowing this. Without using another means of cost accounting instead of pricing "How do they know that there is a correlation between ... costs and their supposed representations in the market economy? One can determine whether such a correlation exists only by measuring one against the other. If libertarians are not prepared to do this then their claim amounts to an irrelevant assertion based on faith, a tautology that only the profit system can ascertain what is 'efficient' when 'efficiency' in their eyes equates with profitability. If, on the other hand, they are prepared to do this then once having done it their whole argument falls to the ground — they will have shown that you can indeed calculate 'costs' in some other sense than market prices for factors of production. " *Libertarian Student*, Volume II, Number Four, n.d.
34. *Ibid.*
35. 'Is Central Planning Compatible With Socialism?', Guildford Branch of the SPGB, December 1981.
36. 'Economic Calculation in the Socialist Commonwealth' in *Collectivist Economic Planning*, p.94.
37. See 'Impossibilism' in *Non-Market Socialism*, pp.87-8.
38. See the brief discussion in Chapter 1 and 'Labour-Time Accounting or Calculation in Kind?' by Adam Buick in *World Socialist*, Number Two, Winter 1984.
39. 'The Practical Nature of Socialism' by Guildford Branch of the SPGB, October 1982.
40. *State Capitalism: The Wages System Under New Management*, p.135.
41. *Non-Market Socialism*, p.142.
42. 'Labour-Time Accounting or Calculation in Kind?' in *World Socialist*, Number Two.
43. *Libertarian Student*, Autumn 1986.
44. In 1984 the FAO reported that using current Western farming methods the world could support a population of about 33 billion people, and with less sophisticated methods, about 15 billion. See *From Capitalism to Socialism*, pp.25-32.
45. 'Economic Calculation in the Socialist Commonwealth' in *Collectivist Economic Planning*, pp.103-4.
46. 'Economic Calculation Versus Production For Use' by Pieter Lawrence in *World Socialist*, Number Two.
47. See 'Practical Socialism' in *Socialist Standard*, March 1990. For more information on the communicative network in socialism see 'The Socialist Breakfast' in *Socialist Standard*, December 1981.

48. Report of the 'Production For Use' Committee, February 1983, p.1.

49. 'Production For Use' Report, p.6.

50. *Socialism as a Practical Alternative* (SPGB, London, n.d.) p.11.

51. For more information see *Socialist Standard*, August 1970.

52. A more comprehensive list is given in *From Capitalism to Socialism*, pp.19-20.

53. 'Production For Use' Report, p.12.

54. *Socialism as a Practical Alternative*, pp.23-4.

55. *Socialism as a Practical Alternative*, p.25.

56. 'Production For Use' Report, p.18.

57. 'Production For Use' Report, p.19.

58. See *Ecology and Socialism* (SPGB, London, 1990) p.27.

59. *Socialism as a Practical Alternative*, p.30.

60. See, for instance, front cover and editorial in *Socialist Standard*, August 1987.

61. *Ecology and Socialism*, p.29.

62. For the Socialist Workers' Party see *The Future Socialist Society* by John Molyneux (SWP, London, 1987). This pamphlet bears all the hallmarks of having been published as a response to the SPGB's persistent arguments about the nature of socialist society. For Militant see *What We Stand For* (Militant Publications, London, 1986) p.24.

Conclusion

From the preceding chapters it can be seen that the SPGB has responded to events throughout the twentieth century in a manner which clearly distinguished it from those political organisations in the wider labour movement. It is also abundantly clear that the distinctive political and economic theories of the SPGB discussed in this work did not emerge from a vacuum — they invariably arose through analysis of concrete conditions utilising the analytical tools provided by the Marxian system, principally the materialist conception of history and the labour theory of value and its related economic concepts.

The Marxian theoretical system was never fully completed or worked out, and its application in the unripe conditions of ascendant nineteenth century capitalism left it open to modification and advancement at a later stage. The fact that Marx and Engels were advocating a theory of world communism which was practically impossible at the time they were advancing it is of particular note, for it was this which led them to take up positions on wars, reforms and other issues which were in many ways seriously at variance with the communist body of theory which they helped build up. Essentially, the task of applying the Marxian analytical method to the more appropriate conditions provided by the twentieth century had to fall to others, and this necessitated a fundamental reappraisal of some of the key Marxian proposals during capitalism's more formative phase. The SPGB explicitly recognised this at its foundation with its break with the reformist politics which had characterised the approach of the Second International, and then with its steadfast refusal to take sides in the Great War of 1914.

The battle against reformism provided the most striking example of the SPGB's application of classical Marxian concepts to new conditions. The justifications advanced for its argument that the problems of capitalism cannot be reformed away have been of special significance, particularly with its attempts to demonstrate how economic crises, unemployment and poverty are endemic to the market system and immune to the attentions of the reformists. As this work testifies, the SPGB's record in both predicting and chronicling the political failure of reform organisations has generally been a good one.

Reformist politics in its various guises undoubtedly provided the most enduring challenge for the SPGB, but the attempt by others in the labour movement to apply Marxian theory to changing conditions has probably provided the most serious. Leninist vanguardism was the most obvious expression of this, and the SPGB's early response to it, with its defence of the positions of more classical and democratic Marxism, must rank as among the most distinctive and fascinating political analysis of the time. Without the pockets of resistance of which the SPGB was such a primary example, Marxism could certainly have been lost forever to the Leninists and their political admirers.

While the SPGB's detractors have been able to point to its small size and possibly a certain sectarianism in its outlook — more evident at some times in its history than others — the responses of the SPGB to what amounts to the dynamic of the capitalist system's own development this century have certainly been deserving of more than fleeting reference. Hopefully, this text has provided a reasonably comprehensive account of the principal political and economic theories of the SPGB, though admittedly not an exhaustive one. As is clear from the preceding chapters, this has sometimes necessitated examining some of the controversies that have occasionally arisen within the SPGB itself. Disputes within the SPGB — their causes, courses and ramifications — could be the subject matter of another work entirely, but such political controversies could rightly only be touched upon here.

The main purpose of this work has been to demonstrate what became ever more apparent during the research, that far from being a moribund sect obsessed with political minutiae, bygone theories and traditions, the SPGB is rather more of a living political organism than many of its detractors have assumed. Above all, it has proved capable of responding to events in an imaginative and distinctive manner while still holding true to its fundamental principles, derived in large part from the classical Marxism of the nineteenth century.

It should also be noted that in developing its own distinctive political platform the SPGB has surely demonstrated something of significance to the world of modern political philosophy — that social democracy was never entirely swamped by the forces of reformism and vanguardism, and that a form of revolutionary social democracy has survived into the twenty first century in the guise of the SPGB itself. Moreover, though it was reformist social democracy which emerged as the primary product of 'democratic classical Marxism' in the conditions of the late nineteenth century, the revolutionary social democrats of the SPGB have, through their various applications of Marxian theories, proved their greater suitability as standard bearers for that political philosophy in the decades after, when Marxian socialism has technically been capable of realisation.

Perhaps revolutionary social democracy can best be understood as the politics of democratic classical Marxism transposed from the backwaters of immature capitalism into the more favourable and developed conditions of the twentieth century and beyond. In this sense alone, the political intervention of the SPGB has been more indicative of an attempt at a bold political and economic leap into the future than a glorification in Marxism's past, and an assimilation of this is vital if the politics of the SPGB is to be de-mystified once and for all.

Against the SPGB's distinctive interventions in the political and economic arena must be set nearly a hundred years of failure to achieve its goal. Mere continued existence through often troubled times has been an achievement of sorts, but the SPGB at the turn of the millennium is not appreciably nearer achieving socialism than it was in 1904. Its failure on this score has not been entirely a product of its own actions, of course — and the failure of the entire left and Marxist movement to achieve a lasting transformation of society testifies to this. So far the weight of 'bourgeois ideology' generated in capitalist society has been more than a match for the propagandism of the tiny SPGB. This lack of success isn't necessarily indicative of a flawed outlook, even though the Party's socialist goal seems unrealistic to some, and it would certainly be dangerous to suggest that the validity of any idea should always be judged by the numbers of its adherents. But the SPGB must bear at least a part of the responsibility for its rather isolated, and in some ways, ineffectual condition. As noted, the SPGB has sometimes exhibited a sectarianism of both political style and content which has only served to harm it and the political tradition which it represents. Furthermore, some of its arguments certainly appear to be in need of further refinement if it is to make any real political progress.

Others in the non-market socialist political sector have often received short shrift from the SPGB and have sometimes engendered an hostility from the Party that has been excessive and disproportionate. The SPGB's assertion that it, alone, is the only socialist party in Britain, has rankled with many, and perhaps justifiably so. Probably the most notable example of the SPGB's intransigence — and coincidentally one of the Party's arguments in need of some further consideration — has been its insistence that only its own 'parliamentary' road to socialism is capable of success. After nearly one hundred years of failure to achieve socialism its claims on this front seem rather hollow. Nor is it entirely clear why parliament and the need to formally take over "the machinery of government" has tended to form such a large part of the Party's revolutionary strategy. The essential prerequisite of a socialist transformation would seem to lie not in the Kautskyite idea of gaining control of parliament, but in a majority of workers from all occupations and none simply organising together to achieve revolutionary change. Therefore a majority socialist consciousness among the working class would seem to be of far more importance than the number of socialist delegates in parliaments and congresses across the world. If and when a majority of convinced socialists is achieved, the formal annulment of capitalist private property rights in parliament would only be a very small part of a massive social transformation which would essentially have to take place outside of the parliamentary arena altogether.

In much of its propaganda the SPGB has hitherto paid a disproportionate amount of attention to the legalistic process of socialist change rather than how a revolutionary movement can transform itself from a propagandist function to a transformative one, at the social and economic as well as political levels. Not only has this held back thinking in the SPGB on the mechanics of revolutionary change, but its rigid defence of the totem of formal expropriation of the capitalists through parliament has won it few friends among those who might otherwise have been sympathetic to its other ideas on, for instance, the self-organisation of the working class and on the future society. As the Party enters the new millennium it does now at last seem that the SPGB has begun to consistently assert the democratic, majoritarian aspect of its case rather than the mechanistic legalism of the 'parliamentary road', so evident in Party propaganda until recent years.

Its somewhat sectarian outlook on this issue aside, there are other potential difficulties looming for the SPGB and its revolutionary strategy. Despite what some might term its parliamentary fixation, the SPGB has never seen a role for leadership in the revolutionary transformation. This is notwithstanding its conviction that a political party is necessary if socialism is to be achieved, as only a political party can organise in a systematic manner to propagate the case for socialism, meet opposition and, eventually, take the reins of political power. The absence of a political leadership will quite possibly cause the SPGB some difficulties if it ever reaches anything approaching a large size, including those problems associated with the rather laborious nature of SPGB internal democracy, at least as it has developed so far. Scrupulously democratic Party-wide polls on the expulsion of members, for example, are practicable in an organisation of a few hundred or even a few thousand members, but when millions become involved, they seem more problematical. If the SPGB grows, its present internal structure will have to become much more devolved than it is at present if the emergence of a 'controlling elite' is to be avoided entirely.

Some theorists, most notably Roberto Michels in his work *Political Parties*, have argued that leadership is a necessary function of all social aggregates. According to Michels, organisation itself causes leadership to appear, and organisation has a tendency to grow, so reinforcing the domination — and eventually the detachment — of leadership groupings. Michels called his particular elite theory the "iron law of oligarchy" and claimed that among the masses there is a psychological need for leadership arising from a widespread apathy towards political and social affairs. Michels formulated these beliefs as a result of his study of the internal workings of the German SPD and much of his supporting evidence was anecdotal. Nevertheless, his argument was a serious one and has some relevance to the politics of the SPGB. It suggests that the SPGB could develop a leadership, and would only be more successful if it did so.

The evidence thus far suggests that the emergence of a leadership within the SPGB, though not impossible, is an unlikely prospect. This is not just because it has yet to happen over nearly a century, though that itself is worthy of note, but because of the underlying reason for this — the democratic consciousness exhibited by SPGB members. Put simply, leadership is unlikely to emerge precisely because the members will not let it — they have, after all, become SPGB members partly due to their opposition to leadership. The SPGB is entirely a voluntary organisation and opposition to political leadership is one of the basic requirements of SPGB membership. The Party membership seems no more likely to ditch this key principle than any other, and applicants to the SPGB who show signs of 'weakness' on this issue are not allowed into the ranks of the Party. The internal structure of the SPGB, based on democratic accountability and the principle of delegated function, is framed to reflect the democratic consciousness of the members, and to stop leadership emerging, whether by design or accident. Thus far, at least, it has worked well enough.

It is worth noting that if the SPGB did abandon its opposition to leadership, or if one emerged despite it, the SPGB would cease to be a socialist party on its own terms. Clearly, if for some reason a leadership did emerge, the problem of 'goal displacement' referred to by Michels would then be a real one, with the leadership developing interests and priorities of its own, separate from — and most likely antagonistic to — those of the wider membership. As was outlined in Chapter 1, this is in part what happened to the SPGB's parent body, the SDF, and the SPGB was not slow to learn the lesson from it.

Given this, the issue of whether the SPGB would be more successful if it developed a political leadership becomes largely redundant. With a leadership, the SPGB would effectively cease to be the SPGB as we know it. Logically, the SPGB transformed into an organisation with a leadership could go in one of two directions — either openly reformist like Hyndman's SDF, or, as is possibly more likely, it could become left communist, conceding to the precepts and demands of democratic centralism. Interestingly, those organisations in the left communist tradition, who share the SPGB's goal of socialism and its opposition to reformism and the pro-capitalist parties, but which have a vanguardist-style leadership, have usually been even less successful than the SPGB itself. One possible reason for this is that their commitment to a democratic, egalitarian future society sits uneasily with their undemocratic practices within capitalism, and few of those attracted by the notion of a stateless, moneyless social commonwealth have been impressed by their methods.

A total collapse in the democratic consciousness exhibited by SPGB members seems very unlikely, but today there are some more immediate and practical problems for the SPGB surrounding this issue of leadership. Media organisations, in particular, frame their coverage of political events to harmonise with prevalent concepts of political leadership, and the SPGB may yet find its currently developing relationship with the media a difficult one, just as the Green Party in Britain did when it disavowed formal leadership and appointed only 'media spokespersons'. As a result of some of the tensions arising from this action, the Greens eventually split between a dominant reformist group prepared to countenance the existence of a leadership, and a more anarchistically-inspired faction resolutely opposed to leadership and centralism.

One was prepared to accommodate to the media world around it, while the other remained hostile to prevailing media norms. It is clear that the tensions which disrupted Green politics in Britain during the early 1990s could possibly infect the SPGB, especially in the age of spin-doctors and soundbites.

If the SPGB's vision of a democratic socialist society is to be achieved, it is necessary that the socialist movement within capitalism prefigures proposed democratic structures in socialism to a degree but the practical problems this raises for a revolutionary organisation cannot be ignored, and the UK Green Party has demonstrated the dangers lurking for radical parties growing up in a somewhat hostile environment. The SPGB at present is not geared towards responding to the demands of the media in the way it might have to be if, and when, it grows. If Michels' "iron law of oligarchy" is not to take root, the SPGB may well have to devise new internal structures which can ensure that there is sufficient specialisation of tasks within the Party for it to be able to cope with the attentions of the media, without inviting the emergence of a formal leadership, possibly based in parliament itself. Although it has been noticeable that some members have exerted more influence within the SPGB than others in the past due to specialisation of function (e.g. writers, editors, speakers), we have already noted that the emergence of a leadership has, at least so far, been avoided, so this task may not be beyond the Party if and when it gets socialist representatives elected to parliament and local councils.

Problems arising from this leadership issue aside, other concerns are currently more pressing still for the Party. Considering its weak position at present, it is worth noting that the SPGB has not, as an organisation, fully addressed itself to the question of why the working class hasn`t yet mustered under the Party's banner in any great numbers, or the related issue of what real incentive there might be for them to do so. As has been seen, the SPGB has made some compelling points about the 'muddying of waters' from the Leninists and others who have made its task even more difficult than it would otherwise have been, but it is far from clear that this explanation of the SPGB`s lack of success is entirely adequate on its own. It was widely expected within the Party that the SPGB would start making greater progress after the mythology surrounding the 'socialist motherland' in Russia had disappeared, but early findings have not demonstrated this and the SPGB's membership has certainly not risen significantly since its position on Russia has been essentially vindicated with the fall of the Kremlin's Empire. The abiding association of 'socialism' and 'communism' with the USSR still looks like being the legacy the SPGB is left with for the immediate future.

The SPGB has been caught in a dilemma over whether its small size is caused in part by a lack of credibility among the working class, or vice versa. Conveniently plumping for the latter option, its members have often assumed that the SPGB's first task is to reach such a size — perhaps a few thousand members — that its political credibility is enhanced and it finally emerges as a serious player in the political field. At this point, it is argued, the SPGB would effectively reach a 'critical mass' when the Party's growth could take off exponentially. But these assumptions, while plausible enough in themselves, seem to neglect the problem of how the SPGB can reach a credible size in the first place, and of how momentum can practically be maintained. The necessary incentive for revolutionary change is an important consideration here and the SPGB has often been content to list the serious social problems that have defeated the reformists (unemployment, poor housing conditions, etc) and to assert that only socialism remains as the solution to them. But if only a minority are touched by these social problems, as is arguably the case in the major industrialised countries, the likelihood of exponential growth leading to mass social revolution is reduced.

Of crucial relevance, the SPGB often seems unsure about the precise role the material interests of the working class play in promoting a revolutionary outlook among the workers. In its early years the SPGB stressed the importance of absolute impoverishment in fermenting working class discontent. With the 'long boom' in Britain of the 1950s and 60s, emphasis on this diminished and the SPGB switched to asserting that while real wages and the purchasing power of the working class had risen significantly, the portion of the social product extracted as surplus value — and hence the exploitation of the working class — had risen even more. In that sense, the prime incentive for socialist revolution for the SPGB altered from being the absolute impoverishment of the workers, as had previously been the case, to relative impoverishment. But relative impoverishment would appear to be a much less powerful stimulus for change, and the period since the Second World War has demonstrated, if anything, that workers are less inclined to make comparisons with the capitalists if their own position is still steadily improving. A return to an analysis based more resolutely on absolute impoverishment would only be credible, of course, if such impoverishment returned in the real world of the capitalist economy, say as a result of a declining mass of profit, as discussed in Chapter 4, but the very high technical composition of capital necessary for this scenario is unlikely to occur in anything but the long term.

While the real income of the working class has increased and undermined the effectiveness of the 'absolute impoverishment' argument, other imperatives have served to usher some workers towards the waiting arms of the SPGB, but only as yet in small numbers. In this category falls concern over war, particularly nuclear war, and the environment. The 'quality of life' issue also rears it head here, and the SPGB has had much to say on the weariness and frustration of working class life in the market economy. Given this, it is perhaps surprising that the SPGB has been rather slow to recognise that the 'worsening material conditions of life' scenario is, judged in its wider sense, alive and kicking even if the absolute impoverishment of the working class is less of a pressing concern in the industrial nations than it was when the SPGB was founded. Certainly on a world basis — and perhaps when judged in countries like Britain alone — the working class appear no more content now than they seemed two hundred years ago, despite increases in working class purchasing power across much of the industrialised world. With rising crime levels, increasing drug abuse, growing insecurity of life and widespread social dislocation in even the most tranquil of capitalist states, other concerns have arisen. Marx's "mass of misery" may yet take on a new significance which the SPGB can turn to its favour, a misery which is widespread and not merely contained in pockets of discontent amid general calm and which is not simply dependent on absolute impoverishment.

It follows that if world social revolution is to be brought about through a recognition of working class self-interest rather than through altruism or other notions, then the various inadequacies and contradictions of the capitalist system are what are most likely to provide the spur. It should therefore be a matter of great importance to the SPGB whether the contradictions of capitalism are sharpening or not. If it is the case that world crises have a tendency to become more devastating in their effect, that capitalism is becoming more unstable and dangerous, that the on-costs of the system such as the welfare state are becoming more burdensome, then the imperative for SPGB-style social revolution would be increased. If it can be demonstrated that this is not the case, then the SPGB's revolutionary strategy would certainly seem to lack force and potential impetus. This should be a matter of supreme interest to the SPGB, and chapters 4 and 6 show that the Party is now beginning to make at least some tentative headway in these fields.

One other area where the SPGB has some work yet to do in developing its political analysis is in relation to its ideas on how future socialist society could be organised. It has already made some important developments here, but still has some way to go if its conception of socialism is to be truly convincing. There are three main causes of concern.

Firstly, the SPGB has not entirely tackled the problem of distribution in socialism. While the incorporation of the stock-control system into the Party's model of socialism has been a definite advance, it does not entirely account for how non-abundant consumption goods in particular could be allocated. The stock-control system would provide signals to produce more of those goods where the demand exceeds the supply, but has no allocative mechanism for dealing with distribution in the interim. Some SPGB members have mooted the operation of a self-imposed system of rationing in the early days of socialism, as noted in Chapter 1, but the success of such a system could not be guaranteed, especially in the period when the weight of bourgeois ideology has not be fully removed from society. One way around this problem would be simply to not produce those goods for which demand could not be met, and transfer resources elsewhere — for instance, socialism might not produce luxury cars at all, only utility models. But this would deprive potentially large numbers of people in socialist society from fulfilling their self-defined needs, and would undoubtedly serve to stifle innovation too.

Perhaps a more likely method of dealing with the problem of non-abundant consumption goods would be to distribute them on a 'first-come-first-served' basis. This would meet as many needs as society could, given the development of the productive forces and existing priorities of production, and would ensure reasonably fair distribution. However, the SPGB has so far not indicated a preference either way, and does not even appear to have given really serious thought to this problem, and this certainly amounts to an omission in its conception of how socialist society could function.

The second potential difficulty for the SPGB on how socialism might be organised relates to its model of democracy. Given that the SPGB has been prepared to suggest what it considers to be a workable model of democratic organisation, the onus is on it to confront the difficulties presented by this model. Foremost among these is the relationship between the local, regional and global bodies of democratic administration. Decisions made at regional or global level would require the co-operation of the local democratic units if they were to be enforced, but there would appear to be no mechanism for ensuring this co-operation beyond the goodwill of all those involved. This would seem unrealistic if it is intended that goodwill would solve all conflicts. For instance, it is possible that socialist society, through say the global world council, would need to rapidly increase electricity supply, and that it would decide to commission nuclear power stations for this purpose. Although a global decision on these lines would be reflective of global opinion on the subject, those areas in the minority and strongly opposed to the project would have their wishes overridden. It is possible that it would be precisely those areas most suited to location of the project which would be those most opposed to its implementation. In this instance, they may choose not to co-operate. What sanctions against this would wider socialist society have? Would it simply give in to the wishes of a vociferous minority or compromise by siting nuclear power stations in less suitable environments? The SPGB, certainly if it ever gets to be a bigger political force than it is today, would need to give consideration to exactly this kind of problem, and would have to be prepared to draw up guidelines to a constitution that could be operative in socialism to minimise these sort of difficulties.

Moreover, if the SPGB is to be really serious about planning for a post-capitalist world, it perhaps should start considering other problems of democracy which would be present in socialism. Foremost among these would be the philosophical problem of boundaries. Where should democratic boundaries be drawn, and who should draw them up? The SPGB, as we have seen, is pledged to the abolition of the capitalist nation state, but this does not mean that socialist fraternity will render distinctions between localities and regions entirely meaningless. How will it be decided, for example, whether the

British Isles shall be one region, or two, namely the old British nation state and the island of Ireland? This would presumably have to be decided through interaction between the other two levels of democratic administration, local and global, though it is not immediately apparent how. Again, when and if the socialist movement becomes much bigger than it is now, consideration will have to be given to this possible area of conflict. No doubt the SPGB would point out that the very idea that conflict could arise over boundaries in socialism would be indicative of a capitalist mentality rather than socialist consciousness but the initial constitutional difficulties, at least, would require some attention.

One particular controversy emanating from the Party's conception of the socialist future has arisen with a vengeance in recent years, and presents the SPGB with its third difficulty. This is the issue of social compliance within socialism and of how socialist society could deal with anti-social minorities in a fair and democratic manner. For much of the Party's existence it has shown little interest in such matters, arguing that to give detail on this would be to give in to utopianism. However, during the 1980s, the Party became much bolder in its declarations about the absence of coercion and force in a stateless socialist world, where — to use Marx's term in the *Communist Manifesto* — "the free development of each is the condition for the free development of all". But these declarations that coercion will be absent in a socialist society have not been supported by all members and this is an issue which now appears regularly on the SPGB Conference agenda. The main problem is this: while the Party has long eschewed the need for capitalist institutions like the police and prisons in socialism, it has been much less clear about what they could practically be replaced with. It would currently seem that the Party is now facing up to the difficulties associated with this position and is in the process of adopting a stance whereby it concedes that democratically arrived-at coercive mechanisms of various sorts would be necessary in socialism, especially in its formative years when the existence of capitalist-inspired social behaviour will still be apparent. Whether it will eventually conclude that a legal system, something akin to prisons, and even a police force of sorts will need to exist in socialism remains to be seen although the SPGB's present recognition of the need for 'regulations' and the 'restraint' of anti-social individuals would seem to be an embryonic statement of this, shorn of the language of class society.

How will the SPGB respond to challenges such as these? With an organisation as small and isolated as the SPGB there is always a danger that it will lapse into mere sectarianism, and a glorification in its traditions and history. In such circumstances the SPGB would become a fossilised relic, far more of a monument than it could ever again be a movement. The danger of this has diminished in recent years and the Party has developed a more outward-looking stance that has been reflected in a refinement of its political positions and most recently of all, perhaps, a more tolerant internal political culture. Crucially, this text would seem to indicate that far from being a rigid sect, the SPGB in essence is capable of modifying its arguments to new circumstances. That it has done this on the nature of the capitalist class, on economic crises, on the welfare state and socialist planning, to name but a few, augers well. For if it is ever to make much headway it may have some tough questions to ask of itself, of capitalist society and of its socialist goal. On balance, it so far seems to have shown itself equal to the task, and a constant questioning of its own programme and its analysis of the capitalist system may one day come to fruition in the shape of a less isolated position within the working class movement and some real progress towards its ultimate goal.

Bibliography

Aside from its monthly *Socialist Standard* (September 1904-) much of the SPGB's written political intervention has come in pamphlet form. The following is a complete list of SPGB pamphlets dating from the Party's foundation to the present day, with dates of publication:

Socialist Party Manifesto, 1905.
Handicraft to Capitalism (by Karl Kautsky), 1906.
Art, Labour and Socialism (by William Morris), 1907.
The Working Class (by Karl Kautsky), 1908.
The Capitalist Class (by Karl Kautsky), 1908.
Socialism and Religion, 1910.
The Socialist Party and the Liberal Party, 1911.
The Socialist Party and Tariff Reform, 1912.
Socialism, 1920.
Why Capitalism Will Not Collapse, 1932.
The Socialist Party and Questions of the Day, 1932.
SPGB Principles and Policy, 1932.
War and the Working Class, 1936.
The Czech Crisis and the Workers, 1938.
The Socialist Party Exposes Mr Chamberlain and His Labour Critics, 1938.
Should Socialists Support Federal Union?, 1940.
Questions of the Day (revised edition), 1942.
Beveridge Re-organises Poverty, 1943.
Family Allowances: A Socialist Analysis, 1943.
Nationalisation or Socialism?, 1945.
Is Labour Government the Way to Socialism?, 1946.
The Racial Problem — A Socialist Analysis, 1947.
The Communist Manifesto and the Last One Hundred Years, 1948.
Russia Since 1917, 1948.
The Socialist Party and War, 1950.
Questions of the Day (revised edition), 1953.
Socialist Comment, 1956.
Schools Today, 1959.
The Capitalist — The Worker — The Class Struggle — Wages — Depression — Politics, 1962.
The Case For Socialism, 1963.
The Problem of Racism, 1966.

Russia 1917-67, 1967.
Labour Government or Socialism?, 1968.
Questions of the Day (revised edition), 1969.
The Socialist Party and War, 1970.
Historical Materialism, 1975.
Socialist Principles Explained, 1975.
Questions of the Day (revised edition), 1977.
Marxian Economics, 1978.
Trade Unions and Socialism, 1980.
Is A Third World War Inevitable?, 1982.
Ireland — Past, Present and Future, 1983.
From Capitalism To Socialism ... How We Live and How We Could Live, 1986.
Women and Socialism, 1986.
Socialism As A Practical Alternative, 1987.
Racism, 1988.
Ecology and Socialism, 1990.
How We Live and How We Might Live (by William Morris), 1990.
Eastern Europe — The Collapse of the Kremlin's Empire, 1991.
The Market System Must Go — Why Reformism Doesn't Work, 1997.

Over its long political life the SPGB has issued hundreds of different leaflets on a wide variety of issues and has a large collection of tape recordings for sale of its debates and public meetings, many of which have proved to be extremely useful indicators of the outlook of SPGB members across a range of topics. The SPGB's internal documents have proved to be a rich source of information for this work too, particularly Conference and Autumn Delegate Meeting reports, together with the many circulars sent around Party branches. Interviews with Party members and other written materials which have been made available by members to the writer have also proved invaluable. From 1952 to 1959 the SPGB ran a well-produced internal discussion journal called *Forum* which provided useful insights into the thinking of SPGB members at a time when the Party was in relative decline and when factional strife was at its height.

Much else — of both direct and indirect interest — has been published by the SPGB's Companion Parties in other countries, though it would be fair to say that some have been more prodigous in their output than others, the more active being able to sustain journals and regularly produce pamphlets. In 1984 the SPGB started publication, on behalf of the World Socialist Movement, of a bi-annual booklet entitled *World Socialist*, which carried contributions with a primarily global theme from members of the SPGB and its Companion Parties. This series ran for seven issues.

It is worth noting that other journals and publications periodically contain interesting material on the SPGB and they have helped inform the thinking of the writer on some issues. Foremost among these is *Discussion Bulletin* (DB Committee, Grand Rapids, bi-monthly), essentially a debating and discussion forum for those situated in the 'non-market socialist' political sector, ranging from socialist industrial unionists and 'world socialists' of the SPGB/WSM variety through to anarcho-communists and left communists. Indeed, the publications of the other organisations in this political sector are always worth some investigation from those interested in the SPGB. Here must be included the small group of members expelled from the SPGB in 1991 over the issues of democracy and reformism who continue to publish their quarterly journal *Socialist Studies* (referred to in Chapter 6) as well as regular pamphlets.

Also of use for this work (and of interest to observers of the SPGB) have been the various publications of the Social Science Association, its offspring the Walsby Society, and the small group of individuals who went on to develop the theory of 'systematic ideology'. The Social Science Association had been formed by a group which had left the SPGB during the Second World War and which had later been bolstered by individuals who had become disillusioned with the Party during its troublesome 1950s. The focus of their work was an attempt to account for the nature and spread of political ideologies. In particular, they expressed the wish to identify and understand possible explanations for what they claimed to be the persistently small number of adherents to radical political ideologies and to explain the limited growth typically encountered by radical political groups. The SPGB was of special interest to them — not simply because of their former membership of it — but because they considered it to be the 'purest' radical or revolutionary organisation of them all, epitomising both the pursuit of theory above 'practical politics' and the lack of success experienced by the revolutionary movement as a whole. The most recent, regular expression of their theory can be found in the journal *Ideological Commentary* (Calabria Press, London), which was published on a quarterly basis from 1979 until its demise with the death of its editor, George Walford, in 1994. Virtually every issue of this journal carried material on the SPGB, some of it insightful, some heavily critical and some convoluted to the point of abstruseness. Additionally, this group published several books and pamphlets, some of the latter of which were concerned solely with the SPGB and its political ideology, with the most accessible probably being *Socialist Understanding: A Study of the Thinking of the Socialist Party of Great Britain* (George Walford, 1980).

Books and Journals

The following books and journals have in most instances been cited in the text or notes. The small number which have not are included as they contain material of direct and obvious interest to observers of the SPGB:

Barltrop, Robert, *The Monument: The Story of the Socialist Party of Great Britain* (Pluto Press, London, 1975).
Barrot, Jean, *Leninism or Communism?* (Wildcat, Nottingham, n.d.).
Bebel, August, *Woman and Socialism* (Socialist Literature Company, New York, 1910).
Beer, Max, *A History of British Socialism* (G. Bell and Sons Ltd., London, 1921).

Beetham, David, *Marxism in the Face of Fascism* (Manchester University Press, Manchester, 1983).

Boudin, Louis, *The Theoretical System of Karl Marx* (Kerr and Co., Chicago, 1907).

Buick, Adam, 'A Revolutionary Socialist' in *The Journal of the William Morris Society*, Volume VI, Number One, Summer 1984.

_____, 'The Myth of the Transitional Society' in *Critique 5*, n.d.

Buick, Adam and Crump, John, *State Capitalism: The Wages System Under New Management* (MacMillan, London and Basingstoke, 1986).

Cahn, Herman, *Capital Today* (Kerr and Co., Chicago, 1918).

_____, *The Collapse of Capitalism* (Kerr and Co., Chicago, 1919).

Callaghan, John, *The Far Left in British Politics* (Basil Blackwell, Oxford, 1987).

Cannan, Edwin, *An Economist's Protest* (P. S. King and Son, Westminster, 1927).

_____, *Modern Currency and the Regulation of its Value* (P. S. King and Son, Westminster, 1931).

_____, *Money* (P. S. King and Son, Westminster, 1923).

Challinor, Raymond, *The Origins of British Bolshevism* (Croom Helm, London, 1977).

Clarke, John, Cochrane, Alan and Smart, Carol, *Ideologies of Welfare* (Hutchinson, London, 1987).

Cliff, Tony, State *Capitalism in Russia* (Pluto Press, London, 1974).

Clinton, Alan, *Post Office Workers, A Trade Union and Social History* (George Allen and Unwin, London, 1984).

Cmd. 827, *Radcliffe Report* — *Committee on the Workings of the Monetary System* (HMSO, London, 1959).

Cmd. 2600, *Report of the Royal Commission on the Coal Industry* (HMSO, London, 1926).

Cmd. 3897, *Report of the MacMillan Committee Into Finance and Industry* (HMSO, London, 1931).

Cmd. 6404, *The Beveridge Report* (HMSO, London 1942).

Cmd. 6527, *White Paper On Employment Policy* (HMSO, London, 1944).

Cole, G. D. H., *The Second International*, Part One (Macmillan, London, 1956).

Coleman, Stephen, *Daniel De Leon* (Manchester University Press, Manchester, 1990).

_____, 'The Origin and Meaning of the Political Theory of Impossibilism', unpublished Ph. D thesis (University of London, 1984).

Coleman, Stephen, and O'Sullivan, Paddy (eds.), *William Morris and News From Nowhere* — *A Vision For Our Time* (Green Books, Bideford, 1990).

Coontz, Sydney, H., *Productive Labour and Effective Demand* (Croom Helm, London, 1965).

Crick, Martin, *A History of the Social Democratic Federation* (Ryburn Publishing, Keele, 1994)

Crump, John, *A Contribution To the Critique of Marx* (Social Revolution/Solidarity, London, 1976).

Davis, Horace, B. (ed.), *The National Question* (Monthly Review Press, London, 1977).

De Leon, Daniel, *Who Pays the Taxes?* (Socialist Labour Press, Glasgow, 1912).

Douglas, Major C., *Social Credit* (Eyre and Spottiswoode, London, 1933).

_____, *The Monopoly of Credit* (Eyre and Spottiswoode, London, 1931).

Drachkovitch, M. and Milorad, M., *The Revolutionary Internationals 1864–1943* (Oxford University Press, London, 1966).

Dutt, R. Palme, *Why This War?* (Communist Party, London, 1939).

Engels, Friedrich, *Anti-Duhring* (Lawrence and Wishart, London, 1954).

_____, *On Capital* (Lawrence and Wishart, London, 1937).

_____, *The Condition of the Working Class in England* (Panther Books, London, 1984).

_____, *The Peasant War in Germany* (Lawrence and Wishart, London, 1969).

Fernandez, Neil C., *Capitalism and Class Struggle in the USSR: A Marxist Theory* (Ashgate, Aldershot, 1997).

Feuer, Lewis, S. (ed.), *Marx and Engels: Basic Writings on Philosophy and Politics* (Fontana, London, 1981).

Friedman, Milton, 'Inflation, Taxation, Indexation' in *Inflation, Causes, Consequences, Cures* by various authors (Institute of Economic Affairs, London, 1974).

Gankin, O. H., and Fisher, H. H., *The Bolsheviks and the World War — The Origins of the Third International* (Stanford University Press, Stanford, 1940).

Girard, Frank, and Perry, Ben, *The Socialist Labor Party 1876–1991 — A Short History* (Livra Books, Philadelphia, 1991).

Glennerster, Harold, *Paying For Welfare* (Basil Blackwell, Oxford, 1987).

Glyn, Andrew, and Harrison, John, *The British Economic Disaster* (Pluto Press, London, 1980).

Gossen, H. H., *The Laws of Human Relations, and the Rules of Human Action Derived Therefrom* (MIT Press, Cambridge, Ma., 1983).

Graham, Keith, *The Battle of Democracy* (Wheatsheaf Books, Brighton, 1986).

Grant, Ted, *The Unbroken Thread* (Fortress Books, London, 1989).

Grossmann, Henryk, *The Law of Accumulation and Breakdown of the Capitalist System* (Pluto Press, London, 1992).

Hands, Gordon, 'Roberto Michels and the Study of Political Parties' in *The British Journal of Political Science*, April 1971 (Cambridge University Press, Cambridge).

Harman, Chris, 'Marx's Theory of Crisis and Its Critics' in *International Socialism 11* (Socialist Workers Party, London, Winter 1981).

Haupt, Georges, *Socialism and the Great War* (Oxford University Press, London, 1972).

Hayek, F. A. (ed.), *Collectivist Economic Planning* (A. M. Kelly, Clifton, 1975).

Hobsbawm, Eric, *Industry and Empire* (Penguin, Harmondsworth, 1986).

Hosking, Geoffrey, *A History of the Soviet Union* (Fontana, London, 1985).

Howard, M. C., and King, J. E., *A History of Marxian Economics 1883–1929* (MacMillan, London and Basingstoke, 1988).

Hyndman, Henry, M., *Commercial Crises of the Nineteenth Century* (NCLL Publishing Society, London, 1932).

International Communist Current, *The Decadence of Capitalism* (ICC, London, n.d.).

Irving, David, *Churchill's War*, Volume I (Veritas, Bullsbrook, 1987).

Jarman, T. L., *Socialism In Britain* (Victor Gollancz, London, 1972).

Jerome, William, and Buick, Adam, 'Soviet State Capitalism? The History of an Idea' in *Survey 62* (Information Bulletin, London, 1967).

Kahn, Richard, F., 'The Relation of Home Investment To Employment' in the *Economic Journal*, June 1931.

Kautsky, Karl, *Terrorism and Communism* (George Allen and Unwin, London, 1920).

_____, *The Economic Doctrines of Karl Marx* (Black, London, 1925).

Kendall, Walter, *The Revolutionary Movement in Britain, 1900–21* (Weidenfeld and

Nicholson, London, 1969).

Keynes, John Maynard, *How To Pay For the War* (Macmillan, London, 1941).

_____, *Laissez Faire and Communism* (St. Martin's Press, New York, 1926).

_____, *The General Theory of Employment, Interest and Money* (MacMillan, London, 1936).

Labour Party, *Report On Full Employment and Finance Policy*, 1944 Conference.

Leaf, Walter, *Banking* (Home University Library, London, 1926).

Leight, Samuel, *The Futility of Reformism* (WWW, Tucson, n.d.).

_____, World Without Wages (WWW, Tucson, n.d.).

Lenin, Vladimir I., *'Left-Wing' Communism, An Infantile Disorder* (Foreign Languages Press, Peking, 1975).

_____, *On State Capitalism During the Transition to Socialism* (Progress Publishers, Moscow, 1985).

_____, *Socialism and War* (Lawrence and Wishart, London, 1940).

_____, *The State and Revolution* (Progress Publishers, Moscow, 1985).

_____, *What Is to Be Done?* (Foreign Languages Press, Peking, 1976).

Lipsey, R. G., *An Introduction To Positive Economics* (Weidenfeld and Nicholson, London, 1983).

Luxemburg, Rosa, *Accumulation of Capital* (Routledge and Kegan Paul, London, 1951).

_____, *Reform or Revolution* (Bookmarks, London, 1989).

_____, *Rosa Luxemburg Speaks* (Pathfinder Press, New York, 1970).

MacIntyre, Stuart, *A Proletarian Science* (Cambridge University Press, Cambridge, 1980).

MacNicol, John, *The Movement For Family Allowances 1918–45* (Heinemann, London, 1980).

Mandel, Ernest, *Marxist Economic Theory*, Two Volumes (Merlin Press, London, 1968).

Martov, Julius, *The State and the Socialist Revolution* (Slienger, London, 1977).

Marx, Karl, *Capital*, Three Volumes (Penguin, London and Harmondsworth, 1976, 1978, 1981).

_____, *Class Struggles In France 1848–50* (Progress Publishers, Moscow, 1972).

_____, *Critique of Political Economy* (Lawrence and Wishart, London, 1971).

_____, *Grundrisse* (Penguin, Harmondsworth, 1973).

_____, *The Civil War In France* (Foreign Languages Press, Peking, 1977).

_____, *Theories of Surplus Value* (Lawrence and Wishart, London, 1951).

_____, *The Poverty of Philosophy* (Foreign Languages Press, Peking, 1978).

_____, *Value, Price and Profit* (George Allen and Unwin, London, 1951).

Marx, Karl, and Engels, Friedrich, *Collected Works* (Lawrence and Wishart, London, 1976).

_____, and _____, *Selected Correspondence* (Progress Publishers, Moscow, 1975).

_____, and _____, *The German Ideology* (Lawrence and Wishart, London, 1970).

Mattick, Paul, *Economic Crisis and Crisis Theory* (Merlin Press, London, 1981).

_____, *Marx and Keynes* (Merlin Press, London, 1980).

McLennan, David, *The Thought of Karl Marx* (Macmillan, London and Basingstoke, 1986).

Michels, Robert, *Political Parties* (Collier, New York, 1962).

Militant, *What We Stand For* (Militant Publications, London, 1986).

Mises, Ludwig Von, *Socialism: An Economic and Sociological Analysis* (Yale University Press, New Haven, 1951).

Morris, William, *The Collected Works of William Morris* (Longmans, London, 1910-15).

Molyneux, John, *The Future Socialist Society* (Socialist Workers Party, London, 1987).

O'Neill, John, 'Markets, Socialism and Information — A Reformulation Of A Marxian Objection to the Market' in *Socialism* edited by Paul, E. F. *et al* (Basil Blackwell, Oxford, 1989).

Pannekoek, Anton, 'The Theory of the Collapse of Capitalism' in *Capital and Class,* Spring 1977 (Conference of Socialist Economists, London).

Panicker, M. J., *20th Century World Socialist or Communist Manifesto* (Panicker, London, 1951).

Pepper, David, *Eco-Socialism, From Deep Ecology To Social Justice* (Routledge, London and New York, 1993).

Philoren, *Money Must Go* (J. Phillips, London, 1943).

Pierson, Stanley, *British Socialists* (Harvard University Press, Cambridge, Ma. and London, 1979).

Pigou, Arthur, *Unemployment* (Home University Library, London, 1913).

Plekhanov, Georgii, *Selected Philosophical Works* (Lawrence and Wishart, London, 1961).

Powell, David, *What's Left? Labour Britain and the Socialist Tradition* (Peter Owen, London, 1997)

Putkowski, Julian, and Sykes, Julian, *Shot At Dawn* (Wharncliffe Publishing, Barnsley, 1989).

Quail, John, *The Slow Burning Fuse* (Paladin, London, 1978).

Radek, Karl, *Socialism From Science to Practice* (Socialist Labour Press, Glasgow, n.d.).

Reed, John, *Ten Days That Shook the World* (Penguin, Harmondsworth, n.d.).

Revolutionary Communist Group, *The Revolutionary Road to Communism in Britain* (Larkin Publications, London, 1984).

Ricardo, David, *The Principles of Political Economy* (J. M. Dent and Sons, London, n.d.).

Rousset, David, *The Legacy of the Bolshevik Revolution* (Allison and Busby, London, 1982).

Rowbotham, Sheila, *The Friends of Alice Wheeldon* (Pluto Press, London, 1986).

Rubel, Maximilien, and Crump, John, *Non-Market Socialism in the Nineteenth and Twentieth Centuries* (Macmillan, London and Basingstoke, 1987).

Ruhle, Otto, *From the Bourgeois to the Proletarian Revolution* (Socialist Reproduction/Revolutionary Perspectives, Glasgow, 1974).

Samuelson, Paul, *Economics* (McGraw-Hill, New York, 1980).

Shipway, Mark, *Anti-Parliamentary Communism: The Movement For Workers' Councils in Britain 1917–45* (Macmillan, London and Basingstoke, 1988).

Shub, David, *Lenin* (Pelican, London, 1986).

Skidelsky, Robert, *John Maynard Keynes — The Economist As Saviour 1920–37* (Macmillan, London, 1992).

Smith, Adam, *The Wealth of Nations* (Black, Edinburgh, 1843).

Smith, Ken, *Free Is Cheaper* (John Ball Press, Gloucester, 1988).

_____, *The Survival of the Weakest* (John Ball Press, Gloucester, 1994).

Social Democratic Federation, Fabian Society and Hammersmith Socialist Society, *Manifesto of English Socialists* (Twentieth Century Press, London, 1893).

Steele, David Ramsay, *From Marx To Mises — Post-Capitalist Society and the Challenge of Economic Calculation* (Open Court, Illinois, 1992).

Stewart, Michael, *Keynes and After* (Penguin, London, 1967).

Strachey, John, *The Nature of Capitalist Crisis* (Victor Gollancz, London, 1935).

_____, *What Are We To Do?* (Left Book Club, London, 1938).

Thompson, E. P., *William Morris: Romantic To Revolutionary* (Merlin Press, London, 1977).

Tsuzucki, Chushichi, 'The Impossibilist Revolt in Britain' in *International Review of Social History*, Number One, 1956.

Walsby, Harold, *The Domain of Ideologies* (William McLellan, Glasgow, 1947).

Walford, George, *Beyond Politics* (Calabria Press, London, 1990).

Waters, Chris, *British Socialists and the Politics of Popular Culture 1884–1914* (Manchester University Press, Manchester, 1990).

Weston, W. J., *A Textbook of Economics* (Pitman and Sons, London, 1930).

Widgery, David, *The Left in Britain 1956–68* (Penguin, Harmondsworth, 1976).

Yaffe, David, 'The Marxian Theory of Crisis, Capital and the State' in *Economy and Society*, Volume II, Number Two (London, May 1973).

Index